Toms and *Dees*

Southeast Asia

POLITICS, MEANING, AND MEMORY

Rita Smith Kipp and David Chandler

SERIES EDITORS

Toms AND Dees

TRANSGENDER IDENTITY AND FEMALE SAME-SEX
RELATIONSHIPS IN THAILAND

Megan J. Sinnott

 UNIVERSITY OF HAWAI'I PRESS *Honolulu*

Library of Congress Cataloging-in-Publication Data

Sinnott, Megan.

Toms and dees : transgender identity and female same-sex relationships in Thailand / Megan J. Sinnott.

p. cm.—(Southeast Asia: politics, meaning, and memory)

Includes bibliographical references and index.

ISBN 0-8248-2741-4 (hardcover : alk. paper)—
ISBN 0-8248-2852-6 (pbk. : alk. paper)

1. Lesbians—Identity—Thailand. 2. Transsexuals—Identity—Thailand. 3. Women—Identity—Thailand. 4. Women—Thailand—Sexual behavior. 5. Gender identity—Thailand. 6. Sex customs—Thailand. 7. Thailand—Social life and customs. I. Title. II. Southeast Asia: politics, meaning, memory.

HQ75.6.T5S56 2004

306.76'8—dc22

2004004668

Designed by Leslie Fitch Design

Text in Sabon with display in Gill Sans

Composition by Josie Herr

Printed by The Maple-Vail Book Manufacturing Group

Printed on 60# Text White Opaque, 426 ppi

CONTENTS

The first time that I saw that person from behind, I thought, "That's right." I looked again and again. His body was very manly, with hair cut short like a teenager. I saw him leaning against and hugging a young woman who had hair down to her shoulders. She had a beautiful face, one that should be cherished. They were holding hands, gazing into each other's eyes, revealing the feeling in their hearts. They were stroking each other so sweetly, enjoying each other like lovers do. . . .

Because of the extent of their affection, it attracted the gaze of those around them, with everybody looking at them with a different expression in their eyes. But when I got closer, the picture was not what I thought, because the "he" that I was looking at was a "she." I looked around and saw another couple, over there another couple . . . oh, it was getting more exciting!

PANWA, "'PHU-YING' KAP THAANG SAAI THII-SAAM"
("WOMEN" ON THE THIRD PATH)

ACKNOWLEDGMENTS

The writing of this book began years ago, starting as fieldwork for my dissertation in anthropology at the University of Wisconsin—Madison. Over the years that followed, as I transformed my field notes into a dissertation and then into a book, countless individuals and organizations have assisted me. To all the *tom*s and *dee*s who patiently answered my questions and told me their life stories, I owe a huge debt of gratitude. I give heartfelt thanks to Sutheera Wongskaew (Phii Mao), whose friendship and support made this project possible. Her enthusiasm, good humor, and willingness to contemplate and comment on my questions and perhaps strange theories of *tom*ness made this research better and more fun to do. I thank Lek Meena, Pearl, Taeng, Naan, Chuy, Joy, Raem, Maew, and all the others too numerous to name here. I also thank the members of Anjaree and Lesla who allowed me to participate in their lives and events.

I am grateful to my parents, George and Arlene Sinnott, whose support, both financial and emotional, made this project possible. My warmest appreciation is for Kevin and Mary-Ellen for being kind and supportive over the years and to Matthew and Isabel for just being there. I owe special thanks to my sister, Eileen, for her care packages, love, and friendship, which maintained my overall well-being and psychological health. I thank my aunt and uncle, Maureen and Michael Torphy, for their loving tolerance of my long stays at their house in Madison.

I am deeply grateful to everyone who read and made useful comments on the dissertation and on the manuscript for this book. I thank Peter Jackson for his insight and excellent research that aided my work immeasurably. I also thank Tamara Loos for her perceptive comments and suggestions that made this a better work. Thongchai Winichakul, Maria Lepowsky, Kirin Narayan, and Ken George—my dissertation advisers and readers—provided invaluable suggestions and advice that greatly improved my work. I owe a special debt to my mentor, friend, and main adviser, Katherine Bowie. She read numerous drafts with almost surreal patience and provided illuminating and constructive comments. My gratitude to her is immense.

I am grateful to Matthana Chetamee, who helped me collect information and whose master's thesis helped me develop my work. I owe great thanks also to Suphecha Baothip for her intelligence and fresh perspective when all I saw was a void. I thank Sandra Pendall, whose outreach project provided valuable information and many memories. I also appreciate the interviews, advice, information, and friendship offered by Somjai Viriyabunditkul, Ubonrat Siriyuvasak, Thamora Fishel, Dararat Mettariganond, Pranee Srikamneard, Santi Svetavimala, Kittisak Pokkati, Sombat Ritklang, Nerida Cook, Mantana Adisayatepakul, Somsonge Burusphat, and the late Surasinghsamruam Shimbhanao. I also owe thanks to all the individuals who allowed me permission to reprint their images.

The Fulbright Foundation and the Center for Southeast Asian Studies, University of Wisconsin—Madison, provided funding for this study, without which it would not have been completed. I thank the wonderful staff at both places, and Michael Cullinane in particular. I also am grateful to the staff at the Department of Anthropology at University of Wisconsin—Madison for their help over the years and would like to express my appreciation especially to Peg Erdman and Maggie Brandenburg. I also thank Rosemary Wetherold for her meticulous editing, and all the staff and editors at the University of Hawai'i Press.

Finally, I thank the person to whom I dedicate this work, Kallayanee Techapatikul. Her endless hours in libraries with me, checking each translation and keeping me emotionally and psychically on track through these past years, will never be forgotten.

Introduction

IN JUNE 1995 a visiting American professor of psychology gave a talk at Thammasat University in Bangkok on the topic of current psychological approaches to homosexuality. Because the audience was mostly Thai, an interpreter was provided. The speaker explained that same-sex sexual behavior does not necessarily lead to a sexual identity. The professor's statement that "some women have sex with other women but do not consider themselves as lesbians" was translated with the Thai word for "men" *(phu-chai)* replacing the English word "lesbians." After murmurings from the disconcerted audience (which consisted of university students, activists, and faculty members) and a discussion between the speaker and the interpreter, the interpreter retranslated the sentence with the English word "lesbians" carried over into the Thai translation. Apparently "lesbian" was an untranslatable, culturally specific term.

The interpreter's original substitution of the Thai word meaning "men" for "lesbians" was no accident. Females who are sexually attracted to "women" are commonly understood by Thais to be masculine beings. The sexuality implied in the term "lesbian" was elided and replaced with an assertion of gender—these females are simply considered "men." The feminine partners of these "men" are linguistically exterior—no reference to them is made in the translation "men." There is a Thai term (*"dees"*) for these feminine partners of female "men," but the exclusion of *dees* from the Thai translation of "lesbian" indicates their ambiguity in the dominant discourses of the Thai sex/gender order, as well as their peripheral status in the Thai articulation of the Western concept "homosexuality" when describing local transgendered practices. In the case of the Thammasat lecture, the presence of Western and Thai feminist activists in the audience made this commonsense translation of "lesbians" as "men" awkward. The Western professor's statement on lesbianism was loaded with cultural implications that snagged and buckled when forced into translation. This incident offers a glimpse at the process of cultural production, in which complex and contradictory borrowings, adaptations, and transformations of categories of gender, sexuality, and self are made.

In Thailand these female "men" who look to "women" for love, romance, and sex are called—and call themselves—*tom*s. The term *"tom"* is derived from the English word "tomboy." Their feminine partners are called *"dee*s," a term derived from the last syllable of the English word "lady." This book is about the way that *tom*s and *dee*s construct their identities and their vibrant, growing, and highly visible communities.[1] It is also about the social discourses in Thai society that form the contours of being *tom* or *dee*. *Tom* and *dee* identities are relatively recent. They emerged in Thailand in the late 1970s, corresponding to profound socioeconomic changes that characterize that period. These identities are new, but they have important links to preexisting cultural understandings of sexuality and gender, which will be explored in chapter 2.

TOMS AND DEES

Although *tom* and *dee* identities are recent linguistic categories of identity, female homosexuality itself is, of course, not new to Thailand or anywhere else. A *tom* is a *tom* by virtue of her self-assumed masculinity, and sexual attraction to women is an assumed extension of being masculine. *Dee* "identity" is the result of having a sexual or romantic relationship with a *tom*. However, *dee* identity is less formal than *tom* identity, and many women involved with *tom*s stated in interviews that they thought of themselves not as *dee*s but simply as women. In contemporary Thailand, *dee* is something less than a fully formed identity and something more than a behavioral description. The term *"dee"* overlaps with other terms, such as "ordinary woman." For example, Pek, a girlfriend of a *tom,* told me that she was a woman and not a *dee*. Pek said, "A *dee* is only for *tom*s, but a 'woman' can be with either a *tom* or a guy. For now, I cannot stand being with a guy because I like [my *tom* partner] so much better."

Some *tom*s and *dee*s said that a *dee* is any woman with a *tom,* while others made distinctions between "real" *dee*s and "fake" ones, saying that real *dee*s would be only with a *tom* whereas fake ones would be with either men or *tom*s. Some *tom*s said that the latter may be true, but they knew of very few "real" *dee*s.

*Tom*s, as transgendered females, share some common discourses of self with transgendered males (*kathoey*s) in Thailand, which will be discussed in more detail in chapter 3. However, there are some notable differences between transgendered males and females in Thai discourse. *Tom*s are not women "passing" as men, whereas *kathoey*s often do make efforts to pass as women, including opting for sexual reassignment surgery.

*Tom-dee*ism is not a category that encompasses all female homoerotic experiences or identities. Not all female homosexuality is as highly gendered as *tom-dee*ism, nor are all female homosexual experiences necessarily labeled or discursively situated; in other words, not all homosexual experiences lead to an identity. Homosexual behavior in Thai cultural logic does not necessitate the same all-encompassing identity and resulting stigma that such behavior in a Western context almost automatically entails. Som's story exemplifies the experience of same-sex relations that are relatively common among Thai women.

Som is a rural woman in her thirties who worked at various factories as an adolescent and lived in factory dormitories for some periods of time. While in one factory dormitory, Som had a sexual relationship with a young woman, Tuk. Som shared a room with Tuk for several years, and they formed a tight friendship. Som said they divided daily chores and lived together "like a couple." Som would clean the house while Tuk cooked the food. As they slept at night, they would touch and caress each other as they masturbated. One day Tuk came home and said that her parents had decided it was time for her to marry and had found a suitable young man in the village to which she would soon return. Som said she was depressed and responded simply, "You're going to get married, huh?" Tuk left, and they lost contact. Som was clearly disappointed and hurt at the breakup but had no language to express her feelings about the relationship—it fit no meaningful category of marriage or building a future together. Som said she did not consider herself or her female partner to be a *tom* or a *dee*, nor did she identify herself with the increasingly recognized term "lesbian." Som married at about age sixteen, and after a few years she had a child, like many of the other young village women. Som's story was like many I collected through the course of my research—I was told of such past sexual experiences while discussing topics unrelated to homosexuality or *tom* and *dee* identities (e.g., factory working conditions). Homosexual behavior does not necessarily lead to an identity, nor does it necessarily constitute a distinct transgression of sexual or gender norms.

Tom identity does not exhaust all possible female masculine identities in the Thai context. Saipin Suputtamongkol's study (2000) of prison life in Thailand describes the female prison world, in which masculine female inmates who are involved sexually with other female prison inmates are categorized as either a *tom* or a *"man."* The term *"man"* is a transliteration of the English word "man" into Thai. *Tom*s are understood to have been masculine, homosexual females before their prison terms, and thus their masculinity is an extension of their "real" life. A *"man,"* on the other hand, is a woman who chooses a female sexual partner and a masculine gender as a survival technique during the time she is in prison, which may amount to several decades. Being a *man* is seen as a temporary, situational gender change as women adapt to the necessities of prison life. Most of these prison women assume that a *man*, upon release, will revert to her previous feminine heterosexuality (Saipin 2000, 206–222).

Som's story and the prison *man* indicate that focusing on *tom-dee*ism as a given and obvious identity by virtue of the sexuality of these women would be misleading. Neither *tom* and *dee* identities nor their imagery in mainstream discourses can be assumed to be a "natural" or obvious interpretation of gendered and sexual activity—they are culturally and historically specific interpretations of both female homosexuality and transgenderism that exist within a range of possibilities.

THAI SEX/GENDER TERMS AND CATEGORIES

The meanings of Thai terms for sex and gender categories have changed over time and are neither static nor homogenous. Even within dictionaries contradictions abound, as writers attempt to link Thai terms to their understanding of Western terms for sexuality within the context of an expanding vocabulary of sexual and gender categories in contemporary Thailand.[2] Thus a Thai word such as *"lakkapheet,"* for example, may be simultaneously interpreted as transsexual, transvestite, and homosexual. A brief description of the key terms and concepts in the Thai sex/gender order follows.

Pheet (Sex/Gender)

Jackson (1997b) demonstrates that Thai terminology reflects the absence of rigid conceptual distinctions between sex and gender, for both are denoted by the word *"pheet."* *"Pheet"* can indicate sexual acts; "to have sex" is expressed as *"ruam-pheet";* and *"pheet"* can also mean "sex," as in "female sex" *(pheet-ying).*[3] *"Pheet-ying,"* like the masculine referent *"pheet-chai,"* can also refer to the gendered identity of an individual rather than specifically to biological status—transgendered males or *tom*s may refer to themselves or be referred to as *"pheet-ying"* or *"pheet-chai,"* respectively, indicating their gendered status as feminine or masculine. A female's statement that she is *pheet-chai* is not a claim to a male body or physical hermaphroditism.

Phit-pheet

The term *"phit-pheet"* can be translated as "misgendered" or "mis-sexed," implying that one is acting against one's normative gender. Thus a *kathoey* (feminine male) or a *tom* (masculine female) may be called *phit-pheet.*

Kathoey

"Kathoey" means an indeterminate gender or a combination of masculine and feminine gender and is commonly translated into English as either "hermaphrodite" or "third sex/gender." *"Kathoey"* can be used to describe any animal or plant that does not have a clearly distinct male or female sex or is infertile. For example, I have heard some mangoes called *kathoey* mangoes, meaning mangoes without fertile seeds,[4] although some Thais have interpreted the phrase as referring to mangoes that are a hybrid of mango types.

"Kathoey" has been used to refer to either males or females who physically have both male and female genitalia, corresponding to the English term "hermaphrodite." More commonly, *"kathoey"* is used to refer to a male or a female who seems to embody the characteristics, or "gender," of the opposite sex, such as "feminine males" or "masculine females."[5] These males and females are presumed to be homosexual as a result of their blended gender. *"Kathoey"* is a blending of *"pheet,"* which can refer to either sexed body (hermaphrodite) or gender (a transgendered *tom*, for example). Not only are homosexuality and hermaphroditism typically considered to be indistinguishable, but erotic interest in the same sex, hermaphroditism, and bisexuality are also linked. An

English-Thai dictionary defines "bisexual" as "having two sexes *(pheet)*, having to do with two sexes *(pheet)*, having male and female genitalia in the same body, being a *kathoey*, and/or having sexual desire for both men and women" (Wit 1994). "*Kathoey*" now refers almost exclusively to males, and masculine females are usually referred to as *tom*s. *Kathoey*s, or feminine men (presumed to be homosexual), are sometimes referred to as "*tut*," which is pejorative Thai slang perhaps translatable as "fag" or "homo."

Gay

Homosexual Thai men who are normatively masculine often identify themselves as "gay," as a way to distinguish themselves from the very visible, feminine, and stigmatized *kathoey*s. Masculine gay men are not highly visible in Thai society, because they do not participate in transgenderism, which is widely held by Thais to be synonymous with homosexuality (with the gender-normative partner of these transgendered males not distinguished from "men" in general). However, many Thais understand the term "gay" to refer to *kathoey*s and feminine homosexual males. Some transgendered males also call themselves "gay" because the term does not carry the same stigma that the term "*kathoey*" does and because it sounds modern and international.[6]

Third Sex/Gender

The term "third sex/gender" *(pheet-thii-saam)* is used in many academic articles, particularly in the field of psychology, and in the press to refer to *tom*s, *dee*s, gays, and *kathoey*s. The term "third sex/gender" is relatively new, and none of the elderly people I interviewed recognized it. Exactly how this term was introduced into Thai discourse is unclear, but it most probably was through academics and psychologists as they introduced Western sexology. The term "third-sex/gender" is closely associated with preexisting understandings of *kathoey* as an intermediary sex/gender category. However, most *tom*s I met did not think of themselves as "third sex/gender." Kralok, an urban *tom* in her forties, explained, "If somebody calls me third sex/gender *(pheet-thii-saam)*, I won't agree with that. 'Third sex/gender' means you are neither man nor woman, maybe some kind of monster. So there isn't any third sex/ gender for me. I am female *(phu-ying)*, but mis-gendered/sexed *(phit-pheet)*. Mis-gendered/sexed means that naturally a man and a woman live together as a family, but if some woman lives with another woman or some man lives with another man, that is being mis-gendered/sexed.

We have only two sexes/genders *(pheet)* in the world." The term "third gender/sex" is now fairly well known among Thai urbanites and the educated middle classes, who have access to both the print media and academic texts.

Rak-ruam-pheet / Homosexuality

The formal, medically derived term for homosexuality, *"rak-ruam-pheet,"* is of relatively recent origin and smacks of academic jargon. "Sexual deviance" *(biang-been thaang-pheet),* like "homosexuality," is a Western-derived academic term that is used increasingly by the media and academics. The term *"rak-ruam-pheet"* is paired with another new term, *"rak-tang-pheet"* (heterosexuality). However, unlike the relatively neutral connotations of the English term "homosexuality," *"rak-ruam-pheet"* tends to carry an inherently negative meaning, according to Thai gay and lesbian activists. The first word *"rak,"* meaning "love," is followed by two syllables that form the word *"ruam-pheet,"* a direct and formal term for "sexual intercourse." So a possible reading of the term *"rak-ruam-pheet,"* in spite of its medical and academic origin, is "loving to have sexual intercourse" or simply "sex-crazed." Explicit associations with sexuality are particularly offensive to Thai women, including *tom*s and *dee*s, and they tend to feel uncomfortable with the term *"rak-ruam-pheet."* Anjaree, a Thai lesbian activist organization, is concerned that this term conveys a negative image to mainstream Thai society by implying that homosexuals are unduly interested in sexual acts. Anjaree has recently suggested a new term, *"rak-pheet-diaw-kan"* (literally, "to love the same sex"), to replace the term *"rak-ruam-pheet"* in academic and journalistic writing. The term "homosexuality" and other Western-inspired academic terms, such as "sexual deviance" *(biang-been-thaang-pheet),* are interpreted by many Thais as referring to transgenderism, consistent with the Thai concept that homosexuality is a form of "gender deviance."

Lakkapheet

In addition to *"kathoey,"* *"lakkapheet"* is perhaps the closest Thai equivalent to the Western concept of an overarching category of sexual and gender "deviance." The term *"lakkapheet"* means literally "to steal another's sex/gender," implying that one is acting against one's "proper" sex or gender. Academics and authoritative-sounding journalists often use *"lakkapheet"* as an equivalent to the Western category of "transvestite." For example, a journalist defined *"lakkapheet"* as people who "gain satisfaction from wearing clothing of the opposite sex" (Ophat 1984a). "*Lakkapheet,*" unlike "third sex/gender," has an inherently negative implication and is almost never used as a positive self-identity.

Thais often use specific terms for homosexual or transgendered individuals, such as "gay," "*tom,*" "*dee,*" "*tut,*" or "*kathoey*" rather than trying to reach for an overarching term that could encompass all these categories, such as "homosexual," "third sex/gender," or "*lakkapheet.*" Thais use the specific terms primarily as references to a gender identity, with homoeroticism as a necessary corollary.

DISCOURSES OF "SEXUAL DEVIANCE" AND THE QUESTION OF "TOLERANCE"

Although this book aims to demonstrate that *tom*s and *dee*s are active participants in constructing the framework and meaning of *tom* and *dee* identities, it is imperative to recognize that *tom*s and *dee*s, and the concepts they deploy, are not free-floating in a sea of semiotic creativity. *Tom*s and *dee*s as individuals are grounded in a social system that often discourages and criticizes their identities and life choices. They exist in a contemporary social situation in which some *tom*s and *dee*s experience oppression, insults, and intimidation regarding their gender and sexuality. Jackson (1999b, 229) makes the useful distinction between "tolerance" and "acceptance" of homosexuality in the Thai context: "Tolerance denotes a preparedness to endure, put up with, or permit to exist, but does not necessarily imply the lack of criticism or the favorable or approving attitude connoted by acceptance. It is possible to tolerate something even while considering it inappropriate, misdirected, or wrong." Although Jackson's discussion focuses primarily on male homosexual and transgender identities in Thailand, his distinction is useful in making sense of attitudes toward *tom* and *dee* identities.

As *tom* and *dee* identities and subculture experience a dramatic popularity and growth, a virulently anti-homosexual/*tom-dee* discourse has been produced by academics and medical professionals under the guidance of the Thai state. Discourses of "homosexuality" *(rak-ruam-pheet),* "misgendering" *(phit-pheet),* and "sexual/gender deviance" *(biang-been-thaang-pheet)* have been disseminated by state-based Thai educational and academic institutions in cooperation with the media, particularly the print media. These hegemonic discourses of the Thai state and its agents are presented in chapter 7.

The coexistence of tolerance and intolerance was evident in many of the interviews I conducted with *dee*s. For example, I was struck by the relative openness with which some women would discuss with me past love affairs with *tom*s or *dee*s. Nok, a mother and wife in her mid-thirties, freely volunteered information about her past love affairs with *tom*s when she learned of my research topic. Nok is a professional, well-educated woman from an affluent family in Bangkok. She seemed to have fond memories of her experiences with several *tom*s in her teens and twenties and said that her family was accepting of, even nonchalant about, her girlfriends and her *dee* lifestyle at the time. Later I decided to interview Nok to get details about her life to include in this research, and a different picture emerged. In the interview, Nok said she always felt unnatural when she was with her girlfriends and was afraid that her friends would not accept her. She said she had little social life at that time for fear of being criticized about her *tom* lover, and she felt that her family was pleased when she finally ended her relationships with *tom*s and married a man.

Many of the *dee*s I interviewed expressed similar feelings of ambivalence about society's attitudes toward them. Many Thais classify *dee*s as "normal women" and therefore believe that *dee*s do not face the same social pressure that transgender *tom*s face. However, *dee*s are not effortlessly incorporated into either the *tom* subculture or mainstream society. *Dee*s often recounted more resistance from family members and others to their choice of taking female lovers than did many *tom*s. Although *dee*s could easily move between relationships with men and *tom*s and were not obviously "homosexual" to outsiders, their lives were full of difficult compromises that both *tom*s and people in general seemed to fail to appreciate fully. Masculine women have long been evident in the Thai system of sex and gender, but the linguistic and social marking of feminine women who are partners of masculine women creates a new and precarious field of identity. *Dee*s, as feminine women, do not fit Thai understandings of "homosexuality." *Dee*s are not as stigmatized as *tom*s are, but they are rendered invisible and collapsed into the category "ordinary women," which does not acknowledge or validate their life choices. In the politics of *tom*s and *dee*s, as will be seen in the following chapters, this instability of *dee* identity allows *dee*s fluid movement in relationships but prevents them from appropriating a discourse that validates their choices in female partners. This is one of the many complexities of *tom* and *dee* identities and relationships that are explored in the chapters 3 through 5.

CHINESE AND THAI ETHNICITY

The *tom*s and *dee*s of this study can be generally placed in two main ethnic categories—Thai and Sino-Thai. Ethnic differences between Thai and Sino-Thai *tom*s and *dee*s are largely subsumed by class differences. One of the significant findings of this study is that although Thai and Chinese traditions differ in the position of women in the family and in models of ideal marital arrangements, the overall result of these cultural differences is less significant than class and social position in determining the life choices of both Thai and Sino-Thai women. When I contrast "Thai" and "Sino-Thai," it should be remembered that this is an ethnic distinction that is relevant only in some contexts, and all the people of this study are Thai in terms of nationality and citizenship. Here I will briefly outline the differences between Thai and Sino-Thai culture regarding women and discuss how these differences play out in *tom* and *dee* identities in contemporary Thailand.[7]

Despite its reputation as a relatively homogenous country, Thailand is home to people with a variety of ethnic, cultural, and linguistic traditions (Keyes 1987). Thailand is typically described as comprising four regions—southern, central, northern, and northeastern. Each region has its own dialect, but the central Thai dialect is the standard national language. Nuanced regional differences in discourses of sex and gender exist, embedded in local myths, rituals, and popular expressions. The ways in which these regional differences influence local constructions of *tom* and *dee,* or of male homosexuality and transgenderism, have yet to be formally described. The general form of *tom* and *dee* identities is fairly consistent, however, and regional differences have become absorbed in a growing national culture of gender and sexual identities. The most significant ethnic differences for Thai society as a whole involve the Chinese/Sino-Thai population and the ethnic Thais.

Although most of the population practice Buddhism, there is considerable variation in belief systems throughout Thailand.[8] The urban Chinese practice Confucian-based ancestor worship, as well as Mahayana Buddhism, whereas ethnic Thais practice a blend of Theravada Buddhism and beliefs involving the propitiation of spirits and deities. The pantheon of deities and spirits is large and includes Chinese deities, indigenous animistic spirits, local ancestor spirits, spirits of historical figures, and Hindu Brahmanistic deities. Sino-Thais have adopted many of the Thai practices, such as sending their children to become Theravadin monks or novices, as well as praying at the shrines of Hindu deities and local animistic spirits. Thais also participate in Chinese ceremonies, such as Chinese New Year celebrations and the traditional lion dance. Thus, although differences still exist between the religious practices of Sino-Thais and Thais, considerable syncretism has occurred.

This Chinese-Thai syncretism is particularly obvious in Bangkok. Bangkok society is largely influenced by Chinese immigrants, whose descendants constitute a significant portion of the urban middle class.[9] Thai and Chinese traditions have become blended, and Bangkok residents often are not clear exactly what constitutes "Thai" and "Chinese" traditions. The ethnic distinctions that are the most relevant for this study of *tom*s and *dee*s concern the position of women in the family and the meaning of marriage for Sino-Thai and Thai families.

Chinese families, influenced by Confucian tradition, tend to place importance on the patrilineage, represented through the clan name. Sons are highly valued as the bearers of the clan name. Ideally, a wife is expected to move into her husband's family home, to serve the needs of her mother-in-law, and, most importantly, to bear a son for the patrilineage. The ideal Chinese family contrasts with the ideal Thai family in postmarital residence patterns and kinship systems. Traditionally, a Thai husband is expected to move into the family compound of his wife and to provide labor for her family before setting up a household nearby, ideally in or near the wife's family compound (Hale 1984; Rabibhadana 1984). The youngest daughter is expected to care for her parents and receives the family house as compensation for her service. The general Thai family structure is characterized by equal inheritance between sons and daughters or inheritance rules that favor women; bilateral kinship reckoning; and postmarital residence patterns that tend to favor matrilocality (Hale 1984, 4). In northern Thailand and parts of the northeast, matrilineal tutelary spirits link generations through females, in contrast to the Chinese Confucian patrilineage (Cohen and Wijeyewardene 1984). In practice, family form does not always follow these ideal forms. Increasing urbanization has forced couples to move away from their extended families, and practical considerations often take precedence in deciding who will live where and with whom.

Like the Chinese, Thais highly value duty to parents. Sons and daughters are expected to repay their debt to their parents *(nii bun khun)* in gender-specific ways. A son performs a highly meritorious act for his parents by becoming a Buddhist monk, thereby transferring merit to his parents, particularly his mother. Thai women thus depend on sons to achieve this merit, which they cannot achieve on their own because women are forbidden from full ordination in Thai Theravada Buddhism. A daughter, barred from monkhood, is expected to be a caretaker of her parents and younger siblings. This caretaking often takes the form of financial support, with professional and wage-earning women sending money to support their parents and siblings (Rabibha-dana 1984; Tantiwiramanond and Pandey 1987). Tantiwiramanond and Pandey (1987) argue that the Theravada Buddhist practice of ordaining only males has led to a preference for sons and to pressure for women to be mothers in order to obtain merit from their sons. This general outline of family structure and social values was borne out in my research. Both Sino-Thai and Thai women were under pressure to help financially support their parents and siblings. Both Sino-Thai and Thai women reported a need to express gratitude to their parents by following their wishes and being responsible for others as good daughters.

Chinese women are often encouraged to marry in order to give "face" to the family. Chinese women explained to me that it is considered embarrassing to have older unmarried daughters. When a woman is married, it means she has been "chosen" and given the status of wife, which in turn gives status to her family. The husband's family will also provide a "brideprice" (*kha-sin-sort* or *kha-namnom* in Thai) for the wife's family as compensation for their raising his wife to adulthood. The brideprice may consist of money, gold, farming equipment, and animals.[10] An unmarried daughter is considered to be a burden to her family and a possible source of shame if she delays marriage and takes a lover instead. In Chinese families a son is also pressured to marry, because it is imperative for him to have a son to carry on the clan name. Jackson (1995) has noted that there tends to be pressure for Chinese and Sino-Thai men to marry, and thus homosexual men find it difficult to pursue relationships with men if it means neglecting their family duty to marry and have children. However, as is discussed in chapter 2, the rising employment rates and opportunities for Chinese and Sino-Thai women have allowed them to postpone marriage or avoid it altogether, while providing economic resources for their family (see Guest and Tan 1994).

Social scientists have described Thai women as having a relatively high status because of their central role in the family structure, and their late marriage rates are evidence of their relative importance in the family (Phongpaichit and Baker 1996). However, Thai women are also pressured to marry in order to promote "face" of the family. Thai and

Chinese marriage ceremonies are less religious ceremonies in the Western/Christian sense than public presentations of face and social ties created between families. Both Thai and Chinese marriage ceremonies involve presenting the brideprice, usually in the form of gold and cash, to impress guests with the status of the husband's family and the value of the wife and, by extension, her family's value (this wealth is often borrowed for the ceremony for the purpose of maintaining face).

The Sino-Thai communities differ from communities in China in that the family cycle in China was typically broken through the act of immigration to Thailand. Notably, the first generation of Chinese immigrants often formed families without the presence of the dominating mother-in-law and other family elders (see J. Bao 1998). Also, Chinese immigrants usually settled in urban areas, engaged in commerce, and achieved relatively high educational levels for the descending generations. The middle-class offspring have greater career and life choices than their elders had, but they often feel indebted to their family and under pressure to follow their parents' decisions concerning marriage. Sino-Thais are presumed by most Thais (and Sino-Thais) to be relatively wealthy, educated, and of high status relative to ethnic Thais. Therefore, stereotypical Chinese physical features, such as lighter skin tone, are interpreted by both Thais and Sino-Thais as reflecting high social status.[11] In contrast, the typically darker-skinned people of the northeast, presumed to be farmers with little education, are often ridiculed as "country bumpkins" (*baan nork* for rural people in general, or *siaw* for northeastern people in particular). These ethnic stereotypes play out in the ways *tom*s and *dee*s present their ideal masculine and feminine types. For example, *tom*s and *dee*s both described the ideal *tom* as having a Chinese appearance, such as light skin, and the corpulence commonly associated with the wealth and prosperity of urban Chinese men.

These cultural differences between Thais and Sino-Thais play out in varying ways in the context of contemporary industrializing Thailand. However, ethnic difference does not clearly structure the social attitudes toward female same-sex relations and transgenderism in Thailand. Class is the more significant factor because women who are financially independent and educated, regardless of their ethnicity, tend to have more options in terms of life choices and marriage. For example, according to census statistics for 1970, Chinese women in Thailand tended to marry later than Thai women, but when educational levels were factored in, the numbers evened out, which was not true for Chinese and Thai men

—regardless of educational levels, Chinese men tended to marry later than Thai men (Chamratrithirong 1979, 31–32).

Marriage is a survival strategy for many families. Marriage of a daughter is a way to get brideprice for both Sino-Thai and Thai families. Andrea Whittaker (1999) and Chris Lyttleton (1999) present evidence that brideprice exchanges are increasingly monetary and expensive in northern and northeastern Thailand, because of greater dependence on wage labor and cash, and a reduction in agricultural land per family. Brideprice is an important source of money for a financially strapped family, can provide the funds necessary for a son's marriage, and may be a way to obtain support and security for a daughter. If other possibilities for income, security, and support are available, such as employment, the pressure for women to marry is less intense. Also, *tom* and *dee* relationships can fit into the survival strategies of poorer families if a daughter is involved with a female partner who is well-off, as the stories in the following chapters will illustrate.

Both males and females from both ethnic groups have faced pressure to marry and to end same-sex relationships. I also found numerous cases where this was not the case for both Thai and Sino-Thai women. No common patterns strictly linked ethnicity to the attitudes of families toward their daughters' decisions to marry or to pursue relationships with *tom*s or *dee*s. However, one common feature of both Sino-Thai and Thai attitudes toward women stood out—the overriding belief that women need to avoid shaming themselves and their families through illicit sexual encounters and promiscuity. This sexual threat was nearly universally defined as heterosexual, and herein lies the main difference between women's and men's experiences of homosexuality in the context of contemporary Thailand. For both Sino-Thai and Thai women, the rumor of illicit heterosexual sex is more dangerous to their position in society than are homosexual encounters and even long-term relationships with other women. Taywaditep, Coleman, and Dumronggittigule (1997) reported that women in northern Thailand used the expression "hit her feet with a hammer" to describe what a wife must do if she has sexual feelings that her husband cannot satisfy. The expression refers to the need to do anything necessary to suppress such dangerous feelings in a woman. Thais have borrowed a Chinese expression that compares a daughter to having a toilet in the front yard, meaning that in being female, a daughter is vulnerable to being disgraced through illicit sex, which would in turn disgrace her family. Thai and Sino-Thai discourse abounds with aphoristic expressions of the shame of illicit (heterosexual) sex for women—movies, soap operas, stories of all kinds, conversations, writings by academics and the print media, and sermons continuously repeat this theme of the shame of a woman's promiscuity. These attitudes toward women's heterosexuality, which are important factors in the way that *tom*s and *dee*s express themselves and structure their relationships, are explored in chapter 4.

UNLEARNING SEX AND GENDER IN ANTHROPOLOGY

To make sense of local Thai discourses that position *tom*s as "men" and as categorically different from *dee*s, an accounting needs to be made of the concepts, terms, and paradigms used within the discipline of anthropology to explain sexuality and gender cross-culturally. Anthropology has long questioned the assumed "naturalness" or "timelessness" of practices, institutions, and beliefs of both the anthropologists' home culture and the culture under study (see Marcus and Fischer 1986). For example, scholars have shown that the characteristic norms of modern Western society, such as the nuclear family, normative heterosexuality, and monogamous marriage, are particular social and historical products, not universal standards.[12] The implicit association between gender and sexuality on the one hand, and changeless truths of human nature on the other, has proven to be difficult to dislodge. Even the preeminent social historians Karl Marx and Fredrick Engels start their study of social history with a presumption of the naturalness of the system of gender distinctions within the family. Feminists and scholars of cross-cultural sexuality and gender have challenged simplistic assumptions of the naturalness and precultural status of gender and sexuality. A sizable literature has been produced on the historical development of sexual practices, family forms, and, in Sherry Ortner's words, "gender hegemonies" (1990).[13]

The pathbreaking work of Gilbert Herdt (1987a, 1987b, 1992) and Maurice Godelier (1986) on semen transmission rituals in New Guinea compelled anthropology to take serious notice of the importance of sexuality in the transmission of culturally significant practices, statuses, and beliefs. Herdt's and Godelier's studies of male same-sex sexual practices in male initiation rituals among cultural groups in New Guinea powerfully demonstrated that even the most embedded assumptions about the naturalness of heterosexuality and "deviance" of homosexuality are culturally defined beliefs of Westerners, not universal truths.

Herdt's study of the initiation rituals of the "Sambia" of Melanesia/ Papua New Guinea describes the practice of boys' ingesting the semen of older men through a ritual cycle lasting years, marking the initiates' entry into the social status of manhood.[14] The semen, ingested through oral stimulation of the older man's penis, is believed to build the masculinity of the initiates. Herdt concludes that homosexual acts do not imply sexual identity or social deviance and must be understood as part of local meanings systems.

The works of Herdt and Godelier were seminal in promoting greater anthropological focus on sexuality as a key cultural practice. However, these works on ritualized homosexuality unintentionally reveal further embedded Western cultural assumptions about what constitutes "homosexuality" and even "sexuality" itself. Deborah Elliston (1995) has critiqued these studies of "ritual homosexuality" by arguing that the concept of "sexuality," as understood by Western researchers, is a cultural discourse, not an objective or neutral category. Elliston notes that anthropologists, including Herdt, have astutely avoided labeling people "homosexual" based on their sexual acts, recognizing that "homosexual" is a type of personal and social identity with a particular history within the Western cultural context. However, Elliston points out that although it is widely acknowledged that observers cannot conclude that certain acts are indicative of a homosexuality identity, there is still an assumption that homosexuality is a behavior that can be identified cross-culturally. The assumption that genital contact and stimulation are somehow analogous to Western conceptions of sexuality is a flaw in the studies of ritual homosexuality, according to Elliston.

Elliston, influenced by Michele Foucault, argues that the Western concept of sexuality as an intrinsic aspect of the individuated self is not applicable to these ritualized expressions in New Guinea. She describes the wider cultural patterns of the Melanesian area in which a variety of symbolic exchanges of substance are performed in the formation of social hierarchy. Therefore, the ingestion of semen by boys through ritual is not any more erotic or sexual than the rituals of nose bleeding or expurgating that also characterize the cultural constellation of which the Sambia are a part. Elliston (1995, 861) emphasizes that "to assume that genitally organized activities between same-sexed bodies signifies eroticism is simplistic." The categorizations of homosexuality that have also been introduced into anthropology are faulty simplifications of the larger contexts in which these acts take place and wrongly imply that these acts are extensions of Western concepts of sexuality, concludes Elliston.

In order to understand what being a *tom* or a *dee* means in the Thai cultural context, the goal of this book is to critically engage preconceptions about gender and sexual categories. Appreciation of local cultural understandings of sexual practices will be lost or subtly skewed if researchers use the categorizations of "homosexuality" and "heterosexuality" without conscious awareness of the implicit cultural meanings embedded within this binary construct. The term "homosexuality" implies a primacy of sexuality in the definition of *tom* and *dee* identity, as well as a sameness between the two based on their sexuality—both problematic assumptions for the understanding of *tom*s and *dee*s. Gender difference is more relevant and important to *tom*s and *dee*s than are notions of sexual identity. Rather than assuming commonality between *tom*s and *dee*s as "homosexuals," this book explores constructed and contested meanings deployed by *tom*s and *dee*s in the creation of their identities, relationships, and communities.

The a priori primacy given to the binary of homosexuality and heterosexuality is so entrenched in Western thinking that it is nearly impossible to discuss sexual practices or forms of intimacy without reference to these terms. For example, Stephen Murray (1992d) has attempted to demonstrate the variety of homosexuality that exists historically and cross-culturally by providing a schema of four categories of homosexuality: age-stratified, gender-defined, profession-defined, and "modern" egalitarian relationships. This pluralization of homosexuality allows for recognition of cultural variation in sexual practices but still asserts "homosexuality" as a category with universal relevance. Cross-cultural studies of this type imply that homosexuality may vary but, underneath the cultural variation, remains a coherent and stable subject. The assumption of a stable, universal homosexual subject is precisely what this study of *tom*s and *dee*s challenges. Also, Murray's categorization refers almost exclusively to men, reproducing cultural biases (both Western and often those of the culture studied) in which women's sexuality, apart from their role as recipients of men's sexuality, is rendered invisible.

The aim of this book is to place *tom* and *dee* identities within their cultural context, including the transnational linkages that form the basis for these categories of selfhood. *Tom* and *dee* identities can be appreciated only with an understanding of discourses of nationalism,

Buddhism, sexual propriety, and gender performances—all topics that are explored in the following chapters.

METHODS

This book is based on research conducted between 1992 and 2001. The primary data were derived from ethnographic research, such as interviews and participant observation with *tom*s and *dee*s, academics, activists, and the staff members of Thai publications. I have gathered information and interviews from more than a hundred *tom*s and *dee*s from fifteen to sixty years of age. As anthropologists have long recognized, understandings of other societies and cultures often comes equally from daily interactions, friendships, informal discussions, and socializing and from the formal interview, complete with tape recorder and question list. I found this to be true for my research as well. The *tom*s and *dee*s I interviewed were usually introduced to me by friends or acquaintances. I developed long-term friendships with some of the people I interviewed, which led to extensive conversations over the following months (and in some cases, years) and further introductions. These interviews and prosaic interactions were the core of my research. I spoke with people from both rural and urban areas; people from working-class, middle-class, and upper-class backgrounds (students, professionals, and housewives); people with university degrees; and some individuals who had never set foot in a classroom.

Most of the *tom*s and *dee*s I interviewed were currently residing in Bangkok. Some had come from rural areas to work in the factories of Bangkok, and others had come to Bangkok for education or employment in the office economy. I also spent approximately a month in several rural villages in Chonburi Province, and this experience has helped me understand dimensions of class and sexuality in rural communities. Interviews were also conducted in Chiang Mai Province. Given the high levels of migration that characterize Thai society, it has proven difficult to definitively categorize individuals as either "rural" or "urban." Many of the people currently living in urban areas are originally from rural areas and still maintain important links to their home villages, often returning to live there temporarily or permanently.[15] Class is a more salient category for understanding differences in life experiences and outlooks among groups of people because it relies less on the ephemeral location of people and more on their social positions. I have located informants according to relative class backgrounds.[16]

The majority of *tom*s and *dee*s in my study were between the ages of twenty and fifty. I had originally intended to talk with elderly women who were *tom*s or *dee*s or had same-sex relationships, but they were difficult to approach. Many of the *tom*s and *dee*s I interviewed said they knew of elderly women in their neighborhood or village whom they called *tom*s or who had relationships with women. Five of the *tom*s and *dee*s in my study said they had an elderly relative who had had a same-sex relationship or was a *tom,* but either they did not feel comfortable about talking to that relative directly about her gender identity or sexuality or the elderly relative was deceased. For example, Ung, a woman in her early twenties who took part in this study, told me of her elderly aunt: "Upcountry I have a very old aunt who lived with another woman who acted like a *tom.* Before, I thought my aunt sent her to school because she thought this woman was a good person—I didn't think that they had any kind of relationship. But now I think back that they did have a relationship for sure. Nobody in the family talked about it, but I think they knew, because when I came home with my partner/lover *(faen),* she would see that it wasn't an ordinary friend I came with. She would be like, 'Oh, is that her girlfriend *(faen)?*' She would ask others but would never ask me directly."

In another example, Nuu, a *tom* in her mid-forties, laughed when she recalled that her elderly aunt was called "iron cunt" *(hii-lek)* by her relatives and neighbors, meaning "untouchable for a man." Nuu remembered that when she was eleven or twelve years old, the elderly aunt asked to meet this niece (Nuu) because the aunt had heard about her. Nuu met her and said that when her aunt smiled, Nuu felt that the aunt was making a special connection to her, knowing that they were alike.

I also collected interviews with twenty men and women in general over the age of sixty about attitudes toward female transgenderism and homosexuality in the past. Most of this material is covered in the discussion of the history of female masculinity and female homoeroticism in chapter 2.

Tom and *dee* identities are a cross-class phenomenon and exist in both rural and urban areas. Some *tom*s and *dee*s are commercial sex workers, and I interviewed several of them. Being *tom* or *dee* is perhaps less stigmatized among sex workers than in mainstream populations because of the different experiences sex workers have had and their different valuations of sex. Most sex workers with whom I spoke have practical attitudes about marriage and sex and see them as tools to gain things that are wanted in life. This does not mean they are callous or that they do not having loving relationships with men. Rather, sex workers are realistic about what is required of them in these relationships and what role these relationships play in their lives. Sex workers acknowledged to me that sex with men was risky in terms of disease and pregnancy and that heterosexual sex could be painful or cause injury. Sex with women was widely understood as "softer" and less risky. It was not uncommon for sex workers to have relationships with each other, in addition to having sex and even long-term relationships with their male clients. However, *tom*s and *dee*s are not particularly or necessarily associated with prostitution in Thailand.

Additional data for my research came from media stories and academic literature on the issue of homosexual/transgenderism in Thailand dating to the mid-1970s. I also consulted material on female same-sex eroticism in the palace in past centuries, collected by Thai historians. I researched the Thai press and its attitudes toward *tom*s and *dee*s by interviewing reporters, columnists, and editors for most major Thai publications (including *Matichon, Siam Post, Khao Sot, The Nation, Bangkok Post, Daily News, Krungthep Turakij,* and *Chiwit Tongsu*) and two DJs from Bangkok's Channel 5 Radio. I interviewed Thai academics in the fields of media studies, law, and political science who have spoken or written about the subject of homosexuality/*tom-dee*ism. This material is discussed throughout the following chapters but is given specific attention and analysis in chapter 7.

I have also drawn on the rich and exciting data of several master's theses in Thai on the subject of *tom*s, *dee*s, and female same-sex sexuality in order to bring this important information to an English-speaking audience. In particular, I have cited material from the theses of Matthana Chetamee (1995), Chonticha Salikhub (1989), and Manitta Chanchai (2003).

Two Thai organizations with *tom* and *dee* membership, Anjaree and Lesla, served as additional research sources. Chapter 6 presents the principles, activities, and strategies of these organizations. Anjaree is a feminist organization established to serve "women who love women," in terms of both lobbying and providing social functions for members. I attended discussion groups, field trips, and parties held by Anjaree and interviewed women who attended its functions and who were members. I have also included material from a WebBoard hosted by Lesla, a relatively new *tom* and *dee* social group. Lesla holds social functions and runs a Web site; its WebBoard has hundreds of recorded discussions among Lesla members. Lesla is not only an Internet group but also a large community of friends who meet and socialize together, so their WebBoard conversations are only one aspect of their relationships. Lesla has grown rapidly since its inception in the middle of 2000, with parties routinely attracting several hundred women.

One of the most striking features of Lesla is that it is composed of mostly young members, and they tend to follow gendered *tom* and *dee* roles strictly. Lesla members often indicate their *tom* or *dee* status on the WebBoard by using gendered terms, such as first-person pronouns (which are gendered in Thai) and other parts of speech that indicate a masculine or feminine speaker. Most of the members are in their late teens and twenties, although some members, including the organizer, are in their thirties. Although most people attending Lesla activities are younger women, older women have participated in the WebBoard chats. Lesla members are mostly urban and almost all are middle-class, as their access to the Internet and expensive group activities indicates. The Lesla Internet discussions are unique in that they are not face-to-face and not edited, which allows for greater openness on sensitive subjects, such as sexual role playing. I have found that face-to-face group discussions on the subject, attempted by Anjaree and myself on occasion, have not been successful, because both *tom*s and *dee*s are uncomfortable talking about these subjects in front of others. I have therefore presented Lesla WebBoard discussions at times where relevant, as well as interviews with Lesla members.

I spent a total of eight years in Thailand conducting the research presented in this book, the last five years of which I was employed as a lecturer at Mahidol University. My conversations with students and faculty over the years provided invaluable information about my topic, and some students volunteered to be interviewed.

Unless otherwise noted, all interviews and Internet conversations were in Thai, and their translations are mine. Most of the names of people interviewed are pseudonyms in the form of Thai nicknames, usually one-syllable words. I have used the real names of people quoted in the press, academics interviewed by me, and other prominent people with their permission, such as the founder of Lesla. As for the spelling of Thai names, I have used the standard romanization of place-names and the preferred romanization of individuals' names. Where no such standard spelling was available, I transcribed the names or terms according to a modified version of the Haas transcription system without the tone markings.[17] There are several systems in use for the transliteration of Thai words into romanized script, and individual Thai words, proper names in particular, can be found transliterated several different ways. Thus my rendering of some names may differ from their spellings in other sources. Following convention, works in Thai by Thai authors are listed by the first name of the author in both the text and the bibliography; works in English by Thai authors are listed by the last name.

The choice of using romanized script for titles of works in the bibliography was based on providing information necessary for those interested in finding the original document. I have translated the names of journals that could be directly translated into English, such as *Journal of Clinical Psychology*. Other journal names were proper names that could not be sensibly translated, so I phonetically transcribed the names into romanized script. In some titles of Thai articles and books where some English words, such as "sex" and "gay," were transliterated into Thai, I used the English spellings in translating the titles.

Some *tom*s use the masculine pronoun *"phom"* to refer to themselves, and I have indicated such usage in my translation because it indicates a purposeful masculine gender term as a self-referent. When *tom*s, like Thai men and women in general, used gender-neutral terms, such as *"phii"* (elder sibling), *"chan"* (me/I), or their personal name, I have not indicated those terms in the text. Therefore, the reader may assume that if no Thai translation is provided for personal pronouns used by *tom*s or *dee*s, the pronouns were not indicative of masculine speech patterns or explicitly feminine speech patterns for *tom*s. Using third-person pronouns when referring to *tom*s is awkward because of the distinction between feminine and masculine pronouns in English. I chose to refer to *tom*s in the feminine form ("she," "her") to reflect the common understanding among Thais that *tom*s are female, and although they are masculine, they are distinct from males. The range of ways in which *tom*s incorporate femininity and masculinity into their sense of self makes this either-or choice of masculine or feminine pronoun seem inappropriate, yet for the sake of consistency in the text, a feminine form has been used for all third-person references to *tom*s.

Although my research would not have been possible without the kind efforts and assistance of many Thais, my topic has not always been a popular one for Thai audiences. One of the Thai organizers of the Sixth International Conference on Thai Studies (held on October 14–17, 1996, in Chiang Mai, Thailand) asked me what topic I would like to present at the upcoming conference. My response of *"tom*s and *dee*s*"* was met with an awkward chuckle, a look in the other direction, and a quick change of conversation topics. I realize it must seem strange to some Thais that Westerners seem compelled to study "unseemly" topics such as homosexuality, *tom*s, *dee*s, or *kathoey*s in Thai society. Recent Thai researchers on these subjects have also faced some degree of disapproval over their choice of topics (although this seems to be changing as more Thai students are pursuing these topics). However, I sense that some Thais feel particularly awkward that "outsiders" are probing the realm of the personal and private and exposing it in a possibly salacious manner to an English-speaking, foreign public. To be fair, perhaps it is strange—this compulsion to tell people what Thai *tom*s and *dee*s are really like. I have to remind myself that I too am fully embedded in a cultural discourse as I expose what I see to be the "truths" of Thai paradigms of gendered sexualities and transgender culture. I may be indulging in what Foucault (1978, 71) labels as a particular Western obsession: "[the] pleasure in the truth of pleasure, the pleasure of knowing that truth, of discovering and exposing it, the fascination of seeing it and telling it . . . of capturing it in secret, of luring it out in the open—the specific pleasure of the true discourse on pleasure."

Perhaps I am motivated to reveal the unsaid "truths" of *tom* and *dee* by critiquing in the following chapters the social beliefs that are responsible for the litany of stereotypes heard about *tom*s and *dee*s. But more than that, my goal is to shed light on a misunderstood, trivialized, and often maligned group of people who have forged gendered and sexual identities in the cultural milieu in which they find themselves.

Global Sex   I

GAY BARS have opened in Taiwan, lesbian organizations within Southeast and East Asia have formed networks, and female impersonator shows are tourist attractions in Bangkok. Some women in Indonesia call themselves "lesbi," while masculine females use the term *"tomboi"* to refer to themselves (Blackwood 1999). In Taiwan, just the first letter "T" is used to refer female masculine identity (A. Chao 1999; Y. Chao 1996). Men use the label "gay" throughout the region (e.g., Boellstorff 1999; Jackson 1997b; M. Tan 1995). Can we say that these identities and behaviors are results of transnationalism and globalism? One could not reasonably deny that Thai society, like the rest of Southeast and East Asia, has been profoundly influenced by transnational socioeconomic forces; the Thai nation itself has been brought into existence through Western discourses of nationhood, ethnic identity, and national boundaries, as Thongchai Winichakul has argued (1994). But does the presence of these strangely familiar terms mean that these identities are products of the globalization of the Western gay/lesbian movement? This question is important. In the postcolonial context, a connotation of being Western is a double-edged sword. Being "Western" can signify progress and modernity and at the same time can symbolize loss of local or national tradition or identity.

The image of homosexuality as a Western intrusion is used in nationalist, anticolonial discourses in developing countries throughout the world. For example, an order from the Zimbabwe minister of information prohibited members of Gays and Lesbians in Zimbabwe from operating a stand at the 1995 Zimbabwean International Book Fair, stating that they would not be allowed to "force the values of gays and lesbians onto the Zimbabwean culture" (Aarmo 1999, 259). In response to international protest of the exclusion of gays and lesbians, President Mugabe said, "Let the Americans keep their sodomy, bestiality, stupid and foolish ways to themselves, out of Zimbabwe. . . . Let them be gay in the U.S., Europe and elsewhere. . . . They shall be sad people here" (Aarmo 1999, 260).

Malaysia's prime minister, Dr. Mahathir Mohamad, also has notoriously linked homosexuality to Western neo-imperialism. For example, in his speech at the United Nations in 1991 he stated, "If democracy means to carry guns, to flaunt homosexuality, to disregard the institutions of marriage, to disrupt and damage the well-being of the community in the name of individual rights, to destroy a particular faith, to have privileged institutions [the Western press] which are sacrosanct even if they indulge in lies and instigations which undermine society, the economy, and international relations; to permit foreigners to break national laws; if they are the essential details, can't the new converts opt to reject them?" (*The Nation,* July 20, 1997).

To avoid adding fuel to these aggressively antihomosexual stances, we must be precise about what we are saying is being globalized when we talk about the globalization of homosexual identities. Is it a kind of sexual desire that has been globalized? Or is it terms and labels? Or is it theories of self? Most scholars on the subject of transnational gay/lesbian identity trace the move as being from "gendered" identities (such as *kathoey, māhū,* and berdache) to sexual identities (such as gay and lesbian).

TRANSNATIONAL THAILAND

Dennis Altman has been a central figure in debates concerning transnationalism and the emergence of Western-style gay/lesbian subcultures. Altman, influenced by John D'Emilio, links these emerging subcultures with economic changes and social transformations: "There is a clear connection between the expansion of consumer society and the growth of overt lesbian/gay worlds: the expansion of the free market has also opened up possibilities for a rapid spread of the idea that (homo)sexuality is the basis for a social, political and commercial identity" (1996a, 1). According to Altman, Western forms of sexuality have spread to the rest of the world, resulting in growing subcultures based on Western archetypes: "The 'macho' gay man of the 1970's, the 'lipstick lesbian' of the 1990's, are a global phenomenon, thanks to the ability of mass media to market particular American lifestyles and appearances. One sees unmistakable signs of American lesbian/gay imagery and self-presentation in almost every part of the rich world. . . . *The Economist* is probably correct in suggesting that the very diffusion of modern homosexual identities throughout the world is part of both economic and cultural globalization" (1996a, 2). Altman's proposal of a globalization of Western homosexual culture has generated controversy as well as efforts among researchers to situate these sexual/gender forms, including Thai *tom*s and *dee*s, in a local context.

Rosalind Morris (1994) has stated that the Thai *tom* and *dee* identities (and the Thai gay male identity) are results of a fundamental shift in cultural paradigms from the Thai "traditional" system of three genders to a Western discourse that posits a sexual binary. Morris asserts that in the past (exactly when is not clear, but she draws her data from Lan Na texts that she says may be based on pre-Buddhist Thai sources), the "Thai"[1] mythic order conceived of humanity as a trinity of genders —male *(phu-chai)*, female *(phu-ying)*, and *kathoey* (intermediate sex or "third sex"). However, Morris believes that this traditional trinity of gender categories in Thailand is being supplanted by the Western conception of sexual categories of heterosexual and homosexual. Morris argues that the category of *kathoey* originally applied to either males or females who exhibited gender behavior of the opposite sex, and the classification came to be seen collectively as a "third gender." The term *"kathoey,"* says Morris, has been since incorporated into masculine homosexuality and is only infrequently used to refer to females at present. This category of masculine homosexuality has been constructed through the influence of Western discourse, which divides humanity into exclusive binary genders (masculine and feminine) and binary sexualities (heterosexual and homosexual). Morris recognizes that the preexisting Thai sex/gender order she outlines is "radically different" from the Western model of sexual categories. She also acknowledges that these two radically different systems coexist in contemporary Thailand: "The present appears to be one of those times in Thailand when different and mutually irreconcilable systems cohabit in a single social field" (1994, 19).

Morris is clearly right in pointing out that contemporary Thailand has incorporated many Western terms and concepts and that new discourses and identities have entered the Thai sex and gender order. However, the popularity of using derivations of English for new identities, found frequently throughout the world, does not mean that the new term carries the same meaning as the original English word. The choice of English words, such as "tomboy," was most likely based on associations with the processes of "modernization" or "westernization," such as industrialization and urbanization. Jillana Enteen (2001) argues persuasively that the use of English terms is a common Thai practice for creating a new word in Thai when no Thai equivalent is available. Enteen describes the historical emergence of the categories "boyfriend" and "girlfriend" to label romantic relationships that did not entail the financial commitments of "marriage," itself a relatively new concept. Thais created the word *"faen"* to label these temporary relationships, derived from the English words "friend" and "fan." Enteen (2001, 103–104) points out that the new Thai-ified word does not hold exactly the same meaning as its English referents. The West and its representative language, English, are commonly held to be synonymous with social change, and any perceived new social category will be tied symbolically to the West through the use of English terminology. Rather than assuming that terms and outward gestures have the same meanings as Western gay and lesbian identities, their local meanings must be studied.

Globalization (less charitably called cultural imperialism) has undeniably had a profound impact on political, economic, and cultural dimensions of Thai society. However, positioning *tom, dee,* and gay identities as products of Western discourse reifies the dichotomous categories of Western/local and modern/traditional and fails to capture the complexity of cultural change and gender. The case of Thai *tom*s and *dee*s and other cases from around the world compel greater attention to questions concerning the transformation of local discourses of sex and gender. How do we explain gender/sexual identities that widely use English terms as their self-referents yet stubbornly retain local paradigms of gender? What if, as in Thailand, these groups are not only members of the Western-oriented Thai middle class but also farmers, laborers, and market vendors?

Tom and *dee* identities are hybridizations of local gendered categories and emergent sexualized identities. This hybridity not only refers to the blending and interaction of cultural discourses (i.e., Western/Anglo, regional, and Thai concepts of sex and gender) but also extends to the ways in which masculinity and femininity are idealized by *tom*s and *dee*s in novel ways. The categories of masculinity and femininity, while often perceived as obvious and stable sets of characteristics or values, in actuality are imbued with contradiction and tension. The term "gendered sexualities" is used in this work to refer to the Thai constellation of gendered identity and sexuality. The Western categories of gay, lesbian, and homosexual, while having their own history of transformation and gendered meanings, are currently dominated by the notion of "sexual orientation." Sexual orientation says little about the perception of one's self as either masculine or feminine, which are the prime categories of identity within the Thai context.

*Tom*s are understood by Thais to be biological females who are sexually attracted to "women" (the term "women" in this context refers to a socially ascribed identity), and this attraction is perceived as a natural extension of *tom*s' masculine gender. Being sexually attracted to women, in itself, does not necessarily constitute a *tom* identity. *Tom*s are unlike *dee*s, who, like all other women, are referred to by Thais as "ordinary women" *(phu-ying thammada)*. *Tom*s and *dee*s are not united in a common identity based on shared sexual orientation but rather are distinguished from each other according to gender difference.

*Tom*s and *dee*s, and their visibility and recent popularity among younger women, are extensions of Thai cultural preoccupation with transgenderism. Thai fascination with transgenderism is evident in the proliferation of media images of cross-dressing males and females. The Thai media relishes informing its readers about the world of *tom*s and *dee*s and transgendered males. Television dramas routinely have transsexual/transgendered characters. Thai transgenderism has fascinated Westerners as well, with an image of a Thai male-to-female transsexual kickboxer appearing in the pages of the *New York Times*. Documentaries have been made and books have been written about Thai transgendered men, called *kathoey*s. *Kathoey* reviews and beauty pageants are popular entertainment for Thais and foreigners alike. *Tom*s, *dee*s, gays, and *kathoey*s are embedded in a cultural system in which homosexuality and transgenderism are equated.

GAY MEN AND *KATHOEYS*; LESBIANS AND *TOMS*

In Thailand, homosexuality, or being "gay," is understood by mainstream society to refer to "misgendered" *(phit-pheet)*, or effeminate, males. To many Thai people, the term "gay" refers to cross-gendered or transgendered identities or, in the very least, to an overabundance of femininity in a man. In support of this concept, current scientific theories about hormone levels or the possibility of a "gay gene" are popular topics in the Thai press. The tremendous visibility of male/transsexual *kathoey*s further supports this dominant view that the term "homosexual" is another word for *kathoey*-like people.

Given this local reality, it does not seem that Thai discourse has been much affected by globalization, if, as Altman asserts, globalization means sexualized identities replacing gendered identities. However, in Thailand there has also been a dramatic growth in numbers of masculine/gender-normative males who are involved in same-sex relations and who identify with the global concept of gayness. These men ("men" in both the social and the biological sense) are not highly visible, in that they do not match the perception that gayness equals effeminacy—they simply fall off the radar for many Thais. Jackson (1997b) argues that *"kathoey"* traditionally has referred to a kind of masculinity that was placed in opposition to "men," and thus "homosexual" encounters occurred between the feminine/transgendered *kathoey* and the gender-normative "man." The category "gay" has introduced a third possible kind of masculinity positioned between normative "men" and *kathoey*s, in that gay men are masculine yet desire other masculine men as sexual partners.

Thai gay men bear some similarity to *dee*s in that they are not particularly visible, nor do they embody the kind of "gender inversion" that marks a person as "homosexual" by mainstream society. Therefore the real transformative effect of modernity on Thai society's sex and gender order is usually invisible—homosexual gender-normative men and women. Both gays and *dee*s are linguistically marked and therefore recognized as specific categories of people who nevertheless have an ambiguous relationship to normative gender categories.

There are crucial differences between the cultural configurations of *dee*s and gay men, however. Thai gay men are keenly aware of the transnationalism of their identity. Through bars, literature, media, encounters with foreigners, and the Internet, Thai gay men are aware that they are part of a larger global community of men with the same sexual identity as they have, and it is precisely this contact that allows their own gay identities to be developed. By contrast, *dee*s are distinctly not part of this global community. *Tom*s and *dee*s both generally disdain the term "lesbian" and its sexual and homosexual connotations: "I am a *tom*. I am not a lesbian. I feel disgusted when I hear that word. It isn't good at all; I don't like it at all. Whoever hears it probably won't like it. Somebody wants to be like that? It [being a lesbian] isn't the same at all [as being a *tom*]. *Tom*s are women who are capable *(khlong-tua)*, a little bit coarse, but not acting like a man, and not sweet and gentle like a woman. *Tom*s can protect women, can show concern for and take care of *(aow-cai-sai)* women very well. This is the most important thing. There is no way a man can understand a woman as well as a *tom* can. And women who are women *(phu-ying thii pen phu-ying)*, they won't like each other either. A woman who is a woman must like a *tom*" (Chonticha 1989, 66). Another *tom* expressed disgust at the sexual connotations of the term "lesbian": "'Lesbian,' huh? It's disgusting *(kliat ca taai)*, like "hysterical" people *(phuak hysteria)*. I am a *tom*, and my partner is a *dee*. Lesbians are like women who sleep with women and can sleep with men. They care just about sex, but *tom*s and *dee*s care about feelings" (Chonticha 1989, 66). A *tom* quoted in a Thai magazine strongly opposed the term "lesbian" as a self-referent because it neglects gendered distinctions between partners: "*Tom*s aren't the same as lesbians. *Tom*s are men and [perform sexually] for women. Lesbians do it to each other. People like to think that *tom*s are lesbians, and it makes me angry. If somebody says this, I'll punch them. It's an insult" (Wiphaan 1984, 59).

An important difference between gay men and *dee*s is that *dee*s are only *dee*s in their relation to a *tom*. The masculine female gives the *dee* her identity, whereas gay men take pains to distinguish their community and identities from *kathoey* identity. Gay men form sexual identities based on their mutual attraction to other men. *Dee*s are a subset of women whose sexual desires are not particularly marked in *tom-dee* discourses of self or in mainstream society's discourses. Also, in contrast to gay men, *dee*s have an ambiguous relationship to the category "homosexual." *Tom*s, *dee*s, and people in general often see *dee*s as necessarily women who are heterosexual but have chosen *tom*s for various personal or social reasons. *Dee*s are consequently not understood by most Thais as "homosexual" in the same way that *tom*s or gays are. In this way *dee*s are similar to gender-normative men who have relations with *kathoey*s. Sexual desire is rarely mentioned by mainstream society as a reason for *dee* identity, that is, being in a relationship with a *tom*. Both mainstream commentators and *tom*s and *dee*s themselves assert that *dee*s are looking for friendship, companionship, and caring from *tom*s. In my research I rarely found a *dee* who would link sexual desire with her *dee*ness. *Tom*s were more likely to be explicit about the sexual desire of *dee*s, but even many *tom*s would avoid the sexualization of both their identities and *dee*s' identities.

The theories and images that have been developed in relation to global gay identities and their local forms are highly gendered because they are almost exclusively based on male subcultures. Larger overarching structural schemes of sex and gender, and dominant meanings of sex and gender, produce some common themes for male and female identities that need to be critically examined. For example, being homosexual is widely understood by both mainstream society and by *tom*s, gays, and *kathoey*s to be an inborn trait, as well as a source of suffering and karmic punishment for wrong deeds; however, this suffering is not associated with *dee*s. The common ground in the discursive constructions of these sex/gender categories and their structural and discursive differences are discussed in the following chapters.

THEORIES OF TRANSNATIONALISM

Dennis Altman states that the global trend is toward a transition from gender-based identities to the increasing acceptance of "sexual orientation" as the basis of identity. Altman recognizes that many societies have had intermediary or transgender identities, such as *banci* in Jakarta, *kathoey* in Thailand, *bakla* in the Philippines, and *fa'afafine* in Polynesia. These identities are used mostly by men and denote a mixed-gender, cross-gender, or transgender status. Thus, Altman concludes, these modern Western forms of the "lipstick lesbian" and the "macho gay" demonstrate the new sensibility in which sexual desire and erotic subjectivity are not rigidly tied to any particular gender identity or to the masculine/feminine binary structure. According to Altman (1996a, 3), the vehicles for Western notions of sexuality are largely the media and consumer-based lifestyles that focus on urban recreation: "With affluence comes exposure to mass media and consumerism, as well as increasing space and time to develop identities and lifestyles which go beyond the expectations of one's parents. It is perhaps symbolic that the massive shopping malls of Southeast Asia have become major meeting places for young homosexuals, both men and women, just as they are potent symbols of the ways in which mass consumerism is transforming certain social and economic relationships." Although Altman acknowledges that local patterns of sexuality and gender, as well as traditional family obligations, structure gay and lesbian identities to a greater degree than many observers, particularly the Western media, seem to recognize, he concludes by asserting that Western consumer culture is the driving force of the creation of these new identities: "Economic and cultural globalisation is creating a newly universal sense of homosexuality as the basis for identity and lifestyle, not merely for behavior" (1996a, 5).

Altman's proposition that Western styles of identity are largely responsible for the growth of these non-Western subcultures has attracted criticism from researchers who urge for more contextualized accounts of local homosexual identities. Peter Jackson (1996a, 1997b, 1997c, 1999a) has argued extensively that these new models of identity, such as "gay" in Thailand, are based on preexisting cultural patterns of transgenderism to a much greater degree than Altman acknowledges. Jackson stresses that although Western discourses of sexuality and identity are popular and widely consumed by Thai homosexual males, these discourses are "indigenized" to fit the local cultural constructions of multiple gender identities rather than adopted wholesale.

Jackson's critique has been echoed by a range of other scholars who question the degree to which Western models have affected local cultural constructions of gender and sexuality. Gary Dowsett (1996) has labeled Altman's theory of Americanized global gay culture as the "political economy model," and Jackson's as the "accommodation model." Dowsett cautions that the growth of these communities is more problematic and involves more conflict and tension than either of these models allows. Dowsett does not expand on exactly what these conflicts and tensions are in local settings, but the myriad examples of antihomosexual rhetoric in nationalist discourses in the non-West is evidence of his point that these identities have not been neatly incorporated into local sexual and gendered systems. Jackson has countered that although these transnational forms are "accommodated" to local meanings, this does not mean they are "accepted," and he gives ample analysis of antihomosexual attitudes in Thailand (Jackson 1989b, 1997a, 1997c, 1999b).

Richard Parker has called for greater inquiry into the specifics of local practices in order to get beyond generalizations of transnational theories of sexuality: "It is only by seeking to interpret the specificities of local sexual cultures as they are caught up within the cross-currents of these global processes of change that we can begin to move past a largely superficial reading of sexual similarities and differences in order to build up a more complex understanding of the vicissitudes of sexual experience in the contemporary world" (1999, 1). Tom Boellstorff's work (1999) is an excellent example of the kind of analysis that can result when simplistic divisions of "Western" (or "transnational") and "traditional" are replaced with a detailed analysis of local discourses and their histories and contexts. Boellstorff argues that the models of "sameness" versus "difference" in characterizing local gay communities distort the more complex interplay between local fantasies of Western sexuality and local patterns of gender and sexuality. Boellstorff explains that there are contradictions in the way Indonesian gay men understand themselves—they are gay and their male lovers hold both their emotional and their sexual intimacy, but marriage (to women) is a positive and desired aspect of their lives. These two contradictory assertions are maintained within their gay identity. Their gay identity is not diametrically opposed to heterosexual relationships in their discourse.

Boellstorff further complicates the dichotomy of traditional and modern by noting that the imperative to marry in Indonesia is not a primordial local remnant of "traditional culture" but rather a result of recent nationalist family-promoting policies. As such, the affirmation of family is an assertion of middle-class aspirations that the gays hold, whether they are economically middle class or not. Thus the construction of gayness in Indonesia is a product of a constellation of forces that include the prestige of the association of the concept of gayness with Western/modern affluence, the rise of the state and its pro-marriage policy, and local patterns of same-sex sexuality. The resultant form of gayness is neither a "traditional" mode of being nor an embodiment of the same meanings or lived experiences as those of Western gay men.[2]

MALE AND FEMALE GLOBAL IDENTITIES

A major shortcoming of Altman's insistence on transnational connections is the lack of recognition of the very different dynamics of male and female subcultures and identities. Gay male communities are studied as if they were gender-neutral formations, rather than as particular manifestations of male privilege. In studies of the globalization of sexual identity, the term "gender" has come to refer almost exclusively to the ways in which different males are labeled, not to the ways that being male structures the relationships of gay men to all the other social factors.

The tendency to assume that similar transnational processes apply to both males and females is unfortunately found in what are otherwise rich and fascinating case studies of local histories of transformation. For example, Richard Parker (1999) provides an illuminating case study of the processes whereby local men adopt and transform transnational discourses of gay identity within their local Brazilian context. Parker analyzes how the shift in Brazil to a new political system ruled by industrial and middle classes rather than rural-based agricultural barons, increasing urbanization and industrial labor, political repression under dictatorships, and then increased democracy have all led to conditions that promote the growth of sexual subcultures. Parker draws connections between the growing freedom found in urban areas and sexual activity outside of family scrutiny. Notably, these distinct gay communities focus on commercial and tourist areas and on public spaces such as parks, where men find sex partners and companions. The gendered use of such recreational and public space, especially nighttime entertainment zones, needs to be explored when analyzing the creation of male or female subcultures. Parker provides no analysis of how women and men are articulated differently into this system of commercial entertainment and how the resulting male identities and labels of "gay," *"travesti," "entendido,"* and *"michê"* are based on specifically male models of identity and male opportunity.

Likewise, in Thailand there is a need to explore the specific histories and contexts of female communities and identities before coming to conclusions about the role of transnationalism in new female identities. In Thailand the growth of urban commercial recreation spots, such as bars, clubs, and other public spaces, has been important for the development of "gay" as a local identity. However, Thai women have different patterns of socializing and attending public or recreational venues. Members of female sexual/gendered subcultures socialize in ways consistent with women's socializing in general in their societies. For example, women's subcultures tend to be much less commercialized than are male subcultures. Furthermore, the female transgender and homosexual community in Thailand has its own history and discursive constructions. Norms that structure attitudes toward "proper" female sexual heterosexuality affect the way female homosexual activities are greeted.

When discussing transnational identities, class is also an important factor in determining who has access to recreational zones, travel experiences, foreign media, or other trajectories of Western discourses. For example, Alison Murray (1999) examines how class affects the way Indonesian women experience being "lesbian." Murray argues that upper-class Indonesian women have greater exposure to international gay and lesbian culture and therefore have greater opportunity to develop a "lesbian" identity. Murray's point that class dictates access to transnational discourses reflects the realities of Thai women as well, because only a few elite women have engaged in the kinds of transnational communities and discourses that seem to characterize urban "gay" male communities to a much greater degree. In contrast, Thai *tom*s and *dee*s are notably a cross-class phenomenon. The discourses that define and structure *tom* and *dee* identities, such as discourses of gender, do not depend on access to English or other modes of transnationalism.

The binary of Thai/Western as a descriptive categorization of sexual and gender forms fails to account for these complex interactions between local understandings of sex and gender, and economic and social transformations brought about by intense interaction with Western or global forces. To capture this complex process, I apply the concept of hybridity, as currently used in the social sciences and influenced by postcolonial theory.

HYBRIDITY

By challenging static or essentialist notions of identity, postcolonial theorists such as Homi Bhabha have encouraged critical analysis of the dynamics of power in the construction of identities, whether they be national, ethnic, or other kinds of identification. Bhabha (1994) asserts that although identities are formed in the matrix of power relations, an ambivalence inherent within them compels their continual reassertion and re-presentation. Bhabha explains that identity—and the stereotypes that support it—depends on a sense of rigidity and permanence and, in contrast, is accompanied by the anxious need to reassert and repeat stereotypical images. These essentialist stereotypes (about racial or national characteristics, for example) simultaneously "need no proof," because of their constructions as natural, and they are not provable through discourse (1994, 66). This ambivalence fuels the dynamic of the continual reenactments of self and other. Thus, for Bhabha, identity is "hybrid" in that it is an unstable assertion of difference dependent on the continual reenactment of oppositional categories.

The concept of hybridity is useful in this study in that it allows the reevaluation of binary assertions and essentialist dichotomies that pertain to the understanding of *tom*s and *dee*s in Thailand. Such persistent binaries include Western/traditional and masculine/feminine. The popularity of the concept of hybridity is due to its use in the analysis of cultural change as an alternative to theories such as "modernization" or nationalist theories that contrast national or ethnic identity with the cultural loss associated with the problematic notion of "westernization." The term "hybrid" originally derived from biological notions of mixed breeds or species and has an infamous history in its use in the social Darwinian debates of race in the nineteenth century and in the field of eugenics in the twentieth century. The concept has since been "rehabilitated" within the social sciences to refer to complex processes of social and cultural interaction.

Robert Young (1995) has noted that, given the long process of cultural interchange, it is surprising how few models there have been for analyzing it within social science and cultural criticism. Young observes that the contradictory and varied results of cultural interaction have largely been left undertheorized, and it is to this lacuna that interest in the notion of hybridity owes its current popularity, despite its unsettling earlier associations with racism and colonialism.

According to Young, historically the two major realms in which cross-cultural interaction have been of sociological interest, and in which the notion of hybridity has been developed, are language and sex: "Both [language and sex] produced what were regarded as 'hybrid' forms (creole, pidgin and miscegenated children), which were seen to embody threatening forms of perversion and degeneration and became the basis for endless metaphoric extension in the racial discourse and social commentary" (1995, 5). It is this dual reference to both sexuality and language that makes the concept of hybridity particularly relevant for the study of *tom*s and *dee*s. The use of English ("tomboy" and "lady") to label these new sexual/gender forms is what marks them as ambivalent and ambiguous cultural forms, somehow both Thai and foreign. As Young has stressed, sex has become the primary site for the struggle over the meaning of cultural interactions, for it is either literally or metaphorically the site where the hybrid offspring originates.

In order to use the concept of hybridity to explore contemporary social phenomena, it is necessary to clarify how the use of the term now differs from its ignominious past. During the nineteenth and twentieth centuries, hybridity became a key concept to justify the ordering of colonial and slave societies in which race was the primary category of distinction. Arguing that hybrid offspring of interracial unions were inferior and ultimately dangerous, colonial regimes and promoters of race segregation asserted that racial distinction was necessary and "natural." Within these regimes, the regulation of sex and the offspring of interracial unions became the primary site of debates over the legitimacy of racial categories (Young 1995, 5). For example, the idea that Africans were of a separate species and thereby suitable as slaves for other "races" depended on the biological definition of "species" and "hybrid"—two members of separate species could not produce a fertile offspring. However, the obvious fact that interracial couples did have fertile offspring was a problem for the "species" argument for the separation of races and slave society. Thus in 1864 the term "miscegenation" was invented to describe the "fertile fusion and merging of races" (Young 1995, 9). The term "degeneration" was also applied to the offspring of interracial unions, meaning that these offspring were of inferior genetic quality, the effects of which might not be noticeable for several generations.

Recently, the term "hybrid" has been disassociated with these racial theories and reclaimed. "Hybridity" is now variously used to invoke a sense of "fusion and assimilation" (Young 1995, 18), as in the coming together of diverse elements to make a new type, or a sense of "contra-fusion and disjunction," as in the degeneration of pure species or types into intermediate types. Thus the concept of hybridity can now be used to portray new, diverse cultural constructions composed of various influences. However, within this model, it is possible to see the sources of a hybrid as "original" or pure types, which became adulterated in the process of intermixture. This way of understanding hybridity ironically reproduces notions of pure cultural essences. For example, arguing that interracial mixture produces hybrid offspring implies that "black" and "white" races are self-evident homogenous entities. Young argues that in the context of identity politics it is necessary to recognize that these supposed pure essences, such as "races," are themselves hybrids, products of dialectical forces that are often presented as pure forms.

Recognizing these contradictory dimensions to the concept of hybridity, Mikhail Bakhtin (1981) introduced the notion of a "double form of hybridity," in which hybridity is divided into "organic" and "intentional" types. Although Bakhtin originally proposed this notion in the analysis of language, it has been used in the study of culture and society and, according to Pnina Werbner (1997, 4–5), is a way of recognizing the lack of essential purity of cultures, as well as their inherently mixed characteristics: "Despite the illusion of boundedness, cultures evolve historically through unreflective borrowings, mimetic appropriations, exchanges and inventions. There is no culture in and of itself." Organic hybridity is a kind of fusion in which disparate elements are brought into a dialectically produced new whole that is at the same time not a "pure" embodiment of any original form. Bakhtin asserts that intentional hybridity, on the other hand, is a politicized positioning of differences against each other, thereby creating the illusion of essential identities or cultures that can be placed in opposition to each other. Therefore, the concept of hybridity contains the discrepant modern tendencies of both increased borrowing and blending, and increased reification and essentializing of ethnic, sexual, and national identities as "authentic" forms. Werbner explains that the Bakhtinian model of cultural interchange dissolves the polarity of hybrid, or mixed, forms versus pure forms, because neither is prior to the other, and both are products of cultural interchange.

Contemporary Thai society is a prime example of these dichotomous processes of "double hybridity"; nationalist culture is promoting a kind of Thai identity and essence that has successfully, for the most part, submerged diverse regional and ethnic affiliations. Thailand has also engaged in an active process of "modernization" in which Western forms of government and administration have been appropriated and transformed into "Thai" forms (here the term "Thai" refers to a conscious product of nationalist discourses). Thailand's open economy and role as a world tourist site also mark it as a particularly appropriate site for the study of cultural interaction and exchange.

The term "hybridity" will be used here to indicate cultural fusions, productions, and reproductions, with varying degrees of deliberateness, of varied cultural discourses into new forms in a dialectical fashion. Young's working definition of "hybridization" is useful: "Hybridization as creolization involves fusion, the creation of a new form, which can then be set against the old form, of which it is partly made up" (1995, 25). A cautionary note is needed here to avoid simply replicating the essentialist binaries that theories of hybridity are trying to transcend. "Hybridity" here does not mean the blending of self-evident "pure" categories that are then transformed into a new form. Rather, it means the process by which competing identities are formed in relation to each other, with each dependent on the other for its own identity, unstable and fractured as these identities may be. Rather than presenting a "traditional" Thai essence that has become transformed through interaction with the West (a replication of Orientalist themes), both Thai tradition and the West/modernity are discursive constructions implied in each other.

Thus new cultural forms are neither implants from the West or elsewhere, nor are they long-enduring cultural entities. *Tom*s and *dee*s are products of intense cultural interaction and exchange and are simultaneously unquestionably Thai. They are composed and understood as consistent with local meaning systems, and they are also products of the complex cultural interactions that have produced the Thai state and its nationalist culture. *Tom*s and *dee*s are new in that there were no such categories exactly like them in the past, although the basic components —female masculinity and recognized forms of female homosexuality— were there.

"Hybridity" has an additional meaning in this work as well. Not only does it refer to mutually constitutive interactions between cultural groups, but, perhaps even more importantly, it contains the idea of the inherent ambivalence of gender itself. Terms like "transgender" and "cross-gender" imply the mixing or crossing over of two reified attributes—masculinity and femininity. These terms assume that a coherent gender exists and is transcended, rather than reflect the process whereby nodes of masculinity and femininity are created and consequently contested, manipulated, and transformed. The idea that masculinity and femininity are self-evident entities (albeit culturally varied) that can be blended, leading to a third gender, reinforces the essentialist binaries that contemporary theorists are trying to deconstruct.

TRANSGENDER, CROSS-GENDER, OR HOMOSEXUAL?

The discursive distinction made between "gender" and "sexuality" is a particular phenomenon of the modern West (see Foucault 1978). In many parts of the world, the central social identity of people depends on their gender, and their sexual behavior is understood as a logical extension of that gender. Within local meanings systems, males who hold a feminine identity are presumed to desire men as romantic/sexual partners. Numerous examples of these "third-gender" or "transgender" identities for males, who are presumed to be sexually involved with normative masculine men, have been compiled in the anthropological literature, such as Robert Levy's study (1973) of the *māhū* role in Tahiti, Deborah Amory's study (1998) of the *mashoga* in eastern Africa, Unni Wikan's study (1991) of the *xanith* in Oman, and Mark Johnson's study

(1997, 1998) of the *bantut* in the Philippines, to name a few prominent examples.

The literature on male homosexuality and transgenderism in Latin America provides repeated examples of this pattern, in which local cultural discourses distinguish the male sexual partners from each other based on presumed gender differences (Adam 1993; D. Bao 1993; Carrier 1985; Epps 1995; Goldstein 1994, 2003; Green 1999; Kulick 1998; R. Parker 1999; Prieur 1998). These studies describe a similar scenario of male homosexuality—males who take the "passive" role sexually and are penetrated *(passivos)* are considered in mainstream society as feminine and, by extension, homosexual, whereas their sexual partners *(activos)* are considered masculine and therefore are not stigmatized as homosexual. As with the cross-cultural examples of transgenderism listed above, in the Latin American context one factor in constructing masculinity (making a "man") is sexual dominance (symbolized through the act of sexual insertion), which can be performed with a feminine partner who can be either male or female. Although actual sexual behavior may vary considerably depending on the couple, the dominant discourse in these societies constructs binaries, such as feminine/masculine, homosexual/man, and *passivos/activos*, within which male homosexual relations are understood. This pattern of labeling the effeminate male as homosexual, distinguishing him from gender-normative "men," is widespread in areas of Latin America, but it is also part of sex/gender orders in other parts of the world as well, including Thailand. In these societies, masculine-normative men, engaging in same-sex eroticism, cannot be easily accommodated in Western categories of "homosexual" or "heterosexual." Even the category "bisexual" fails to account for the primacy of their masculinity in their social identity—within local meanings systems these men are defined according to their masculine gender, not the sexed bodies of their partners. "Gay" identity has been appropriated by local males in these areas partly as a rejection of the cultural logic in which male homosexuality is linked to male effeminacy. However, gay identity is embedded in the local cultural understandings of passive/active *(passivo/activo)* and masculine/feminine, and mainstream society may not make the same distinctions that gay men often insist on between gay men and transgendered males (see Jackson 1995, 1997b; R. Parker 1999).

The anthropological literature gives us much less information on female homosexual and transgender communities. However, based on the relatively scant information collected so far, it appears that similar gender pairings occur or have occurred, in which masculine females are paired with gender-normative women. Two cases in the anthropological literature stand out regarding the social roles of transgendered females—the practice of female-female marriage in Africa and the case of the berdache of North American native cultures. In general the African institutions of female-female marriages are ways for both married and unmarried older women who have not had a child, particularly a son, to acquire an heir (Carrier and Murray 1998; Krige 1974; Oboler 1980; O'Brien 1977). The younger woman married to the older "husband" will be expected to provide children (through an arranged encounter with a selected man) for the older woman. Researchers have noted that these relationships are not primarily sexual but are formal kinship relationships. Also, these older women do not take other masculine social roles outside of their status as "husband" (see also Murray and Roscoe 1998). However, Saskia Wieringa notes that homosexual women might also have utilized these relationships and therefore we should not assume all female husbands are restricted to formal kinship arrangements (Blackwood and Wieringa 1999, 5). Thus the case of African female-female marriages is ambiguous and does not seem to indicate the existence of a category of female masculinity that can provide a comprehensive social identity.

The Native American berdache was a more integrated and complete appropriation of a masculine social role for females. By examining early ethnographies, Evelyn Blackwood (1984) convincingly argues that the practice of females appropriating masculine gender roles was widespread among North American native cultural groups.[3] Unlike Europeans who strictly enforced gendered differences based on the physical body, these Native American groups allowed a culturally approved masculine role for females who expressed a proclivity toward masculine-defined activities.[4] Rituals recognizing the female berdache's masculine status were found in some societies, as was socially sanctioned marriage to women. Clothing, body decorations, duties, social roles, and subsistence tasks were in accordance to the berdache's masculine status.[5] Blackwood argues that a berdache and her feminine marriage partner were known to have sexual relations (1984, 35). From Blackwood's evidence, it appears that women who were not part of the masculine/feminine binary (masculine berdache/feminine woman) did not engage in socially recognized sexual relationships. In other words, masculine berdaches did not marry other berdaches. Feminine women married masculine partners, either berdaches or men. Similar to the examples of male homosexuality in Latin America, the gender-normative partner—in this case, the feminine woman—was not marked as "homosexual" or stigmatized.

If we shift attention away from transgenderism and focus on same-sex erotics, we find patterns of female homosexuality that are not structured by the masculine/feminine binary. The most in-depth collection of studies of contemporary female same-sex eroticism is Evelyn Blackwood and Saskia Wieringa's edited volume, *Female Desires: Same-Sex Relations and Transgender Practices across Cultures* (1999). One important theme to emerge from this volume is that same-sex sexual practices do not always or necessarily indicate a gender or sexual "identity." For example, Gloria Wekker (1999) presents her study of working-class Creole women in Paramaribo, Suriname, and the practice of *mati* work. *Mati* work refers to the sexual relationships between women, many of whom also have children and have ongoing relationships with men. *Mati* work is a kind of activity and not an identity. No particular stigma is attached to *mati* work, and Wekker suggests that it has been practiced for at least the past century and probably much longer. Wekker argues that these sexual practices are not constitutive of an identity—neither a gender identity (e.g., berdache) nor a sexual identity (e.g., lesbian).[6]

HYBRID IDENTITIES

Niko Besnier (1993, 2002) and Deborah Elliston (1999) have explored the existence in Polynesian societies of a complex web of pre-existing third-gender categories, as well as newer hybrid identities based on both sexuality and gender. Besnier (1993) lists the range of terms and linguistic borrowings for "gender-liminal" men, such as the Samoan term *"fa'afafine,"* and the contemporary Tonga terms *"fakaleiti"* (*"lieti"* is derived from the English word "lady") and *"fakafefine."* Although Besnier focuses on gender-liminal men, he notes that gender-liminal women are known and are called *fakatangata* in Tongan and *fa'atama* in Samoan. According to Elliston, the Tahitian traditional third-gender category of *māhū* coexists with the newer sexualized identities of *raerae* and *petea*. French terms are also used, such as *"lesbienne"* and *"travesti."* Although same-sex sexuality is implied in the newer terms for identity, they are still based on gender identity—for example, a *raerae* is a feminine male who is presumed to be sexually attracted to a normative masculine male (Elliston 1999). Studying mostly males, Besnier asserts that what makes a male fall into one of these categories is not his sexual behavior per se but his association with the social role of women. *Fakaleiti* and *māhū* are known to do women's work, such as domestic chores and, more recently, clerical work, demonstrating the flexibility of traditional categories to incorporate contemporary cultural models, such as "pink-collar" work, in their traditional formations of gender.

Like Thailand, Taiwan has experienced the recent growth and development of a female same-sex subculture in which women are paired into masculine and feminine identities. Antonia Chao (1999) has studied these *T* and *po* identities of women in Taiwan. Like the Thai word *"tom,"* the term *"T"* is derived from the English word "tomboy," and *"po"* is derived from the Chinese term for "wife." These masculine women are presumed to be homosexual and are expected to pair off with feminine women called *pos*. The gender-neutral term *"bu-fen"* has been introduced by a Taiwanese feminist organization but has not been widely adopted by Taiwanese women. Taiwanese *T*s and *po*s slightly predate Thai *tom*s and *dee*s, emerging in the 1960s and gaining widespread popularity in the 1980s.

Blackwood (1999) describes a similar gendered subculture of women in contemporary western Sumatra in which English has been used by locals to refer to the newer constellation of sex/gender meanings. Masculine women are called *lesbi* (derived from the English term "lesbian") or *tomboi* (derived from the English word "tomboy"). Like Thai *dee*s, the feminine partners of *tomboi*s are not discursively distinct from women in general and often have had previous relationships with men or find male partners after the end of a relationship with a *tomboi*. The use of English in the creation of local terms, such as *T, tomboi,* and *lesbi*, raises complex questions about the relationships among Western cultural forms, transnational movements, and local cultural change.

New subcultures and identities, such as the *T,* the *tomboi,* and the *fakaleiti,* demonstrate that "traditional" and "modern," and "local" and "global," are not clearly defined, mutually exclusive categories. Lenore Manderson and Margaret Jolly (1997) argue for the need to avoid simplistic assumptions of sameness or difference in relation to the West when studying gender and sexuality transnationally. If difference (from the West) is emphasized, the subject is exoticized and positioned as "other" in an Orientalist-like discourse. Conversely, if sameness (with the West) is emphasized, historical and social processes are often ignored or simplified. Manderson and Jolly believe that the either/or approach misses the actual complexity of sexuality and gender. Border crossings, erotic imaginings, colonialism, and cultural intersections all influence and structure the emergence of sexual and gender forms. Rather than choosing a particular culture as a bounded contiguous unit or choosing a kind of sexuality as a preconditioned subject (such as "homosexuality"), Manderson and Jolly use the concept of "sites of desire" as their analytical unit. They explore those points of crossing—those moments of interaction when a gendered or sexual form emerges within cultural, social, economic, and political contexts. Migration, tourism, and erotic imaginings of foreign others all produce sites of cultural hybridity that cannot be simplistically categorized as either transnational/Western or local/traditional. Analysis of these newer gendered and sexual identities in non-Western settings requires a careful reflection on the issues of the nature of cultural interaction and "westernization."

In discussing these complex constellations of sexuality and gender, terminology becomes a problem. Kath Weston argues for an inclusive term that recognizes the multiplicity of possible sex/gender orders: "To cross genders is to move from one to the other of two fixed positions; to engage in transgendering opens up as many possibilities as there are gender categories" (1993, 354). "Transgendering" can thus be understood to indicate transcending normative models of the man/woman binary. However, the degree to which these identities, or social categories, escape the binary and constitute a "third sex/gender" is unclear. Western studies of sexuality currently tend to label forms of non-normative gender as "third gender" in order to destabilize the entrenched Western sexual ideology of two exclusive genders. Weston (1993, 354) has identified this labeling conundrum: "Scholars remain unclear about what makes a particular classification qualify as a discrete gender. At what point does *berdache* stop being an instance of gendered ambiguity, or a variant of masculinity or femininity, and start becoming a gender in its own right?" There does not yet seem to be any consensus on what terms should be used to describe particular phenomena, and a degree of confusion over categories remains; what was once described as "cross-gender" (e.g., Blackwood 1984) may now be termed "third-gender" (e.g., Roscoe 1993) or "transgender" or "gender-variant" (e.g., Bolin 1993). Will Roscoe (1993) has provided a cogent argument for recognizing distinct third-gender categories in his work on the North

American berdache. Roscoe asserts that the berdache is a "third gender" that is not perceived as a crossing between two distinct and mutually exclusive genders ("cross-gendering") or as a blending of two genders ("transgenderism"). However, there seems to be no way to explain or describe berdaches without resorting to the masculine/feminine binary —there simply is no language to capture the gender of a third gender other than the language of the dual masculine/feminine gender system.

Currently in the West, particularly in the United States, "transgenderism" is a word that is commonly preferred as a self-referent by individuals who are intersexed in a physical sense (what is technically called hermaphroditism) or by individuals who feel that their sexed body does not reflect their gender identity. "Transgendered" is an increasingly popular alternative to "transsexual" in these Western communities as a term of self-referent because it rejects essentialist notions that there are only two "correct" genders and only two acceptable forms of the sexed body.[7] For the present study, I did not collect medical information on the physical status of the transgendered women I interviewed and therefore do not know if any of them would be labeled as "intersexed" according to Western medical standards based on external genitalia, reproductive organs, and chromosomes. Unlike many males in Thai society, Thai *tom*s did not express a desire to alter their bodies surgically, even though Thailand is a world center of male-female sex reassignment surgery. Therefore, in this study the term "transgendered" should not be taken to mean transsexual or hermaphroditic in the physical sense.

Given Roscoe's influential distinction, I refer to *tom*s as "transgendered" in that they both appropriate and transform normative discourses of gender. The term "transgendered," as used here, reflects the hybridity of these gender categories in that it problematizes the assumed naturalness of masculine and feminine as distinct self-evident categories. Weston (1993) describes two different approaches to the study of non-normative gender. One approach examines the gender categories that fall outside of the man/woman binary, specifically "third sex/gender" categories (e.g., Herdt 1993; Roscoe 1988, 1991). The other approach examines the variety and subtle distinctions within gender categories (Weston 1993, 354). The latter approach would best describe the present work and embody the sense of hybridity used here. *Tom*s are an extension and manipulation of both masculine and feminine genders that must be understood within the context of the sometimes overlapping categories of *dee,* "ordinary woman," *tom,* and "man." Don Kulick's work (1998) on *travestis* in Brazil perhaps best illustrates the possibilities of understanding gender and sexuality as hybrids that transcend simplistic Western labels of either "homosexual" or "transgender."

According to Kulick (1998), *travestis* are males in urban Brazil who simultaneously embody femininity and reject femaleness. They could be described as "transgendered" in anthropological literature because they have a feminine outer appearance, such as their clothes and use of makeup. However, the *travestis* say they are feminine in order to attract masculine lovers, not because they are feminine, or women, in some inner personal sense. Their male lovers engage in an obvious fantasy that these *travestis* are "real women" so they can deny their own homosexuality, according to the *travestis*. The *travestis* value their male bodies as indicators of their perceived innate superiority to women, but they acknowledge that men prefer female bodies for sex. The *travestis'* male bodies allow them to transcend the gender binary by being both receptors and inserters sexually, embodying through the sex act the symbolic markers of femininity and masculinity. Their feminine gender is a strategy deployed in service to their homosexuality, according to Kulick.

Kulick's study alerts us to the inadequacy of simplistic assertions that transgenderism is the result of a desire to "cross genders." The *travestis'* femininity is not an attempt to achieve "normative" femininity or female status, nor is it a rejection of masculinity and maleness. Kulick's account of this transgenderism is useful to bear in mind as we explore the transgenderism of Thai *tom*s, with their simultaneous appropriation and rejection of masculinity, and the ambiguous category of *dee* as "ordinary woman."

Gender and Sexual Transitions

2

*T*OM AND *DEE* identities are new Thai cultural categories, but they share similarities with local traditions in which female masculinity and female same-sex sexuality have been recognized and practiced. The transformation and persistence of gender and sexual norms formed the social context for the emergence of *tom* and *dee* identities as recognizable cultural categories in the 1980s. However, social change in Thailand in a tricky topic. To avoid replicating tired clichés about westernization and loss of Thai tradition, an examination of approaches to the topic of sociocultural change is necessary.

In both popular and academic discourse in Thailand, there is a strong tendency to position cultural change as a recent phenomenon resulting from westernization. Thai cultural tradition is typically rendered a timeless, bounded entity that has been penetrated and corrupted by a powerful alien force. This force is labeled "the West" but is largely left undefined as an amorphous signifier of the foreign otherness. In this pervasive discourse, the concept of social change in Thailand is telescoped down to a singular event—contact with the West—so that all change is reduced to a reaction to Western powers. For many Thais, the emergence of new forms of sexual and gender identity, embodied in *tom*, *dee*, and gay identities, has become emblematic of this perceived effect of Western values and culture on Thai society. Thais have frequently associated homosexuality in general, and *tom-dee*ism in particular, with vaguely defined "materialism," loss of Thai tradition, and adoption of Western values. For example, in a magazine article about the new phenomenon of *tom-dee* and *gay* identities, Parliament member Suthas Ngernmeun associated homosexuality with modern materialism: "People who take responsibility for the country overvalue the importance of material things. . . . They don't value spiritual things and the culture of the people. Therefore the problem of homosexuality has increasingly spread all over. It is a problem the whole world is experiencing these days" ("From Gay to *Tom-Dee*," 24). A discursive structure in which a traditional pure Thai culture is positioned against a corrupting West is so dominant in discussing social change in Thailand that it becomes difficult to discuss social transformations without repeating this binary of the West as opposed to an "authentic Thai-ness."

An alternative model for understanding social change relies on the concept of hybridity. Robert Young (1995) recognizes the dual manner in which identities (cultural, national, or sexual, for example) are established and solidified; he asserts that they are preexisting, eternal, and self-evident categories. In other words, "Thai-ness" is created through its discursive positioning as a timeless and coherent social entity. Therefore the emergence of transformations in local praxis (the lived embodiment of meanings systems) of sexual/gender norms and discourse is not a moving away from an authentic Thai tradition but a part of the evolution and production of Thai-ness itself.

While striving to resist the dominant binary of the West versus Thailand, I will explore the emergence of *tom* and *dee* identities by tracing points of historical continuity in discourses of sexuality and gender in the Thai context. My aim is to provide a sensible context for the changing sex/gender categories and identities that are being witnessed in contemporary Thailand. The emergence of *tom* and *dee* identities is contextualized within socioeconomic changes over the past three decades; interviews with people sixty-five to eighty-seven years old demonstrate that Thais have recognized both female masculinity and female same-sex sexuality before *tom* and *dee* identities came on the Thai scene. In addition, Thai scholars have located references in Thai discourse to female same-sex sexuality *(len pheuan)* that date back to the eighteenth century (Anake 1999; Kittisak 1993).

Socioeconomic changes in Thailand in the past three decades have created the social space necessary for the preexisting understandings of sexuality and gender in Thailand to become transformed into *tom* and *dee* identities. Women's ability to develop relationships and communities outside the setting of their families has allowed additional sexual experiences to occur and relationships to develop. Availability of employment away from the family setting has provided the economic and social space necessary for women to find alternatives to marriage and motherhood, to embrace masculine identities and same-sex relationships, and to form communities around these identities and relationships. *Tom* and *dee* identities became possible because of a constellation of these socioeconomic changes and long-standing local traditions.

FEMALE SAME-SEX SEXUALITY: *LEN PHEUAN*

The available historical record on female same-sex sexuality and transgenderism in Thailand is sketchy, largely based on documents of the royal courts. These scattered sources show that female same-sex sexuality was a recognizable phenomenon in the palace communities of concubines. The Thai term for female same-sex sexual behavior—*"len pheuan"*—predates the Western category of homosexual, which has been dated to the late nineteenth century. According to Kittisak Prokati (1993, 90), a law historian, the term *"len pheuan,"* or "playing [with] friends," dates to the Ayuthaya period (1350–1767), when King Borommatrailokanat issued a law forbidding concubines from *len pheuan*: "Any woman having sex with another woman like a man has sex with a woman will be punished by being whipped fifty times [and will] be tattooed on the neck and paraded around the palace."[1] Further written evidence that *len pheuan* was a widely known concept in royal circles is a letter from Rama IV to his royal children in 1856 in which he warned them not to violate proper behavior. For males, the king warned against smoking opium and fraternizing with "bad women." For females, the king warned against *len pheuan* (Anake 1999, 41; Kittisak 1993, 90). Both Kittisak Prokati and Anake Nawigamune conclude that if the king mentioned *len pheuan* in a formal letter, it must have been a well-known practice.

Tamara Loos (n.d.a) demonstrates that in a palace oath of loyalty, concubines swore to refrain from all sexual infractions, including *len pheuan*. Such prohibitions against female same-sex sexuality in the Siamese royal court were part of a larger effort to control the loyalty of the king's court and to maintain political alliances that were established through marriages; therefore all illicit sexuality was forbidden to the concubines. Loos asserts that the prohibition against *len pheuan* should not be considered statements about "homosexuality" or even female same-sex behavior in general. Rather, these admonitions and prohibitions were embedded in a politics of alliances and loyalty involving persons in palace circles and were not discourses of sexual repression or sexual "deviance."[2]

Another historical source that acknowledged the presence of *len pheuan* is the epic poems of the famous Thai poet Sunthorn Phu (1786–1855), who wrote most of his work during the reigns of Rama II and Rama III. His classic work *Pra-aphaimanee* includes a story of *len pheuan* in his make-believe city of Romacak. Sunthorn Phu uses the term *"nak-leng-pheuan"* to refer to the concubines. *"Nak-leng"* means "expert," and so the phrase *"nak-leng-pheuan"* means "someone expert at *len pheuan*" (Kittisak 1993, 90–91). The poem tells of concubines seducing women from another kingdom, called Karaweek, who did not know about *len pheuan* before. Afterward, however, the women from Karaweek were so impressed with the *len pheuan* of the concubines that they refused the advances of all young men. At the end of the poem Sunthorn Phu says, perhaps sarcastically: "In our city we have never had *len pheuan,* so do not go crazy and fall for it, for it is not the real thing. The women of Romacak and Karaweek had the scandalous passion and competed with each other over lovers" (Kittisak 1993, 90–91).

Historical mention of female same-sex sexuality can also be found in an epic poem written in the court of Rama III (1824–1851) that

Concubines touching each other in a sexual manner, referred to as *len pheuan*. Wat Khongkharam, Ratchaburi Province.

Photo by Matthana Chetamee.

Palace concubines in sexual poses with each other. Wat Khong Kharam, Ratchaburi Province.
Photo by Matthana Chetamee.

Palace concubines being punished for the sexual transgression of *len pheuan*. Wat Khongkharam, Ratchaburi Province.
Photo by Matthana Chetamee.

describes *len pheuan* among concubines. The poem, *Morm Pet Sawan,* was written in 1841 by Khun Sawan, a female servant of Rama III's ailing daughter).[3] The poem is based on historical figures, and the anecdotes about the concubine Morm Pet Sawan are most likely intended as comic relief to the tragic story of the chronically ill princess. The poem describes the romantic relationship between Morm Kham (teasingly called Morm Pet Sawan, or "heavenly duck," referring to her waddle as she walked) and Morm Sut, older widowed concubines of a son of Rama I who became servants to this princess when the prince died. The poet wrote that one night, after reading to the princess and thinking that she was asleep, Morm Sut put out the candle, took a blanket, and put it over herself and Morm Kham, who was sleeping at the feet of the princess. But the princess was not asleep; she saw their lovemaking and gave Morm Sut a new nickname, "Morm Mong" (masked one).[4] The story of Morm Pet Sawan and Morm Sut was written as an inside joke for palace residents and most probably aimed to entertain its elite readers with a comic portrayal of older female lovers. The poem also may hold some insights into how female same-sex relations were perceived at that time.

The two protagonists are subtly portrayed as a gendered couple. Morm Sut is described as having typically masculine attributes. For example, the poet tells the reader that Morm Sut "speaks loudly without fear" (*fii paak dii,* p. 8) and is so skillful in her joking banter that even the male teachers could not outperform her.[5] In traditional Thai society, skill in witty banter is linked to a man's ability to seduce and impress women (see Klausner 1987 and Lyttleton 1999). Morm Sut is also described as sharp-witted and clever and "reads fluently like a man" (*nangseu thai arn-khlong-thamnorng chai).* She gently chucks the chin (*chorn-khang*) of Morm Pet Sawan, who sits on Morm Sut's lap (p. 8). The poet refers to Morm Pet Sawan in a feminine diminutive, "little Bet" (*morm pet noi,* p. 12), while Morm Sut is called "older sibling" (*phii*), mirroring terms used between male and female lovers. Morm Pet Sawan is also described as acting in a fawning manner (*sam-oi orsor palor,* p. 12), evoking a stereotypical image of passive and flirtatious femininity. These descriptive phrases used by the author set up binary of "active" masculinity and "passive" femininity familiar to modern Thais and perhaps demonstrate that gendered female couples have been part of the imaginary landscape in Thai discourse before this century.

Visual images of concubine *len pheuan* can be found in the temple mural, approximately two hundred years old, at Wat Khongkharam, Ratchaburi Province (Napat and Gordon 1999). The mural includes scenes of palace life, such as daily activities of servants, royalty, and war slaves. Several scenes depict women being punished for *len pheuan* in the palace, including being held in cages suspended from the ceiling. There are also scenes of women surreptitiously flirting with each other, with hands on each other's breasts, a sign of sexual intimacy.

Len pheuan is distinct from *tom-dee*ism in that len pheuan is a description of a sexual behavior and is not an identity. However, its presence in the Thai vocabulary and its depiction visually demonstrate that female same-sex sexuality has been a recognizable entity within Thai discourse for at least several hundred years. The historical records are largely limited to royal sources, so the lives of ordinary people and the discursive fields through which they perceived the world are largely absent from the historical record.

FEMALE MASCULINITY

Until twenty-five years ago there was no explicit category for female masculinity in Thailand, such as *tom*, but some women were understood to be "like men."[6] As one Anjaree member wrote in a letter to *Anjareesaan,* "I was a *tom* before there was the word *tom*." These masculine women were also understood to be sexually involved with other women. Elderly men and women whom I interviewed discussed masculine women and female same-sex relationships of the past, making little distinction between contemporary *tom*s and these older women.

Ing was a seventy-eight-year-old woman who spent the first fifty-eight years of her life in a rural village in Ayuthaya, a province eighty miles north of Bangkok. She moved to Bangkok to live with relatives about twenty years ago and, at the time of the interview, worked selling snacks on a street corner near my house in Bangkok. Ing described a male-identified woman, whom she called Naa Jian, in her village when Ing was a teenager (approximately seventy years ago). Ing called the masculine woman Naa Jian, and her "wife" Ee Iat. "Naa" means male or female younger maternal sibling and can be translated as either "aunt" or "uncle." In this case it is best translated as "uncle." "Ee" is used before women's names. "Ai" is used before men's names, and Ing referred to her relative as Naa Jian but called her Ai Jian when remembering what other people said about her. Ing described Naa Jian as "like a man" and as being a respected member of the community. Ing recalled Naa Jian's relationship with Ee Iat:

> If Naa Jian were a man, he would have children and grandchildren by now because these two were together for so long. They were together like husband and wife, like that. Nobody could flirt with Ee Iat, because Naa Jian would get angry. If Naa Jian was angry, she would drink alcohol. She could drink a lot, but she didn't get drunk. Naa Jian is the one who supported them. Ee Iat was a housewife and cook. They were together until I was over forty years old. At first they had a houseboat together. Then they had a big house and a rice field together. Then Ee Iat's nephew asked Ee Iat to go and live with him in another district for company. Naa Jian almost cried herself to death. Naa Jian said, "This house is for us to live in together. If you're going to leave, this land and house are mine. If you want to go, you just take yourself and get out of here." Naa Jian gave Ee Iat fifty thousand baht, and Naa Jian said, "Okay, now we're broken up. You don't need to come back anymore. If I die, I'll give all the rest of my property to the temple." Later Ee Iat came back to find Naa Jian, but Naa Jian didn't take her back and said she didn't mind being alone.

Naa Jian was "like a man," according to Ing: "She had breasts, but her mannerisms were like a man's. Before this, Naa Jian had a husband, but no children. Whenever her husband got drunk, she would beat him. She never gave in to him [she always had her own way]. So her husband broke up with her and got a new wife. Naa Jian said, 'Go ahead and leave. I don't want you anyway.'"

Throughout the interview, Ing frequently described the breasts of masculine women she talked about. She said that sometimes they seemed bound or she could see the brassiere of a *tom,* thereby knowing she was not a man. Breasts symbolized the female physiology of these women who claimed masculine identity. The *tom*s I interviewed also mentioned their breasts as markers of their femaleness. Some *tom*s complained that *dee*s would not accept that *tom*s, in fact, had breasts. These *tom*s said that *dee*s would be contemptuous of any evidence that *tom*s were not men and were women like themselves. Breasts stood as a constant reminder that *tom*s stood in physical distinction to men. Naa Jian, like contemporary *tom*s, was not "passing" as a man. As with the other masculine women Ing spoke of, Naa Jian's femaleness was acknowledged.

Ing said that she thought Naa Jian was like a man because it was "just the way she was," not because of any social factors. Ing suggested that it was an issue of karma *(bun/kam),* not an issue of fashion or any other concept currently used to describe transgender identity as "deviance." Ing's linkage of female masculinity with karma was also similar to the ways contemporary *toms* interpreted their transgenderism. Many *toms* said they were born a *tom,* or an "incomplete man," because of actions in past lives. *Kathoey* and gay men also frequently use this discourse in which they portray their lives as gay or *kathoey* as a source of suffering, caused by misdeeds in past lives. Female masculinity did not seem to be particularly "deviant" for village society, and Ing could think of no words to describe Naa Jian that were negative, such as "sexual deviant" or other words popular now. Ing said that the villagers accepted Naa Jian: "Naa Jian is still alive. She must be in her eighties or nineties now. The villagers don't say anything negative about her. The call her 'Ai Jian.' Ai Jian did all men's work—fished (with a net), did farming, all the heavy work."

Ing also recalled a more recent same-sex female couple in her village. Ing described the couple as being in their twenties when they got married in her village twenty years ago: "They got married formally. They married like a man and a woman. They had the other villagers help with the wedding too. They had a fancy wedding. They had a brideprice ceremony and a ceremony to pay respect to the spirits too!" Ing stressed the ceremony for the spirits. Permission from the family spirits for sexual relationships is required, and those couples who do not have a ceremony before having sex are often perceived as having offended the spirits. Therefore Ing's emphasis on the spirit ceremony was probably to make the point that this couple was seen as being comparable to a heterosexual couple. The government has tried to encourage people to register their marriages with state officials, but many heterosexual couples refrain from doing so. Also, there is no standardized Thai ceremony for marriage, and couples may include or exclude any of a number of ritual practices in a marriage celebration. Buddhism does not regulate and validate marriage in Thai custom either, so marriage does not have the same religious or spiritual significance that it does in Western/Christian traditions.[7]

Ing referred to the couple as "the woman" and "the one who was like a man": "The 'woman' was very beautiful. Both of their parents had the 'woman who was a man' move into the woman's family house. The family of the 'woman who was a man' had money. The 'woman who was a man' told her parents, 'If you don't give me money to marry a wife, I'll sell my rice field to somebody else. If you give me money, I'll sell my fields back to you.' Then she sold her fields to her mother to get married." Ing described the reactions of the villagers to this wedding ceremony: "The villagers helped with the ceremony. They helped with the food preparation. Nobody gossiped. Just teasing, 'Ai Tia!'—Ai Tia is the husband *(phua),* to put it plainly—'Ai Tia, you're married; how are you going to do your wife?' They laughed together. Nobody said anything negative or mean to them. Ai Tia dressed just like a man that day. Ai Tia wore a suit and tie, like a man. She had breasts, and they were big too. But that day I don't know what she did, but they were flat. *[Laughs.]* Maybe she used an elastic bandage to keep them flat. When they got married, they hugged and kissed. My son told me about this. On that day my son said to me, 'Mom, come see Ai Tia get a wife!'"

Ing commented that there seemed to be more "women like men" now, but she did not make a distinction between the case of Naa Jian and these younger couples. Most of the older people I interviewed had some recollection of same-sex couples in the past. My interviews with older people indicate that the presence of masculine women and female-female couples in the past were not particularly anomalous events.

FEMALE MASCULINITY AND SPIRIT MEDIUMS

Spirit possession is a site of ritual transgender performance in Thai society.[8] Most Thais, in addition to adhering to Buddhism, have a range of beliefs and practices concerning a complex pantheon of territorial, historical, and ancestral spirits. Spirit possession is a common feature of local belief systems, particularly in northern and northeastern Thailand, where extensive research has been conducted on the subject (see Cohen and Wijeyewardene 1984 and Tambiah 1970). Mediums become possessed by spirits during set ceremonies. These spirits may be ancestral spirits (usually matrilineal); guardian spirits of territorial units, such as spirits of particular villages, districts, towns, or provinces; or spirits of real or presumed historical figures. These possessing spirits are usually male. The mediums, on the other hand, are usually female. Walter Irvine

(1984, 315) reports that 84 percent of the mediums he studied in northern Thailand were female.

The female spirit mediums perform as masculine beings while under the influence of their spirit. The mediums demonstrate the identity of their particular spirit in set ways, such as drinking alcohol, smoking, and wearing men's clothing—all of which are masculine signifiers. While in a trance, the mediums are available to the spirit's believers for advice (Taywaditep 1997). Women thus temporarily attain masculine status through spirit possession. The association of spirit possession with transgenderism extends to the few male spirit mediums as well. Taywaditep, Coleman, and Dumronggittigule (1997) and Irvine (1984) have noted that many of these male mediums are *kathoey* in their everyday lives. In contrast, these female mediums do not have a transgender identity outside of their ritual performances. However, female mediums' claims to a more pervasive masculinity as a result of their exposure to their powerful male spirit are an increasing trend in spirit-possession practices in northern Thailand, according to Irvine (1984).

Irvine asserts that before the 1960s the association of female spirit mediums with masculinity was passive; the women were temporary vessels or receptacles for the powerful male spirits. However, since the 1960s Irvine has noted the trend of women making more explicit claims to their spirit's masculinity. For example, Irvine reports that some female mediums say that their spirit has stopped their menstruation. One woman stated that she had a headache because of "exposure to women's underclothes," thereby adopting Thai Buddhist notions that women's undergarments are toxic sites of spiritual pollution for men, especially monks (Irvine 1984, 320). Irvine notes that female mediums' explicit claim to masculinity in terms of spiritual power is relatively new and presents an inversion of usual gender dynamics, in which men are considered spiritually superior (see also McMorran 1984).

Both masculine women, such as Naa Jian, and the female mediums share a cultural tradition of transgenderism, although the implications of that transgenderism for personal identity differ. The female spirit mediums do not claim a masculine identity independent of their spirit. They are often married, have children, and have a normative gender identity in most ways. On the other hand, Naa Jian and other masculine women like her position themselves as women who cannot be feminine and who occupy a masculine role in their day-to-day life. Many *tom*s with whom I spoke said their masculinity was a natural and unchangeable part of themselves, not a product of an external force. Spirit mediums, in contrast, obtain their masculinity in a more partial way by claiming an association with a male spirit.

Another important difference between masculine women and spirit mediums concerns sexuality. The masculinity of women like Naa Jian and contemporary *tom*s is closely linked to their sexual relations with women. Female spirit mediums, however, are not perceived as being homosexual. Spirit mediums may renounce sexuality in order to obtain spiritual purity according to Buddhist monastic traditions. Married mediums may discontinue sexual relationships with their husbands, and these husbands may take on the role of "ritual officiant" to their wives while the wives are in trance (Irvine 1984, 320). In contrast, *tom* identity is not spiritual but rather highly sexual.

Transgenderism is a pervasive aspect of Thai cultural symbolism. A cursory review of Thai publications at a newsstand would easily demonstrate the fascination that Thai society has for transgenderism in all its forms, from congenital hermaphroditism to gender identities such as *tom* and *kathoey*. These studies of spirit possession suggest that transgenderism is an entrenched aspect of spiritual practices. The near obsession with stories about *kathoey*s, gays, and *tom*s and *dee*s found in the contemporary Thai media belongs to a longer cultural tradition in which transgenderism is a key part of ritual and performance. The increase in media attention to transgender/homosexual stories is logically related to the emergence and development of these specific subcultures and to the increase in nationalist discourses about sexuality and morality. However, these transgendered patterns are not in themselves new.

KATHOEY AND TRANSGENDER IDENTITY IN THAILAND

Before the word *"tom"* was coined to refer to masculine women, women who did not seem to fit expected gendered roles were called *kathoey*s. Western terms like "homosexual" have been translated into Thai as *"kathoey,"* and vice versa. The term *"kathoey"* has often been translated as "hermaphrodite" but can be used to refer to an emotional or psychological blending of gender, rather than the actual sexed body. Western categories, such as "homosexual" *(khon rak-ruam-pheet)* or "sexual deviant" *(khon biang-been-thaang-pheet)*, have been introduced in Thailand by academics and the media but are interpreted according to Thai notions that these sexual labels are products of transgenderism. In the emergent mainstream discourse, to be "homosexual" or a "sexual deviant" means in the Thai context to be "misgendered" or "missexed" *(phit-pheet)*. The term *"phit-pheet"* can be translated as either "misgendered" or "missexed" because there is virtually no linguistic distinction in Thai between sex (as in body) and gender (as in masculinity and femininity).

Women who acted or appeared masculine were referred to as *kathoeys* in the past, according to *tom*s and *dee*s I spoke with. Even now, older people and people living in some rural areas refer to masculine women as *kathoeys*. Som, a working-class woman in her early thirties, grew up in several rural villages in Surin, a province in northeastern Thailand, following her peripatetic parents as they sought wage-labor harvesting. Som recalled that, as a child of around twelve years old, she liked to wear male sarongs *(pha khao-maa)*, to cut her hair very short, and to play rough games with boys. Som laughed as she remembered the villagers playfully calling her *bak-ham noi*, a northeastern Thai term literally meaning "little balls [testicles]." Other villagers would call her *"kathoey,"* the term used in central Thailand. Som did not take these labels as a reference to her sexuality and did not believe that others intended to imply she was a *tom* or a homosexual by calling attention to her masculine behavior. She did not hear of *tom*s until she was in her twenties (roughly ten years ago). Female same-sex experiences in Thailand are by all reports common. Thai girls and women often share rooms and beds, and it would be considered strange and unfortunate for a girl or woman to live or sleep alone. These spaces of female intimacy make sexual experiences likely, and such experiences are usually associated with "innocent" female intimacy. *Tom* identity, on the other hand, is a clear identity based on a sense of masculinity, with homosexuality an implicit dimension of that masculinity. However, association with this tradition of female intimacy often leads *tom*s to be understood as sexually nonthreatening.

The centrality of gender in understanding what Westerners consider "homosexual" identities extends throughout Southeast Asia. Mark Johnson (1997, 1998) has noted the cultural weight given to the imagery of male transvestites or transsexuals throughout the region. Johnson (1997, 25–32) summarizes documentation of transvestite men performing ritual duties in the Indianized states of Southeast Asia as far back as the sixteenth century. In his work on transgender men in the Philippines, Johnson discusses the transformation of "third-gender" categories, evident in ceremonial roles, into contemporary markers of ethnic and national identity. In Thailand, *"kathoey"* is currently used almost exclusively to refer to the highly visible subculture of transgendered males (who are often transsexual as well). Since the 1970s, homosexuality activity *(len pheuan)* and *kathoey* gender identity have been conflated and transformed into *tom-dee* identities, with both the gender-crossing *tom* and her feminine partner discursively marked.

THE ARRIVAL OF WESTERN CONCEPTS OF SEXUALITY AND GENDER

In arguing that *tom* and *dee* identities have local cultural origins, I am not asserting that Thai discourses of sexuality and gender have remained unchanged as pristine forms. All evidence points to the contrary, and there has been extensive state intervention in developing new gender and sexual models. Western discourses of sexuality and gender have been selectively appropriated and modified by the Thai state and professional classes since the early twentieth century. Western concepts have been blended with and adjusted to fit local understandings of sexuality and gender. A brief review of some of the trajectories that Western discourses have made in the Thai configuration of sexual and gender meanings follows.

Tamara Loos (1999, 238–301) has studied the Thai state's appropriation of Western anthropological categories of kinship and family during the early twentieth century. According to Loos, Western discourses of the family and of sexual morality associated with the family became useful tools for Rama VI and his maneuvering against restless domestic political enemies. Rama VI's reign (1910–1925) corresponded to increasing political pressure from young elite men for a more inclusive, power-sharing style of government. Loos explains that Rama VI discredited political opponents by claiming that they had violated supposed authentic Thai traditions, embodied in the family and sexuality: "The institution of the family became the site of cultural specificity and authenticity in early twentieth-century Siam. As a result, family law began to symbolize what was authentic about Siam in a period of radical legal and administrative reform. The significance of the function of 'family' as the space in which Thainess originated had obvious political advantages for the king, who could use laws on family to construct and stabilize a national identity that was founded on loyalty to the absolute monarch" (1999, 239). Loos points out that social practices concerning sexuality and family structures are typically presumed or asserted to be "traditional" and therefore static aspects of Thai tradition. However, she argues that, on the contrary, family and the proper sexuality associated with it, as constructed through law, were "a site of innovation" for Rama VI. Loos' work demonstrates that contemporary nationalist discourses that critique excessive or inappropriate sexuality as harmful to the nation have a history dating from at least a century ago.

Rama VI also used the emerging concept that women's status was a marker of civilization. In other words, civilized nations would be identifiable by the high status of women in that society (Loos 1999). He changed the law on nationality and some family laws, making them strikingly similar to Western laws on citizenship and family. For example, all people were required to adopt a family surname (1913), fathers passed their nationality and family names to children (1913), and women were required to use the title of "Miss" *(nang-sao)* or "Mrs." *(nang)* before their name and to take their husband's surname upon marriage (1917). Only after the absolute monarchy fell was a monogamy law passed (1935). Even then, polygyny was not criminalized, nor was the monogamy law rigorously enforced (Loos 1999, 251). These family laws are still in effect, although there is a movement to remove laws concerning the requirement for taking a husband's name and the title of "Miss" and "Mrs."

Thailand has been exposed to Western understandings of "sexual deviance" and homosexuality for a century. The concept of "sodomy," or "unnatural sex," appeared in the Thai legal reforms of the late nineteenth century. During that time, Rama V enacted a series of legal reforms in an attempt to make Siamese laws "modern" and acceptable to Western powers so that extraterritoriality provisions in treaties with European countries could be eliminated. As part of this general project of westernizing Siam's laws, in 1898 [2441], Rama V promulgated a law against sodomy and rape of a woman other than one's wife, with punishment of up to ten years' imprisonment.[9] This law, borrowed from Western sodomy laws, prohibited "unnatural sexual intercourse" *(khwam-phit thaan kratham-cham-rao phit-thammada-look)* (Kittisak

1993, 93). The law was updated in the criminal law codes in 1908 (R.S. 127 in the Chakri dynastic dating system), with punishment ranging from three months to three years and with the crime relabeled as "sexual intercourse against human nature" *(khwam-phit thaan kratham-cham-rao phit-thammada-manut).* These laws were established not in response to general public opinion or scandal involving "homosexuality" but as part of the general effort to bring Siam's laws in accordance with Western jurisprudence, in which sodomy was regarded as a crime, an assessment derived from a Judeo-Christian tradition.[10]

In 1956 [2499], during the regime of Field Marshal Plaek Phibun Songkhram, the law was canceled; the reasons cited were that the law "ruined the dignity of the nation" and that no cases had been brought to court (Kittisak 1993, 94).[11] These legal codes were attempts to modernize the legal system based on the Western system, and Kittisak (1993) states that they did not reflect local understandings of sexuality and the law. Indeed, Loos (1998) clearly demonstrates that sexual crimes before the legal reforms of the 1890s, and to a degree afterward, were defined according to violation of a man's rights over women—in particular, royal concubines or wives. Sexual crimes were defined relationally, depending on the hierarchical status of the participants (Loos 1998, 93). No legal codes against homosexuality have been enacted since the repeal of the sodomy law in 1956.

Although Western notions of bourgeois respectability were appropriated by the emerging Thai middle class starting in the early twentieth century, Western sexology did not become a standard discourse in Thai academia until the 1970s (Jackson 1997c).[12] Western sexology texts are now widely cited in the fields of clinical psychology and social work in Thailand. Discourses of "homosexuality" *(rak-ruam-pheet)* and sexual/gender deviance *(biang-been-thaang-pheet)* have developed alongside the growth of the *tom-dee* community. The introduction of these pathologizing Western discourses in Thailand has led Thais to assume that *tom*s and *dee*s are and have always been "deviant" and against cultural norms. It is difficult to compare attitudes toward *tom-dee*ism at present with those of the past, because these new Western discourses in which *tom*s and *dee*s are criticized as "deviant" are relatively recent, as are *tom* and *dee* identities. Although female homosexual activity certainly occurred and even masculine women were present before the 1970s, there were no *tom*s and *dee*s who could be either "accepted" or "oppressed."

SOCIOECONOMIC CHANGE IN THAILAND AND THE GROWTH OF *TOM-DEE*ISM

Approximately three decades ago, Thai cultural understandings of *kathoey*s, female masculinity, and female homosexuality were transformed into distinct gendered categories for women—*tom* and *dee*. The newness of *tom-dee*ism is striking to Thais themselves. In the early 1980s, newspapers began reporting on the presence of this new group of women. One journalist began her series of interviews with *tom*s and *dee*s at a Bangkok shopping mall as follows: "All the publications these days are talking about the behavior of this group of youth [*tom-dee*] until I couldn't stand it anymore and had to report on it for the readers of *Khruu Thai*" (*Khruu Thai* [Thai teacher], August 1984, 58).

During the following decades, *tom*s and *dee*s became known to the general public through the mass media, academic studies, and their visible presence in society. Unlike masculine women in the past, *tom*s were openly recognized as a distinct category of female. Like their predecessors, *tom*s dressed in men's clothing and used masculine pronouns. The *tom* identity, however, has become formalized as a distinct alternative to normative femininity. Rather than being referred to as "females who are like men," they have now become a recognized social category—*tom*s. In addition to the linguistic labeling of masculine females, what makes *tom* and *dee* identities strikingly different from their predecessors is the linguistic distinction given to feminine partners of *tom*s—*dee*s. Although in general not as firm or distinct a category as is *tom,* the identity *dee* is becoming more solidified, so that now women can and do claim to be "born to be *dee*s." Furthermore, these identities have become central enough to *tom*s and *dee*s that they have formed communities and subcultures around them, unlike individual or isolated masculine women in the past. Thai women now have a readily available cultural model for either female masculinity or same-sex love that was not available before approximately twenty-five years ago.

As recognized and possible identities, *tom*s and *dee*s date from the 1970s. Pop, a fifty-year-old *tom,* says that in her all-girl secondary school in the mid-1960s there were no *tom*s or *dee*s except for herself, and she did not adopt a *tom* label until later. Her parents had commented on her masculine behavior since she was young and called her a tomboy (directly borrowing the English pronunciation), but *tom-dee* was not a recognized concept at that time. Women who started secondary school in the 1970s and later, on the other hand, recall an active and widely recognized *tom-dee* teenage subculture in their schools. Women without secondary education, such as many of the village women I spoke with, did not encounter the *tom-dee* subculture until they entered factory work or other forms of work in Bangkok or provincial centers, again dating from roughly the mid-1970s.

*Tom*s and *dee*s appeared on the scene conspicuously close to the era in which Thailand experienced rapid economic and social change. Industrialization in Thailand is often dated to the first National and Social Development Plan (1961–1966), which vaguely encouraged private industry through a poorly defined laissez-faire governmental stance (Muscat 1994, 86–100). The relative failure of the loose import-substitution policy, an effort to substitute local goods for imported ones, led to a shift in emphasis in the late 1960s and 1970s to developing export-oriented industries and attracting foreign investment, which have remained the focus of development until the present (K. Soonthorndhada 1991). These export-oriented industries have depended on employing almost exclusively young, unmarried women with low levels of education (Arnold and Cochrane 1980, cited in Soonthorndhada 1991, 3).

The economic changes of the 1970s were accompanied by a range of far-reaching social changes in Thai society. Of course, economic change and development had occurred in Thailand before the 1960s. In the first half of the twentieth century, large numbers of Chinese immigrated to Thailand, establishing commercial centers in urban areas, particularly Bangkok. Thai agriculture became increasingly oriented to international markets, especially with products such as rice and rubber. These economic developments before the 1970s were notable to social scientists because the economic changes did not cause dramatic demographic shifts (D. Wilson 1962). Thailand's transformation into an industrialized economy from the 1970s onward, on the other hand, affected the population in significant ways, which were evident in dramatic demographic shifts.

From the 1970s, rates of women migrating to urban areas for employment in industry and the service sector increased dramatically, even surpassing the rates of male migration (Phongpaichit 1982; Tantiwiramanond and Pandey 1987; Thaweesit 2000).[13] The rate of migration, especially to urban areas to obtain industrial employment, is notably large in Thailand, even in comparison with other developing countries (Curran 1994). By 1985, industry had surpassed agriculture, long the economic mainstay of the Thai economy, in terms of share of gross domestic product (Muscat 1994, 103). This growth in the manufacturing sector is the primary source of the increases in migration rates in Thailand. The number of people employed in manufacturing doubled from 2 million to 4 million between 1986 and 1996 (Thaweesit 2000, 61). By the 1980s, women constituted 80 to 90 percent of the labor force in five leading export industries: electronics, textiles, food processing, jewelry, and footwear (Sunteera [Suteera] and Maytinee, cited in Thaweesit 2000, 63). Women moved to the cities to find work in factories, bars, and restaurants, living in flats or dormitories with other female workers.

The growth of a dynamic and powerful Thai middle class is perhaps the most remarked-upon feature of the Thai political and economic landscape of the past several decades. Benedict Anderson (1998, 142) describes the class structure of Thai society before the socioeconomic changes of the 1960s and 1970s as "a political system completely dominated by a largely self-perpetuating, modernizing bureaucracy." Thai middle classes (including small-scale business owners, white-collar employees, and well-educated professionals) have since gained a hegemonic hold on the direction of the Thai economy and, by extension, a hold on political processes and social values (Girling 1996). The Thai middle class has doubled in size from the 1970s and now constitutes one-fifth of the working population (Girling 1996). Phongpaichit and Baker (1996, 92, 106) report that the number of white-collar jobs in Thailand grew from approximately 500,000 in 1960 to 4.5 million by the 1990s, increasing fourfold over the 1980s alone. The political radicalism of the 1970s and the antidictatorship activism of the 1990s in Thailand were largely fueled by these new middle-strata classes (Anderson 1977; Conners 1997; Girling 1996; Laothamatas 1997). Underneath the dramatic political upheavals were steady and pervasive demographic shifts, evident in the increased migration rates and the shifts to industrial labor, as well as rising tertiary education rates and lowered fertility.

The middle classes are a product of expanded business opportunities and tertiary education. During the 1970s alone, the number of Thais with a college education increased fourfold, from 180,000 to 720,000, and the number of workers with college education increased tenfold from 1970 to 1991. Salaries for professional classes were high, and jobs in both the industrial and the service sectors were abundant from the

1980s onward (Phongpaichit and Baker 1994, 108). The rise of urban professional classes and the growing rates of women obtaining higher education have produced a generation of well-educated young urban women with professional white-collar and "pink-collar" jobs. Many of these women delay marriage or do not marry at all. They often live away from their families, at least for a period, in rented flats or school dormitories.

The main factors that have opened the social space for the growth of the *tom-dee* subculture are the changes in marriage trends, rates of education, and rates of employment in occupations away from family, including industrial labor, service work, and professional occupations, as well as the development of a Thai middle class. Although not all *tom*s and *dee*s are economically or spatially independent of their families, these factors contribute to the dramatic increase of these identities in recent years, especially among younger urbanites, whether they be factory workers, middle-class students, or office workers.

URBANIZATION, INDUSTRIALIZATION, AND "WOMEN'S STATUS"

There is no consensus within feminist and anthropological literature over the effects that industrialization has had on women. On the one hand, in industrial economies women earn money independent of their family, and their jobs often take them from the confines of their family's supervision. On the other hand, women usually enter the workforce in lower, poorly paid positions and are subjected to forms of capitalist discipline.

Modernization literature supposed an increase in women's opportunities with industrialization, based on increased access to education and cash income from new employment opportunities. Ester Boserup (1970) critiqued this widely held assumption, arguing that development has worsened the economic situation of women in many parts of the world because of biases that give males preferred access to education and employment in most national development plans. More recently, totalizing theories of advancement or greater repression of women in industrial development have given way to ethnographies of contradictory effects in local settings.

Marjorie Muecke (1984) asserts that the status of women in northern Thailand traditionally depended on children and a female-centered social structure, represented through ancestral spirits. Fertility levels have dropped dramatically in recent years, and migration has separated women from their families, who were traditional sources of support. Belief in matrilineal spirits has declined under accusations of being "unmodern." Also, the spirit cults are difficult to maintain when the followers migrate to other areas for work. Muecke notes that although these traditional sites of women's authority have declined, women are finding more opportunities in wage labor and have benefited from legal changes concerning divorce and property rights, for example. Susanne Thorbek (1987) supports Muecke's assertion that women living in urban areas have less access to traditional sites of status and are more dependent on men for money. Thorbek gives a less optimistic appraisal of women's opportunities in the capitalist economy than Muecke does, noting that women have become more dependent on men and men's wages and lose the support of the village family structure when they migrate to look for work.

Until the last several decades, upward mobility in Thai society was usually acquired through the institutions of the military, the governmental bureaucracy, and monkhood, all exclusively male institutions until recently (Keyes 1987; D. Wilson 1962; Wyatt 1994, 207–218). Even now, monkhood is an exclusively male domain, and the military nearly so. The bureaucracy's upper positions and political positions are heavily dominated by men.[14] Women's main access to the new economy is through wage labor in factories or the service economy or through jobs as urban professionals, which require an educational background that most women outside the middle and upper classes cannot afford. Women's upward mobility has traditionally depended on liaisons and marriages with men. For many women without education, marriage and liaisons with men are the best means of bettering their position, a fact that has fueled the commercial sex business and the phenomenon of women taking the role of "minor wives" *(mia-noi)*.[15]

Women who do not have access to higher-paid jobs or professional positions often spend time engaged in wage labor away from their families before they get married. Living in factory dormitories and in flats with other workers is a time of independence from family scrutiny and an opportunity for women to explore their sexuality. Some women maintain independence from their families, and while often sending money home, they continue working and living in urban areas. Other women continue close ties to family and their rural homes and return home to marry. For women with few economic options, marriage or other relationships have been important ways of getting security and status.

Thai women have had traditional responsibilities to care for parents (Hale 1984; Mills 1993; Potter 1977). This expectation has fused with economic opportunities to encourage women to seek wage work in order to send money home to parents and siblings (Mills 1993, 1999). Sara Curran, in her study of women's migration patterns, quotes a conversation with an older woman about the value of daughters as wage earners. The interviewer asked, "When the children go to live in Bangkok, they send money to you. Is there a difference between sons and daughters?" The respondent answered, "If girls make 5,000 baht, they will send you 5,000 baht. The boys would not send us any money! He would not send us any money! He would not send any to his mother. They do not even make enough for themselves. You cannot depend on sons" (Curran 1994, 69–70). Thus daughters are encouraged to work, and the rapid expansion of industrial and service employment has provided them jobs to go to. Women have gained greater independence and opportunities from this employment on some level, but they are also expected to do what is necessary to ensure the security of their parents, whether that requires working in factories or bars or marrying.

Tom and *dee* identities have emerged within this context of class-stratified options. *Tom*s and *dee*s have flourished in the environments established by these economic transformations: factory dormitories, urban workplaces, tourism/service workplaces, schools, and universities. My most productive "field sites" were the coffee shops and food stalls in front of these dormitories, where I inevitably found some *tom*s or *dee*s willing to sit and talk with me. The possibility of supporting oneself away from family and the consequent trends of later and fewer marriages have allowed women the option of exploring sexual and romantic relationships to a greater degree than was possible before. This area of independence is partial and conditional. Like Thai women in general, *tom*s and *dee*s live in tension between family expectations and their own individual choices and needs.

Nit's story illustrates the conflicting pressures facing Thai women. Nit worked as a cashier at a "beer bar" in North Pattaya. Pattaya is a beach resort town in Chonburi Province, a short drive from the east of Bangkok. Its proximity to Bangkok, its highly developed prostitution economy, and its beaches, fancy hotels, scuba diving sites, and honky-tonk atmosphere have made it a popular destination for both foreign tourists and local Bangkokians looking for a weekend getaway.

My first impression was that Nit was shy and quiet—she had a vulnerable quality, being small and slender, her long hair drifting over her face as she bent down to fill glasses of beer and push checks across the counter. This beer bar was like most others—semi-outdoors, consisting of a roof and a long bar with barstools along the sidewalks. Ten or so women worked there at any given time as freelance sex workers, mixing with the customers, laughing and entertaining them, and eventually leaving with a customer after a small "bar fine" had been paid. Nit quietly worked in this atmosphere of rowdy laughing, ribald joking, and yells of the workers to passersby: "Yes, please come and sit dooooown." Nit shared a room with a couple of the sex workers, in the dorm-style houses in the gravel lot behind the bar, and she sent money home to her family regularly. I got to know some of the more outgoing workers right off, as they told me of their lives and loves, including their lives as a *tom* or a *dee*. Nit took a while longer to get to know and would not usually talk to me directly but would talk to a friend while I sat close by, listening.

Nit had a *tom* lover she had met working at a factory several years ago. She did not want the others to know about her *tom*, but they mostly did anyway. The bar owner would warn the workers not to get involved with *tom*s, "because everyone knows they are violent and emotionally unstable," repeating well-known stereotypes perpetuated in the media. Nit's family upcountry were very upset about her relationship with a *tom* but were apparently accepting of Nit's employment in Pattaya, because they needed the money. After months went by, Nit's family became angrier at Nit's affair with the *tom*, saying it was a "waste of time." Nit recalled that her mother said that if she did not break up with the *tom*, she would lose her brothers and sisters. Her brother periodically came to Pattaya to talk to her, and Nit would send money back home with him. He reported that her mother had said that Nit was a girl, so why wasn't she looking for a husband instead of a *tom*? A few weeks later, I heard that Nit's mother had burned Nit's clothes in anger and made her brother come and demand that she break up with the *tom*. Nit said she agreed to break up, and the *tom* cried and protested. Meanwhile, some of the bar workers had agreed to help Nit sell her virginity. They said they could negotiate a price of at least

20,000 baht (approximately US$500) so that Nit could help pay for her brother's ordination as a monk, which was to be accompanied by a large celebration in her village.

I lost touch with Nit for about six months, and when I went back to the bar in North Pattaya, the bar workers said Nit never did sell her virginity, had married a man chosen by her mother, and had gone back to her village. Nit had had the opportunity to live away from her family, where she met and had a relationship with a *tom*. However, her mother's demand that she not "waste time" with a *tom* persuaded Nit to return home and marry to please her family. According to bar workers who knew Nit, her mother felt that having a family with a man would be the best way to have a stable and secure future, a view commonly held by people I talked to. Nit's experience as a *dee,* therefore, was temporary and ultimately ended when she acquiesced to her mother's demands.

In contrast to Nit's story, other women are able to live as *tom*s or *dee*s without protest from their families. Many women make compromises, such as visiting with other *tom*s and *dee*s but not engaging in any serious relationships that would upset their parents. These stories will be told in later chapters, but suffice it to say here that the opportunities for women to engage in *tom-dee* communities depend on a range of personal and social factors. As females, *tom*s and *dee*s face different family expectations from those that Thai males face, and thus any generalization about the Thai "gay-lesbian" scene would need to account for these important differences between being male and being female in Thai society.

Women are still expected to provide for parents and siblings but may be able to do so within *tom-dee* relationships. *Tom* and *dee* relationships and identities can be acceptable, and often are, if they meet family expectations. For example, many of the rural, semirural, and urban *tom-dee* couples whom I met lived with the acceptance of family members. If the *tom* or *dee* could support herself or her partner could provide for her, the relationship might be embraced.

The relationship between Khaek, a thirty-four-year-old *tom,* and Ying, a village woman in her early twenties, illustrates the importance of status and economic position in acceptance of *tom-dee* relationships. Khaek ran a tour company in Phuket, a prosperous southern province awash with tourist income from its famous beaches and resorts. I met Khaek and her partner, Ying, on a boat trip run by Khaek's tour company when I traveled to Phuket with a group of friends, including Nuu, a *tom* from Bangkok in her forties. Khaek's close-cropped hair, men's shirt and slacks, and masculine speech made her *tom*ness obvious to us. When Nuu saw Khaek board the shuttle bus to the pier, she exclaimed happily, "We have a *tom* tour!" Nuu spoke to Khaek as we rode along, asking her to turn off the air conditioner and to stop for a bathroom break, using "*khrap,*" the masculine speech particle, which Nuu otherwise rarely used, to "let her know we are of the same group." When we boarded the boat, we saw Khaek with Ying, who was wearing jeans and a jacket. Ying was helping pass out water and seat the guests on the boat. Nuu quickly befriended Khaek, who told us that Ying was her "wife" *(mia)*. As the boat sped along to James Bond Island, Nuu asked Khaek about her life and her girlfriend. Khaek was open and friendly, playfully bantering with Nuu about being with a younger woman. Nuu asked about their sex life, and Khaek laughed and said they "wash the cock's face," a saying that means "to have sex first thing in the morning."[16] As they joked, Ying seemed a bit shy at Khaek's dirty jokes, blushed, and looked away. However, their relationship seemed open and obvious to all the staff, and they made no efforts to be secretive or discreet about being a couple.

Khaek explained that Ying was from a village family who had little money. Khaek had Ying help her with the tours so that Ying could make some money, rather than just giving her money directly. Khaek said she planned to marry Ying and had already talked to Ying's family. After the tour, we arranged to have dinner together in town, and Khaek suggested a local restaurant. As we ate together, Nuu mentioned the issue of economic support between couples and said she was tired of always having to support *dee*s. Khaek and Ying exchanged an awkward glance. Khaek said that she saw Ying's family frequently, and they accepted her because they could see that Khaek was responsible and able to take care of Ying. Khaek was also very invested in maintaining a strong masculine image. For Khaek, being accepted as a respectable suitor for Ying was linked to her full enactment of masculinity—she was a provider and a leader, taking care of her younger partner in a way that men are expected to care for women in the eyes of many Thais. Khaek was a successful business entrepreneur and, though not rich, was financially comfortable and independent. Khaek said that she and Ying had already discussed the brideprice. Economics and social position overrode other possible objections to the relationship. Being *tom* or *dee* can be integrated into existing social structural arrangements, such as expectations of sons-in-law and daughters-in-law, and financial independence makes this easier to accomplish. These new identities and relationships exist in a delicate balance between family expectations of daughters and the mobility and relative independence that are increasingly available to women in an industrializing economy.

MARRIAGE TRENDS

The point that economic and spatial independence from families allows women to pursue love interests and sexual experiences that may not have been allowed in the preindustrial family environment is not specific to *tom-dee* relationships, however—it is also true for heterosexual relationships. According to Philip Guest and Jooean Tan (1994), Thai women have been marrying later since the 1970s, and more Thai women are not marrying at all. Guest and Tan's data show that the higher the educational attainment of Thai women, the greater the chance they will remain unmarried.[17] As educational levels for Thai women have increased steadily from the 1970s through the 1990s, women have married less and later. Twice as many women with university education remained unmarried than men with the same educational level. Guest and Tan found that employment factors also affected marriage rates for Thai women. At least four times as many women remained unmarried who were employed in the industrial production, professional, and service sectors as women in the "unpaid family worker" category, unemployed women, and women with little or no education.

Guest and Tan (1994) link these marriage trends to socioeconomic trends in Thai society from the 1970s to the 1990s—namely, increased female migration to urban areas for industrial work, greater employment of women in service and professional sectors, and greater educational parity with males. Although these changes in marital patterns are significant, they are not as dramatic as changes in female marital patterns in other developing countries with similar socioeconomic changes. Guest and Tan note that the increase in unmarried women is less dramatic because Thai women have traditionally married relatively later than women in other developing countries as a result of a host of cultural factors. For example, Thai women have had relative freedom in choosing spouses and therefore tend to marry later than women in societies in which parents have a strong role in choosing spouses (Sumalee

1993). Matrifocal kinship structure has also kept daughters close to their parents and active in family farming and businesses, which has also delayed marriage for women (Guest and Tan 1994). The traditional tendency for later marriages, combined with recent socioeconomic changes in Thailand, has resulted in Thailand's having the highest rates of single women in Asia.[18]

The ease with which Thai women have been able to engage in *tom-dee* relationships must be understood within this context of a relatively relaxed attitude toward marriage for daughters, and the recent trends toward later marriage or no marriage at all. Spending young adulthood with "friends" and female companions before getting married in one's late twenties or thirties is consistent with Thai norms and marriage patterns in general. *Tom-dee* identity is increasingly popular with younger girls and women (in their teens and twenties), as a foray onto *tom-dee* Web sites or into Bangkok clubs and discos will demonstrate. During my seven-year stay in Thailand I have witnessed increasing numbers of communities of and organizations for *tom*s and *dee*s, with younger *tom*s and *dee*s feeding this growth.

These changing socioeconomic factors have also had an impact on social values and attitudes toward marriage and sexuality. Financial independence also seems to affect women's attitudes toward male sexuality. Chanphen Saengtienchai et al. (n.d., 11) report that the greater the financial independence of women, the less likely they were to accept the common attitude that Thai men had a need for and a right to extramarital sex.

Research indicates that urban women are more likely to engage in premarital sex than rural women, although both urban and rural women are reported to be three times as likely to believe that "premarital sex is sinful" than are males. This research indicates that urban women are more likely to seek sexual experiences outside of marriage than are rural women, many more of whom were reported to be living with family and parents (Pramote et al. 1987, 13). However, both rural and urban women are influenced by cultural dictates that women should avoid sexual activities outside of marriage, dictates that are based on the belief that extramarital heterosexuality is dangerous for a woman's reputation and will lead to "social problems" (Pramote et al. 1987). Under these social conditions, women engaging in nonheterosexual sexual activity such as *tom*s and *dee*s, particularly those living away from home, fit with general social patterns.

According to the research discussed above, women are living with their husbands away from the families of origin more often and are more frequently living alone or with friends when not married. *Tom*s and *dee*s have similar patterns. In Chinese families, it has been traditional for women to move in with their husband's family, whereas the traditional Thai pattern (for nonelites) was for husbands to move into the wife's family compound.[19] However, in practice currently there is tremendous variation in residence patterns of both heterosexual and homosexual couples. Few of the couples I interviewed lived with their family (parents, siblings, other relatives) on a permanent basis, although most visited their family frequently, stayed with them for short periods of times, or resided in homes owned by their family. In terms of couples, only two couples among the ninety-eight women I interviewed lived with their family permanently, and both of those couples were from wealthy families. Individual *tom*s and *dee*s who did live with their family on a permanent basis were less likely to have a committed relationship with another woman. These *tom*s and *dee*s felt generally uncomfortable having their family witness their love life in a daily way. Several *dee*s said they were not "allowed" to see *tom*s or men (although they were in their twenties), and some *tom*s said they did not want to disappoint their parents by obviously demonstrating their homosexuality. Thus the opportunities of living independently or semi-independently of family have influenced the ability of *tom*s and *dee*s to form relationships and live together.

URBANIZATION AND THE GROWTH OF SEXUAL IDENTITIES

Chang, a twenty-six-year-old *dee* from rural southern Thailand, described a masculine woman in her village: "There is an old *tom* in my village. She is about fifty years old, and she doesn't have any breasts. I think she must bind them. She also looks like a *tom* and has never gotten married, but she has never had any girlfriend either. She stays there quietly, and she hardly ever talks to the other villagers. So the people ignore her. She dresses like a *tom*. But she never has had a girlfriend, so I feel sorry for her. I don't know why she has never had one. I'm a little bit confused about how she can imagine what a *tom* is. How can she know that being a *tom* means she has to dress like that? Actually I wonder if she knows that acting like that is what we call a *tom*?"

Scholars have argued that the processes of modernization—

economic development and expanded education and urbanization—
have led to the expansive growth of Western gay and lesbian identities.
John D'Emilio (1983, 22) argues that socioeconomic forces led to the
possibility for men and women in the United States to form sexual identities and to form communities with others with the same identity: "On
the eve of World War II, contradictory forces structured the phenomenon of same-sex eroticism in America. On the one hand, cumulative
historical processes—the spread of capitalist economic relations, indus-
trialism and the socialization of production, and urban growth—were
shaping a social context in which homosexual desire might congeal into
a personal identity."[20]

Although much less research has been conducted on female sexual
identities in the West than has been conducted on male sexual identities,
the same linkages between industrialization and urbanization are found
for females. Lillian Faderman (1991) has asserted that the growing economic independence of women in the urban industrial capitalism of the
twentieth century freed them to develop sexual identities outside the
constraints of their family (see also Kennedy and Davis 1993).

Thai *tom-dee* identities were made possible by, but not created by,
socioeconomic changes that sent women out of villages and family
homes into a larger, generally sex-segregated world where sexual exploration could take place free of family scrutiny. The development of a
masculine identity for women was also possible under these conditions,
which allowed women to choose to remain unmarried and to find
employment to support themselves.

Gender Ambivalence in *Tom* and *Dee* Identities 3

KOT, A *TOM* in her mid-thirties, brought some friends to meet me at Utopia, a bar for "gays and lesbians" set up in Bangkok by an American man. Kot had an outgoing personality, laughed easily, and seemed eager to see what this new American "gay bar" was all about. She wore the kind of clothing that makes one clearly identifiable as a *tom* or at least leads others to assume one is a *tom*—men's trousers and a button-down shirt with a white undershirt—and she had short-cropped hair. Kot was from a modestly middle-class family in Bangkok and seemed to be doing well financially. After college, she had taken an office job and eventually opened her own small business. Kot explained to me what she meant by saying that she was a *tom*. "I always wanted to be a boy and even knew how to pee standing up," she joked. She said she had told her parents that she wanted a sex change. Kot said that her old girlfriend once slept with Kot's brother. The girlfriend then went back to Kot, enraging the brother, Kot claimed. Her brother angrily shouted that Kot was a *kathoey*, referring to a transgender or third-sex category. According to Kot, her mother then humorously said that since her brother did not seem to be using his penis very much, why not exchange sex organs with his sister? Kot laughed and said that her mother's comment had shut her brother up. Kot told her brother that "a fish can see only the water and a land animal only the land, but I am a turtle and can see both." Kot expressed herself as someone between categories, neither fully one nor the other but having the qualities and vision of both. Kot did not see being a *tom* in only positive ways, however.

Kot had a girlfriend, Tee, with whom Kot said she was very much in love. Tee had many boyfriends whom, according to Kot, Tee would not even attempt to hide. Kot sighed and said she thought it was inevitable that they would have to break up someday. She suspected that Tee was just looking for a rich girlfriend to support her, and Kot would not be able to be that for her. Kot said she could not give Tee much in the way of material things, and Tee needed somebody to take care of her—preferably somebody rich. Tee did not reciprocate sexually for Kot, making Kot wait until Tee wanted to have sex and then demanding sex the way Tee wanted it. Kot was somewhat resigned about this dynamic, however, explaining that that was how women were. For Kot, Tee was an "ordinary woman" *(phu-ying thammada)* who could be attracted to either a man or a masculine woman and was not the same kind of person as Kot and her other *tom* friends. Kot's social world consisted of other *tom*s and their girlfriends, who would come and go from the circle of *tom* friends.

After sitting for a while and telling me these stories, Kot and her friends stood up from our table and wandered over to the bookshop at Utopia, looking at the glossy photos of musclemen and Western lesbian icons like k.d. lang and Ellen DeGeneres splashed across the covers of the imported magazines. Kot picked up the small Thai-language newsletter of Anjaree, a Thai lesbian rights organization. The newsletter discussed what the labels of *"tom"* and *"dee"* meant to Anjaree members, and it carried current events related to *tom-dee, kathoey,* and gay identities, including local and international stories of gays and lesbians. Kot read the newsletter for a few minutes, then brought it over to the counter and paid for it. She turned to me and asked what *farang* (Westerners) are like: "Do they have *tom*s and *dee*s too?" I said that as far as I knew, there were not such strong gender identities anymore, not like *tom* and *dee* in Thailand. Kot and her friends looked at me blankly at first, then glanced at each other, seemingly at a loss for words, and started giggling. "How do you know what to do then?" one chortled.

As I started my interviews, I approached women who looked like *tom*s, and the women with them, at bars and clubs and asked them to explain to me what it meant to be *tom* or *dee*. One of the first nights of my research, I went to Utopia. I met a small group of *tom*s who were smoking cigarettes and drinking beer. I sat down next to one *tom* who was maybe in her forties or fifties. I awkwardly asked her if she was a *tom*—a stupid question, considering that she looked more butch than any man in the room, with her slicked-back short hair, men's trousers, and nicely creased man's shirt. She smiled and explained, "Look, I am a man *(phu-chai)*." The other *tom*s also referred to other people present as either "*tom*s" or "women," making a distinction between the two categories. The practice of *tom*s and *dee*s referring to each other as "men" *(phu-chai)* and "women" *(phu-ying)* was jarring to me, because it seemed to deny their obvious shared femaleness, which none actually denied.

Over the next several years, I learned that *tom* and *dee* were much more fluid and contested categories than I had originally understood. To *tom*s, being a "man" did not mean that they thought of themselves, or were thought of by *dee*s, literally as men or as embodying the same masculinity as they understood biological men to have. As I learned about *tom* and *dee* identities, I had to adjust my own thinking about the nature of sexual identity and gender by not assuming that *tom*s and *dee*s felt that they shared a commonality as women with a common sexual identity. Although there are *tom*s and *dee*s who prefer this Western paradigm of identity based on sexual preference, it is far from common in the Thai *tom-dee* scene. In fact, when I reviewed my data for the one

A *dee* poses in the office of Anjaree, an organization that promotes the rights of "women who love women" *(ying-rak-ying)*.

A *tom* crawls out of the mosquito net to start her morning.

A *tom* poses on her "chopper."

hundred interviews I conducted, I found that none of my informants exclusively identified herself as lesbian. Four or five used the term "lesbian" to describe themselves over the years I knew them, but not in total exclusion to a *tom* or *dee* identity.

(NOT?) BEING DEE

Here I must make a clarification. I have been using the term "identity" to categorize *tom*s and *dee*s, but *"dee"* is not exactly an "identity." Women exhibit a striking ambivalence about identifying themselves as *dee*. In spite of the trend within anthropological theory to move away from overessentialized or rigid portrayals of subjectivity, "identity" still implies a sense of self that obtains a level of coherency when it is enacted (see Kondo 1990).

The degree to which *"dee"* is not an identity was made clear in the recent defense of a master's thesis in the Sociology and Anthropology Department at Thammasat University on the topic of the development of *dee* identity. Manitta Chanchai (2003) realized, after completing her fieldwork, that in fact women involved with *tom*s did not have a clear self-identity as *dee,* which required a rethinking of her thesis topic. Among the thirteen women she interviewed who had *tom* partners, only five categorized themselves as *dee,* while all of them referred to their partners as *tom*s. The rest of the women called themselves "women" *(phu-ying),* said they were not sure how they should categorize themselves, or were not sure about the meaning of the word *"dee."* "Dee". was more frequently a label that *tom*s used to refer to their feminine partners. Out of the ten masculine-identified females Manitta interviewed, all identified themselves as *tom*s, and eight said their partners were *dee*s. One *tom* said her partners could be either "women" *(phu-ying)* or *dee*s, depending on whether they also had male lovers (and would thereby be a "woman"). Like two of the *"dee*s" interviewed, one *tom* was not sure what the word *"dee"* meant (Manitta 2003).

The term *"dee"* is not as well known as the term *"tom"* among Thai people in general. Manitta interviewed a random sample of Bangkok residents about what they thought the words *"tom"* and *"dee"* meant. A housewife answered, "A *tom* is a mischievous *(kaen)* girl who acts like a male; the kids will call a girl who acts like a male a *tom*" (Manitta 2003, 50). The housewife typically attributed childlike qualities to female same-sex relations. When asked if she knew what a *dee* was, she said she did not know. Manitta asked her what she would call a partner of a *tom,* and the housewife answered, "I'd call her a girl/woman *(phu-ying),* that's all" (Manitta 2003, 50).

In contrast to the idea of *tom*s being "transgendered" or feeling like a man's mind in a woman's body, most *tom*s and *dee*s positioned *dee*s as "ordinary" women. Even women who consistently chose *tom* partners tended to refer to themselves as "ordinary" women who liked *tom*s. Some *tom*s and *dee*s distinguished between "real *dee*s" and "fake *dee*s," saying that real *dee*s would be only with *tom*s, whereas fake *dee*s could be with either *tom*s or men. Ung, a woman with a *tom* lover, resisted being labeled a *dee* herself and described *dee*s as follows: "*Dee*s aren't the same as other women at all. Some *dee*s aren't real lesbians. They can be a man's woman too. But there are some people who, even though they are married, try to have a female lover. One can't tell if someone is a woman's woman or a man's woman from exterior appearances. From within the heart is where you can tell if she likes women *(phu-ying).*" Some *dee*s I spoke with called themselves "one-hundred-percent *dee*" or "a woman for *tom*s, not a woman for men." Not all *tom*s and *dee*s I spoke with were sure about this distinction, though. Most *tom*s said that *dee*s were "ordinary" women who might prefer a *tom* for a variety of reasons, but they were not a different category from women who were with men. Given that *dee*s were closely associated with "ordinary women," the masculine-feminine dynamic of *tom*s and *dee*s therefore depended on *tom*s performing their gendered difference.

*Dee*s are understood by most Thais to be "ordinary women" because *dee*s are ostensibly feminine; their sexuality or sexual object choice does not usually mark them as different from women in general. In Thai mainstream discourse, homosexual desires are largely attributed to being "misgendered" *(phit-pheet),* which means having a transgender identity such as a masculine female *(tom)* or feminine male *(kathoey).* The gender-normative partner of a transgendered male or female is not typically stigmatized as homosexual and is expected by most Thais also to engage in heterosexual relationships. A *dee,* then, is not usually considered "homosexual," since she is feminine in dress, demeanor, speech, and all other markers. Even sexually, a *dee* is understood as being attracted to masculinity, thereby rendering her "ordinary" in the dominant discourse. When I have listened to, participated in, or stimulated discussions of homosexuality, most Thai people exclusively discussed *kathoey*s (transgendered/transsexual males) and *tom*s. Only when I said "What about *dee*s?" did Thais sometimes agree that *dee*s too might be homosexual. Most times Thais would explain that *dee*s were only temporarily interested in *tom*s or were interested in *tom*s only because of disappointment with men, so therefore they were not really homosexual—a position that was often repeated by *tom*s and *dee*s themselves. In Western discourse, by contrast, a woman's sexual interest in other women, regardless of whether she considers herself to be masculine or not, is the single most important determinant of a "sexual identity." In Western discourse, one's sexual behavior may mark one in significant ways as "deviant" in psychological discourses and is the basis of legal and religious restrictions, although this discourse has been challenged in the past decades. For Thais, sexual behavior such as female same-sex sexual behavior, in itself is not highly significant in any of these ways.

Gender difference structures relationships between *tom*s and *dee*s, and shared biological femaleness is explained in various ways by *tom*s and *dee*s—as either an aspect to be ignored or a source of the intimacy between the couple. Most *dee*s I spoke with said they chose *tom*s because *tom*s were particularly sensitive and caring and were better partners than men were. Other *dee*s made no distinction between *tom*s and men. Whether *dee*s distinguished *tom*s from men or not, all distinguished *tom*s from *dee*s.

The ways *dee*s understood their masculine partners structured the ways they understood themselves. *Dee*s who made little distinction between their *tom* lovers and men consequently made little distinction between themselves and "ordinary women." For example, Euy, a *dee*, drew few distinctions between her *tom* partner of nine years and men. Euy was in her mid-forties and had a certain masculine quality to her. She kept her hair short and wore jeans and a flannel shirt. When she showed me the picture of her partner, I was surprised because I had originally mistaken Euy for a *tom*, but in contrast to her *tom* lover, she did indeed look the *dee*. Euy explained that many people mistook her for a *tom*, and she said she had to dress that way because she had a job driving a truck. Euy said she was a woman and wanted to be with a man, and she did not care if her lover was a woman who was like a man, or a man. She said her lover was tough and sweet, but in a way that "men are sweet, not women." Euy did not make any radical distinction between being with a *tom* or a man in terms of her own identity. She agreed she was a *dee* when pushed to identify herself (by the pushy anthropologist), but the term *"dee"* was not strongly resonant for her.

Other *dee*s made sharp distinctions between their *tom* lovers, or *tom*s in general, and men. When asked what qualities it was about their *tom* lover that attracted them, most *dee*s listed a series of stereotypically feminine qualities: soft *(num-nuan)*, gentle, being a good listener, caring, and attentive. This intriguing ambivalence of gender expressed in *tom* identity is perhaps the key to understanding the *tom-dee* subculture. "*Tom*" and "*dee*" are relational identities, defining each other through their mutual opposition, yet failing to conform to any simple categorization of gender.

TOM MASCULINITY

Jiap was a good-looking working-class *tom* in her late twenties, whom I met at a coffee shop with a group of *tom*s and *dee*s outside their dormitory in downtown Bangkok. Jiap had no job and survived through the support of various girlfriends, one of whom, Tii, was there at the coffee shop. Tii worked as an "escort" at a high-class club and gave money to Jiap, who liked to play cards, with some rather horrendous losses. Jiap seemed happy with her life, and when asked if she could choose to be a man or a woman, she answered that in her next life she did not want to be a "man or a woman, but a *tom* again," just one "richer and more handsome."

Most *tom*s positioned themselves as situated between ideal masculinity and femininity, strategically accessing claims to both genders, yet simultaneously distancing themselves from both "men" and "women." The sense of blending of masculine and feminine categories has been inherited from Thai understandings of *kathoey*s, who are often seen as being a blend of both sexes. Contemporary *kathoey*s, or transgendered and/or transsexual men, are often explicitly positioned as embodying a balance of gender traits. For example, in a newspaper interview Professor Wirot Tangwanit repeated the common Thai belief that *kathoey*s are creative because they have both "male and female dimensions within themselves." Wirot noted: "The most capable people in the world are *kathoey*. They have both *yin* and *yang* in themselves, so I want to see them use their positive power in a useful way" (*Matichon*, January 26, 1997, 20).

Some *tom*s explicitly declared their femininity and commonality with *dee*s. Kaew, a middle-class *tom* from Bangkok, said: "I have women lovers because it is easier to be close. We understand what we want because women cooperate. Men, if they're Thai, just think of themselves; they only know what they need. They don't care what women want. But women together can understand each other." Kaew blended her sense of shared femaleness with a distinct masculinity that served to distinguish her from her feminine partners and from *dee*s in general. She linked her desire for relationships with women with a sense of being "in charge" and masculine, defining herself as something both different from men and different from women.

Other *tom*s articulated a sense of being in between the categories of *tom*s and "normal women." Khem, who called herself a *tom*, described her self-identity: "*Tom*s must dress coarsely. I think that *tom*s are womanizers; they drink and take drugs. *Dee*s are normal women *(phu-ying thammada)*. As for me, I am a *tom* because I don't like to wear skirts [and] I have short hair. Frankly, I want to be just a bit of a *tom*, like a fake *tom (tom plorm)*, because sometimes I want to be a woman. You know that there are *tom*s and *dee*s—these *tom*s are totally like men, but I am not. Sometimes I want to be strong, but I have a weakness at the same time. To sum it up, I am a blend, in the middle, but I'm more *tom*-like because I like to serve" (Matthana 1995, 129). Kaew is a *tom* who appropriated a sense of herself as masculine and as essentially different from "normal women," a category that includes *dee*s. She also stressed she was not a man and could not abide those *tom*s who thought they were. During my interview with her, she complained: "They need to accept the truth that they aren't men. They have no way to be men— they can't stand when they pee, do you understand? *[Laughs.]* They think of themselves as men, but in fact they aren't. I don't hate them; I just don't want to be close to them, because I don't like that way of acting [like men]. I think it is disgusting, and so do others."

*Tom*s often stated that they were "not women"—that is, that they were of a different nature from their female partners and all other "ordinary" women. Although they usually accepted that they shared a common physiology with *dee*s and other "women," contemporary Western discourses of "gay hormones" were also mentioned at times, leading to a partial claim of physical difference from *dee*s. However, *tom*s who were highly invested in masculine identity also positioned themselves as not "real men" *(phu-chai thae)*, that is, not equal to fully physically realized males. Fon, a thirty-nine-year-old *tom* from Pattaya, illustrates this paradoxical positioning of both valorizing masculinity in the self and denying full appropriation of manhood status by constructing an image of an idealized and unattainable manhood. Fon wore me out with her rapid conversation and seemingly boundless enthusiasm. She sold papaya salad by the side of the road in North Pattaya and lived in a rented room behind a string of go-go bars, beer bars, and restaurants catering to foreign tourists. Fon shared the rented room with her partner, Nee, a sex worker eleven years older than Fon. Nee had a five-year-old child fathered by a long-gone client. Fon visibly appropriated masculine identity, with her closely cropped hair, men's trousers and shirt, and use of masculine speech pronouns and sentence particles *(phom, khrap phom)*. I asked her how she felt about being a *tom*, and she replied that she did not want to be this way: "I'm talking about being female. My mind is a man's. A woman's mind *(cit-cay)* is not in my head. I am like a man who has a woman [partner] and must take responsibility for her, like that." Fon linked her masculinity to the normative masculine social roles of "taking care" of her "wife" *(mia)*, while also acknowledging a certain dissatisfaction and feelings of resignation about being a partial man.

The *tom* Kot, mentioned above, described herself as having the ability to see both land and water, unlike "real men" who were trapped in their biological destiny as males. Kot and other *tom*s believed that they transcended and transgressed hegemonic parameters for femaleness, without totally rejecting or abandoning the femininity. *Tom*s openly acknowledged feeling that *dee*s were with them because, as *tom*s, they knew how to please and satisfy *dee*s. That attribute is what they had to focus on in order to compete with men, who the *tom*s felt could offer families and social respectability. *Dee*s described *tom*s as soft *(num-nuan)*, tender, intuitive, and understanding. Many *dee*s have told me that *tom*s have the ability to understand them in ways that men cannot, a sentiment shared by *tom*s. Ning, a twenty-four-year-old urban middle-class woman, said that she liked being a *tom* because she felt strong, as if she could take care of her partner and give her sexual pleasure. *Tom*s are better for women, said Ning, because *tom*s are soft *(num-nuan)*. Interestingly, Ning described both being strong and being soft as qualities that typify *tom*s. The flexibility of incorporating masculinity and femininity in the construction of the *tom* gender allowed for creative family relationships.

Fon, mentioned above, raised her lover's child as her own, providing most of the daily childcare. She felt very strongly about her responsibilities to her family and vowed that, no matter what happened, she would stand by her wife and child. Fon called herself a man, used masculine speech, and combined familiar rhetoric about male responsibilities for supporting a wife and children with an unconventional family arrangement. In her own view, Fon was both the masculine head of the family and the person lovingly responsible for the childcare of a girl fathered by an unknown client of her wife, while her wife earned the money to support the family. Fon said, "This is Pattaya. We have our own society here."

Although most *tom*s said that being only partial men caused them suffering, they also perceived this partial status as being positive. For example, although Fon clearly invested a lot in claiming a masculine identity, she also made it clear that she was not like men in other ways: "Lots of men are assholes (*hia*—literally "monitor lizards"), but *tom*s aren't assholes too much. *Tom*s still have good hearts (*cit-cay dii-ngaam*), are more compassionate than men. Men don't feel compassion for women. They think they are stronger and can force a woman, like that."

*Tom*s distinguished themselves from *dee*s by joking about having sex with each other. For example, in a scene that I have seen repeated in various settings throughout my study, a group of *tom*s were sitting around chatting at a friend's house, with a few other *dee*s. The subject of finding new partners came up, and the *tom*s began joking that maybe they would just have to be lovers with each other. To play along with the joke, one *tom,* Ging, walked up to her *tom* friend, Buu, and began to act in typically affected feminine manners, pawing her friend fawningly and looking away shyly while pursing her lips. Buu stayed stiff, made a face to show her disgust, and pushed Ging away, to the laughter of everybody else. Performances like this illustrated the absurdity of such a same-gendered pairing in the eyes of many *tom*s and thereby served to naturalize the masculinity of the *tom*s by naturalizing masculine-feminine pairings.

LOVING THE SAME GENDER? THE IMPOSSIBILITY OF TOM-TOM AND *DEE-DEE* RELATIONSHIPS

For Thais in general and for *tom*s and *dee*s in particular, an activity that is recognized as sexual must by definition include gender opposites, that is, masculine and feminine. Sexual activity between young girls or feminine women is considered play or is simply inconceivable; it is not labeled as "sexual" by many Thais.[1] The requirement for opposing genders in a relationship is widely held by *tom*s and *dee*s and is a point of ongoing contestation in the emergence of new understandings of sexual identity. Thus, *tom-dee* relationships are infinitely more recognizable to Thais as sexual than, say, sexual desire between two *tom*s—a suggestion that *tom*s said made them feel uneasy and awkward.

Same-gendered sex *(dee-dee, tom-tom)* is considered by *tom*s and *dee*s to be almost as "deviant" as same-sex sexuality is positioned within homophobic discourses in the West. For a *tom* to be sexually attracted to a *tom* holds a similar meaning as for a Western man to be sexually attracted to another man, except that *tom*s who desire other *tom*s have no subculture or alternative identity to provide them with support and validation. Both *tom*s and *dee*s usually said they felt it was "unnatural" to change from a *tom* to a *dee* or for two *tom*s or two *dee*s to be in a relationship, although some had heard of such cases. Chang, a twenty-six-year-old *dee* who recently moved to Bangkok from southern Thailand, described the clear-cut distinctions that she and others made between *tom*s and *dee*s:

> I have never had any lover who is a "woman" [*"phu-ying,"* meaning that she never had a *dee* lover]. I usually met *tom*s. I don't know why I usually have a very *tom* lover. I think it may be because our society thinks that *tom*s have to be with *dee*s. I've never seen any *dee* being with a *dee*—I don't think there are any. I think that ninety-nine percent are very *tom* and very *dee*. My twenty or thirty friends are all *dee*s and *tom*s. I saw two *tom*s together, but one *tom* changed herself to be a *dee*. Once I saw an older friend at one of Anjaree's parties. She had her hair cut short and didn't put on any makeup, but she had no bra and dressed like a woman. I was confused at first, but finally I saw her with a *tom*, so I knew that she actually was a *dee*. I remember that at first she was a *tom*, but when she loved a *tom*, she had to change herself to be with her *tom* lover. She looks happy. If one is very *tom* and then she totally changes herself to be a *dee*, I think that would be too much! I don't think I could handle that. I saw some *tom*s in Lesla group who sleep around with *tom*s. These young-generation *tom*s are like that—sleeping around. I think now most people [in Lesla] are against the idea of *tom*s being with *tom*s and *dee*s with *dee*s. So I will feel uncomfortable if I have a girl-friend who is not a *tom*.

Other *dee*s also expressed either hilarity or discomfort with the suggestion of having a relationship with a woman who was not explicitly male-identified. Khwan, a stylishly dressed professional woman in her early thirties sat at a table of friends and told us about her past *tom* lover. Khwan did not hesitate to discuss sex and arguments with her *tom,* and she seemed forthcoming and frank, with a lively sense of humor. I asked her if she could ever be interested in a woman who was not a *tom.* She laughed and said, "No way," adding that she could never be the "active" partner in or the initiator of sex *(faai-ruk).* Khwan explained that *tom*s were the ones who took the initiative in sex and that she, as a *dee,* was naturally "passive" *(faai-rap).* To switch roles and become the "active" partner seemed strange and even unnatural to Khwan. Her friend Jaeng, a *dee* who was sitting nearby, said that she felt a bit differently. Although having sex with a woman other than a *tom* would be bizarre—and she giggled with Khwan at the thought— she said she could be active and enjoy it, but only with a *tom.* For Khwan the sexual dimension of *tom-dee* relations defined her as *dee,* or feminine. Jaeng, on the other hand, expressed sexual flexibility but insisted that gender identity distinct from sexual roles was the key factor in determining who was an appropriate partner. Both agreed that a *tom* was the only conceivable sexual partner, regardless of whether they defined *tom*s as necessarily and exclusively sexual initiators or not.

HEGEMONIC MASCULINITY AND IDEAL *TOMS*

*Tom*s are measured by *dee*s and by other *tom*s according to general social standards in which men are supposed to be good providers, protectors, and leaders. Thai hegemonic masculinity is encapsulated in the concept of *chai-chatrii* (see Taywaditep, Coleman, and Dumronggittigule 1997, 1197–1199). Ideal manly qualities are also represented in the term *"nak-leng."* To be a *nak-leng* or a *chai-chatrii* implies that a man is brave, daring, risk-taking, and fair. The popular meaning of *"nak-leng"* has transformed in past decades and now implies that a man is something of a gangster—tough, loyal to allies, and a playboy who has numerous sexual affairs with women (Taywaditep, Coleman, and Dumronggittigule 1997, 1197–1199). *Tom*s often strive to display these qualities. They were often described by *dee*s and by Thais in general as having this blend of positive and negative masculine traits, such as being tough, knavish *(kee-ree),* and flirtatious, implying a tendency to be unfaithful to partners. *Dee*s often said that their ideal *tom* would have none of these traits, similar to what women in general say about their ideal male partner. A woman wrote in a personal advertisement in an Anjaree newsletter, "I want to meet a *tom* who is 100% *tom* in both her body and her mind, who really dresses like a man, has short hair and the personality of a leader" (*Anjareesaan,* July–December 1996, vol. 3, no. 18, 31). The advertisement also specifically requested a *tom* who did not engage in the baser masculine activities (such as smoking or drinking).

Both *tom*s and *dee*s described ideal *tom*s to me as embodying the characteristics of high-class Chinese men, such as pale skin, small features, and wealth—all supposed attributes of ethnic Chinese urban business elite. The most sought-after *tom*s were often Chinese and wealthy. One woman who had had previous relationships with *tom*s, and had since married a man, described her husband as "not very attractive." She described him as tall, dark, and slender. Surprised, I asked her to describe her ideal man, and she responded, "He would be short *(tia),* fat *(uan),* pale *(tua khaao),* with a flat Chinese face *(naa-baen baen baep ciin).*" The other women present nodded their heads in agreement. These were physical signs of wealth and social status embodied in the *sia,* or wealthy Chinese man.[2]

Students have explained to me that the image of the ideal Thai man as portrayed in Thai movies has also been transformed over the past several decades. Several decades ago, movie heroes were dark-skinned "tough guys" from the countryside, who looked rough and were good fighters. The new ideal man is the fair-skinned *"luuk khreung,"* or person of Thai-European descent. He looks "pretty" and is well dressed, well mannered, and well educated. This ideal male partner, informed by local class and ethnic parameters, was reinscribed in *tom-dee* relationships. These qualities were sought after in *tom* partners, and *tom*s compared themselves with other *tom*s in terms of these desired attributes.

The ideal *tom* is therefore expected to provide financially for a *dee.* In reality, being a *sia,* for both men and *tom*s, is an ideal, a point of comparison rather than a description of real behavior. The *dee*s I interviewed often supported *tom*s, and *tom*s often withheld support of *dee*s because they resented what they felt were opportunistic tendencies of *dee*s. Nevertheless, both *tom*s and *dee*s agreed that the wealthy, usually older *tom* was an ideal partner for most *dee*s. Ideal *tom*ness is an extension of this image of being sophisticated and elite, which is demonstrated through acts of caring for a *dee.*

TOMS AND CARETAKING

The principle of caretaking is central to *tom* identity. Being a good host, by taking out a *dee* and her friends and family to nice restaurants, was important to many women as a sign of a good *tom*. Many women also considered caretaking as the ideal quality for men. Interestingly, *tom*s and *dee*s often used the English expression "take care" to refer to this principle in their relationships, rather than the Thai equivalent, *"duu-lae,"* which they used on occasion. I asked *dee*s and heterosexual women about what they would like from a man they married, and almost all said they wanted a man capable of caring for them as a leader and a protector. However, the kind of caring that was expected from *tom*s, and that *tom*s offered, differed from hegemonic masculinity.

*Tom*s were expected to care for women not only financially but also emotionally and sexually to a much higher degree than was expected of men. For many *dee*s, caretaking was the defining quality of a *tom*, the quality of *tom*ness to which they felt the most attracted. Um, a *dee* and a professional woman from Bangkok in her mid-thirties, described her past affairs with *tom*s by listing the ways they took care of her, such as serving her food, driving her around, taking her on trips, and picking her up at work or school. When asked if *tom*s take care of women like men do, Um answered, "Yes, it is like men, but men take care of me less than *tom*s do and also not as well." For Um, this quality of caretaking was more significant than any other feature of *tom*ness, including dress. Um explained that *tom*s and *dee*s were happy to be together and did not need to be excessively obvious to outsiders about their identity and relationship. For Um, being a *tom* was not so much a sexual role as a social role expressed through constant attentive care. She defined *tom*s not in terms of appearance or sexual desire but in terms of the need to protect and care for women: "*Tom*s don't want to be with men, because they don't want to be with anyone stronger than they are. They want to be stronger than their partners are, so that they can feel like they can protect them."

For Um, the definition of *"dee"* also resided in this caretaking dynamic. When asked if she could ever see herself attracted to a *dee*, she answered no, that she would not enjoy taking care of a woman: "Women seem like they cannot take care of themselves. If I had a *dee* girlfriend, I wouldn't want to bother taking care of her. I wouldn't like it. It's annoying—they are so fussy. If I have a *tom,* she will take care of me and be worried about me. She will find nice presents for me and pay a lot of attention to me. . . . I can be friends with *dee*s, but I don't want to be lovers with them; it wouldn't be fun. *Tom*s are fun. *Tom*s will take me out, take care of me—that's fun. They will help me carry things. When I went abroad with that *tom,* it was such great fun both times we went. She drove me around. I didn't have to do anything. If I had a *dee* lover, I would have such a burden. But I wonder why *tom*s like to take care so much?"

Um further described the qualities of the "most successful *dee*s": "*Dee*s who are successful in being *dee*s have to be helpless. They need to need help. For example, they should not like to drive, so that *tom*s have to pick them up every day, so they are together every day. They don't like to go anywhere by themselves; they need someone to take them out every day. So the *dee* cannot be without a *tom,* and that is what a successful *dee* will think." Um explained that this situation would require the couple to be together a lot of the time, which would lead to a closeness and a good relationship. She also said that that kind of closeness could be suffocating, and the caretaking by *tom*s, while attractive, could lead her to feel as if she could not do anything on her own. Cot, a *dee* in her mid-twenties, exemplifies Um's description of "successful *dee*s" by describing why she likes to be with *tom*s: "I like them because I feel that they are strong, and I can depend on them. I feel that I am weak, and so I want somebody who is strong." Um clarified that *dee*s like herself also took care of *tom*s, but in different ways; "I took care of her feelings. For example, if she was sad, she would turn to me, like I was the only one who could help her. Even though she looked so tough on the outside, she was really soft. Sometimes I feel she is weaker emotionally than I am. She is more sensitive."

Chang, a *dee*, positioned *tom*s as a blend of masculine and feminine characteristics. She said they were strong but also were able to care for her in ways that men would not, such as performing women's typical household tasks: "I understand that a *tom* is a woman, so they don't have to do everything like a man. I don't like *tom*s who act like a big bully or drink or smoke. That's why I prefer older *tom*s who are more mature. So many friends of mine are *tom*s, but they can do housework and don't have to act like a man. Actually my *tom* [*tom khorng chan*] now is doing my laundry at home, and she can do everything like a housewife. But she takes care of me and acts tough outside the house." When asked to define *tom*s, the first thing Chang said was, "*Tom*s have to be caretakers, and *dee*s have to be taken care of and to pay attention to *tom*s." Although labeling *tom*s as caretakers, Chang reversed Um's logic by saying that *tom*s take care of emotions while *dee*s take care of routine household chores (although her *tom* does the household chores).

The kind of caretaking expected by *tom*s was curiously similar to the kind of "service" that Thai women are expected to provide their husbands and others in general. Women are traditionally expected to place the needs of others, especially their husband, above their own. Women's caretaking of others is evident in the everyday activities of Thai women, who are trained from early childhood to feed those around them and make them comfortable. When I have heard *tom*s and *dee*s describe the attentiveness and caring that *tom*s give (or are expected to give) their *dee* partners, the lyrics to the Thai Girl Scout song comes to mind:

> Service, service is our work,
> We do it regularly and never think to hesitate . . . Hey!
>
> *Borikarn borikarn ngarn thii phuak-rao tham*
> *Pen pracam rao tham pai mai khoey khit ruan-ree hee!*

The Thai Boy Scout song, in contrast, is about Thai nationality and loyalty to the founder of the Thai scouts, King Rama VI.

The performance of *tom* masculinity is thus woven into hegemonic notions of masculinity but is not isomorphic with it. Ironically, even though the *tom*s I interviewed avowed masculine status, those qualities that most defined *tom* masculinity were stereotypical Thai feminine traits, such as caretaking and sensitivity.[3] *Tom* identity is crucially dependent on being positioned as different from *dee* identity, even though both share dimensions of hegemonic femininity. *Tom*s and *dee*s must differ in some specific ways, although what exactly these ways are vary widely, according to the *tom*s and *dee*s I interviewed. For a *tom* to be a *tom* and not an "ordinary woman" *(phu-ying thammada),* she must demonstrate that she is not like an "ordinary" woman, by selectively disassociating herself from *dee*s and women in general.

The issue of male identification in *tom* subjectivity is sensitive and complex. Ting, a thirty-year-old social activist and a self-identified *tom*, complained of seemingly sympathetic research on *tom*s and *dee*s that facilely equates *tom*s and men (or masculinity). For Ting the crucial issue was how *tom*s were not like men and how *tom-dee* relationships provided an alternative to compulsory heterosexuality. Ting, unlike some *tom*s, did not idealize or romanticize manhood but instead resented what she perceived as male dominance secured through oppression of women. Ting's avowedly feminist interpretation of gender contrasted sharply with many other *tom*s' sense of idealized manhood. For Ting, being a *tom* allowed greater freedom of sexual expression, as well as a rejection of social strictures on women's behavior and sexuality. Ting's discomfort at automatic equations of *tom*s and men cautions against any essentialist reduction of *tom*s to a singular or unified category, and against assumptions of any stable or simple conception of masculinity for *tom*s. The importance of the idiom of masculinity to *tom* identity is crucial to recognize, but the meanings attributed to masculinity by *tom*s are paradoxical and inconsistent.

SUFFERING AND *TOMS*' INHERITANCE OF *KATHOEY* TRADITION

Although a few *tom*s envisioned a *tom* identity that was not tightly linked to masculinity or notions of being "like men" (such as Ting's above), most perceived their close identity with masculinity as inborn and indicative of their disappointingly partial status as men. They discussed their identity within Buddhist paradigms of karmic retribution, implying that their masculine gender was inevitable and unchangeable. A *tom* named Duang described her situation:

> I think that in my previous life I was a man who was a womanizer and was not good to lots of women, so in this life, by being a woman who loves women, I must deal with the negative karma that I built up. I must be disappointed with love. It's just like *tut* [feminine homosexual males, *kathoey*] that in a previous life were women who deceived lots of men, so that in this life they have to be a man who loves men. . . . Although women can be couples, these couples aren't ideal. For couples who are together for a long time, until they die, it is because they built up merit together. We have had many lives; we don't know what we did in what life. Whatever happens is the result of our actions *(kaam)* in our previous lives. To be really ideal, a couple must consist of a man and a woman. That is natural, because women with women, or men with men, cannot have children. Look at women who want to change to be men; [they] can't do it. Even if they have an operation, they are not complete like real men. (Matthana 1996, 109)

*Tom*s share with *kathoey*s, male transgendered/transsexual males, a discourse of "suffering" from an inability to achieve true maleness or femaleness. Thai gay men have also appropriated this discourse of suffering to describe their difficulties in finding social acceptance and satisfying relationships (see Jackson 1995, 79–86). This shared discourse marks an important point of commonality between Thai males and females in the way they access Thai cultural paradigms, such as Buddhist notions of karma and suffering, to frame their experiences and self-identity. Also, mainstream Thais reiterate this theme that homosexuality and/or transgenderism (usually understood by Thais to be intertwined phenomena) are a form of suffering resulting from past misdeeds, thereby eliciting sympathy for *kathoey*s, *tom*s, and gays. *Dee*s notably fall outside this discourse and are not understood by most Thais, including *tom* and *dee*s, to be suffering karmic retribution.

The explicit assertion that to be "misgendered" is a source of suffering resonates with the fundamental principles of Buddhism. The first Noble Truth of Buddhism states that suffering (*dukha* in Pali and *khwam-thuk* in Thai) is an inescapable part of existence. Craving and desire are the sources of suffering, and consequently the cessation of desire, want, and need will reduce and ultimately eliminate suffering: "When craving ceases entirely through dispassion, renunciation, and nondependence, then suffering ceases" (Robinson and Johnson 1982, 24). Many *tom*s who reported that to be a *tom* is suffering and that to relinquish *dee*s in order to marry men is a meritorious action linked these ideas to their Buddhist beliefs.

The idiom of suffering allowed the *tom*s I interviewed to position their masculinity as inborn and therefore "natural" *(thammachaat)*. For Nuu, suffering was an inescapable quality of *tom*ness. On one of her frequent trips upcountry she met a group of middle-aged *tom*s, and as is Nuu's way, she immediately befriended them and asked them how they felt about being *tom*s. They said they were happy living alone and that they too were tired of being exploited and abandoned by *dee*s. They said they were happy and content now with pets instead of partners. Nuu told me she did not believe them when they said they were fine; she insisted they were in denial: "Thais are really good at being able to deny themselves things and at not recognizing their own pain." Nuu and other *tom*s described being a *tom* as an inescapable karmic fate.

When I met Piin, a *tom,* one day for our usual tennis game, she gave me a mischievous smile and exclaimed, "I hit her!" She added in

English, "I didn't hurt her . . . maybe I should have." Piin, in her late thirties, is from a well-known wealthy Bangkok family and lives in the center of a vibrant *tom-dee* community in Bangkok. The recipient of Piin's blow was another *tom*, several years her junior, who had taken up with Piin's girlfriend.

Every time I met Piin, she had a new entourage of women with her, both *tom*s and *dee*s. I had never met anybody with such a flair for social organizing. I went to a party she arranged at a local *tom*-owned restaurant, expecting the usual *tom-dee* party: shy and awkward women huddled in small groups, nervously eyeing other groups, until they all went home. Piin's party, however, was a spectacle—hundreds of women were crushed into the restaurant, on the dance floor, and along the bar, laughing, drinking, and carousing. Piin moved easily among all the groups with a bottle of liquor, pouring shots, introducing newcomers, and making sure everyone had somebody to talk to. In spite of Piin's popularity and near-celebrity status within the Bangkok middle-class *tom-dee* world, she could see only loss recently. Every time I saw her, our conversation never strayed far from her angst over the loss of Joy, the beautiful flight attendant who ran off with another *tom*.

Piin had many girlfriends, though; her friendly sociability, gentle doting care, and high-style living were an attractive combination. Her apartment was on an upper floor of a high-rise and, though not wildly luxurious by Bangkok standards, seemed to outline the main theme of Piin's social life—entertaining women. Piin and the rest of her visiting friends laughed as we toured her bedroom and saw her huge luxury bed placed in front of a plate-glass window nearly as big as the wall, providing a spectacular view of the lights of downtown Bangkok. Another friend smiled and dragged me to the bathroom, saying I really had to check something out. Piin had a jar for toothbrushes with about ten or so brushes in it. Many had labels taped to the handle, identifying the woman who owned the brush—all Piin's "girls." In fact, I rarely saw Piin without one of her numerous girlfriends, who would usually quietly sit beside her and smile shyly as Piin garrulously laughed and chatted, easily switching from Thai to English.

Piin was gloomy and listless for a while, even with her usual cast of "girls" surrounding her. She was clearly bitter, telling me again how the one who ran off was a flight attendant. Nuu, our mutual friend, seemed impressed, because "flight attendant" equals exceptional feminine beauty in the minds of most Thais. Nuu stressed to me again later,

"Her girlfriend is a *flight attendant*." Time passed and Piin seemed to be distracted with a series of girlfriends, this one too jealous, that one asking for too much. But then one day Pin had run into Joy and her new *tom* lover, back from traveling abroad, at a restaurant that was one of Piin's favorite hangouts. Piin told me that she had hit the *tom* once and that the *tom* had cowered in fear as Piin's friends pulled Piin her off her. Piin seemed upset at the incident and was not her usual energetic self. Nuu stepped in to comfort and make sense of things, a talent she had shown for all her friends, myself included, when they felt depressed. Nuu said that in life we all do silly things, like hitting others over some woman.

Nuu proceeded to relate a hilarious story about her own brawl with a *tom* many years earlier. Nuu said her friend Jai, a *tom*, had started seeing Nuu's girlfriend. One day Nuu saw Jai get out of an elevator with the girlfriend, and Nuu made a fist and swung at Jai with rage. Nuu described Jai's agile contortions to avoid the hapless blows, as Nuu's fist slammed into a wall and generally missed its target. Jai then frantically kicked Nuu in self-defense, and Nuu chortled that she did not think that kicking was allowed. Nuu said she felt so ashamed later, because Jai had been her good friend. Nuu had apologized to Jai, but it took many years for Jai to forgive her. Nuu's story had us all in stitches, as she mimicked her clumsy swings and the way the slender Jai had jumped and ducked. Piin still seemed depressed, quietly listening. Nuu turned to Piin and gently comforted her, saying, "You must know that to be a *tom* is suffering."

Tao, a thirty-three-year-old professional *tom* in Bangkok, described her relationship with her lover of several years, Puu. Tao said she would not keep Puu from leaving her for a man, because that would be better for Puu (Puu did not agree and after several years is still with Tao, running a small business together). Tao said that she had heard a monk on the radio say that "third sexes" were caused by poor karma created in a previous life. She said she must have been a man who had committed a sin, probably adultery, and this was her karmic punishment, to be born an incomplete man incapable of lasting love. Unlike many *tom*s, Tao's sense of *tom*ness did not reside in any outward expression of masculinity. Tao looked feminine, with shoulder-length hair and feminine work clothes. Nevertheless, she described her *tom*ness as innate, inescapable, and generally pitiable.

Likewise, Kralok, a forty-five-year-old middle-class *tom* said, "If I could choose, I would be a man. Because if we look at [Buddhist] religious beliefs, it was because of sin [bad karma] that I was born like this. No matter how much good I might do, people will always see us as violent. And our love lives never last long. So I believe that in our past lives we did something wrong or had an immoral affair. It is about karma, like somebody born crippled. I'm Buddhist, so I accept the way I am. If we look at it from a scientific perspective, I think I have a lot of male hormones."

Kralok used both Buddhist and scientific discourses to position herself as unalterably a *tom* and as pitiable. Luat, a middle-class *tom* in her forties, repeated the message of the sorrowful life of *tom*s by telling me of her first girlfriend, whom she met at college:

"I was with her for four years. She was studying at college. The first day I hugged her, she didn't think anything about it, because we were women. She had only had boyfriends before. She was very confused. She was surprised . . . no, she wasn't surprised, but she was having a problem with her boyfriend. She was pretty and had a good figure. I invited her to live with me. I knew she had only a little money from her family, and I had a little and wanted to help her out, so we stayed at her dorm together. I didn't dare ask her if she loved me. She never spoke about love . . . she didn't love me and she didn't want to lie about it. She cooked and did the housework and cleaned. Sometimes I felt tense with her, not really warm. I thought that not having anyone is better than to have someone like this. I told her I wanted to be alone and that she should go home upcountry, and she was glad to go see her family because she had just graduated. On graduation day she didn't want me to come to the university. She was embarrassed, and we didn't take pictures together, even after being together four years—and I paid for it all. This is life—crying. *[Laughs.]*

*Dee*s often agreed with *tom*s that to be a *tom* was suffering and that this suffering did not extend to *dee*s. Bua, a thirty-year-old urban office worker, told me about her relationship with the first *tom* lover she had, when she was in high school and college. I asked her if she thought her lover, Tum, had a tragic life as a *tom*. Bua answered succinctly, "I am sorry about it, but that's her problem." I asked her if she felt that she was different from Tum. She replied: "I feel I am normal, but she is abnormal and I feel sorry for her. I am with her to be friends, to help her. I want her to feel she can have a partner like anybody else. I am normal, part of society. She is the one I must take special care of, because she is delicate and has lots of problems, which makes her abnormal. Sometimes I think she is like a man, because sometimes she treats me like a man would—takes care of me, is very gentlemanly. I just want her to be a real man, so I could be with her all our lives. I was afraid people would know [we were lovers] and then not like me. I was afraid nobody would help me then. But now I don't think like that anymore. Now I know I can help myself."

Bua implied that she felt freer now to be in a relationship with a woman, because she was not as dependent on society's judgments as she used to be. Bua also did not say that having a relationship with a woman is abnormal, because that was precisely what she herself was doing. She saw her partner's inability to express normative feminine gender as the main point of difference between them and as a source of suffering for the *tom.* Bua did not see herself as "deviant" or essentially different from any other woman. She described herself as "caring" for a loved one in a way that is expected and approved of for women by society. I asked her if she thought of herself as a lesbian, and she said no, that she could love a man too. Bua did not feel she needed to apply any label to herself, although she recognized the label of *"dee"* as an adjective to describe women like her. However, the term *"dee"* had no great significance within her identity.

The main source of the suffering of *tom*s, according to both *tom*s and *dee*s, was the supposed tendency of *dee*s to break off relationships with *tom*s in order to be with men. Chang, a *dee*, agreed with *tom*s that being a *tom* was difficult and even tragic because of *dee*s' fickleness. Chang said that "fake" *dee*s would be likely to turn to men for social approval and comfort and thus disappoint *tom*s. However, Chang distinguished between these women and "real" *dee*s: "There is a good chance that the *dee*s who are not real *dee*s will dump the good *tom*s to have a boyfriend. But I think they are women, so if they want to have boyfriends, just let them go and be happy, since it's their nature and it's the right way for them, and society will accept that. The old and good *tom*s will be hurt by this more seriously than the young *tom*s because the young ones just like to play around anyway. I think there are so many *dee*s now who will change and have boyfriends, so I say you shouldn't make a promise to a *tom* [to be together] if you are not sure you are a real *dee*. But I know myself that I don't want men, so I can guarantee myself."

In the course of my research, I met many *dee*s who were in long-term relationships, and some *dee*s would list these couples as proof that *dee*s were sincere with *tom*s. Um, a *dee* in her thirties, describes her *tom-dee* friends as having stable relationships. Like Chang, Um suggested that older *dee*s are less likely than younger *dee*s to switch from *tom*s to men: "My friends have committed relationships, like they will live and die together. . . . I think that if you are a *dee*, when you turn thirty years old, you won't change after that. You will be a *dee* forever. But if it is during school age, like high school or university, they might have a girlfriend, but when they graduate, they all get boyfriends."

Although some *dee*s did not agree that being a *tom* was tragic, most agreed that *tom*s had been abandoned by *dee*s—through no fault of the *dee*s, because it was usually considered to be their "nature" too. Other *dee*s, however, disagreed strongly with the idea that *tom*s suffered at the hands of *dee*s; according to their experience, it was usually the *tom* who abandoned the *dee* for another woman. This portrayal rather closely matches hegemonic discourse in which men are portrayed as abandoning wives for younger women. In any case, *dee*s would sometimes scoff loudly at the idea of *tom* suffering, saying that *tom*s are promiscuous and flirtatious, just like men.

"RELEASING" A PARTNER

*Tom*s often emphasized their partial male status by renouncing claims to women as long-term partners. These *tom*s said they recognized that they were not really men and therefore were not suitable for "normal women" as long-term partners. Although this position seemed to reflect negative self-understandings, it also validated the choices that *tom*s made to lead independent lives. The statements *tom*s made concerning their willingness to renounce love and sexual pleasure resonated strongly with Buddhist principles in which physical pleasure and desire are perceived as worldly attachments ultimately leading to suffering.

Lung, a forty-year-old middle-class *tom* with her own small company, struck me with her self-effacing comments on the undesirability of being a *tom*. Lung was the envy of other *tom*s—she was attractive and always stylishly dressed in cleanly pressed slacks and designer button-down shirts. Lung's gentle polite manners and obvious middle-class status enticed considerable attention from both *dee*s and emulating *tom*s. She evinced the typical *tom* pathos, however, commenting frequently on her sad fate of being born a *tom*. Lung said she did not want her younger sister to be with a *tom*, because it would mean an "uncertain future." Her sister had men who were interested in her, with good career potential, so she should not waste time with a *tom*, according to Lung. I questioned Lung on the point that she categorically declared *tom*s to be unfit future partners, because she herself seemed to have a good, secure life and was clearly affluent. She replied by switching gears a bit, saying that she knew that sleeping with men would be more satisfying for the *dee* than being with a *tom*. In response to her negative portrayals of *tom*s, I asked her whether she would prefer having been born as a man rather than a *tom*, if that were possible. Lung said no, because being a *tom* meant more "freedom" *(isaraphaap)*.[4]

Phorn, a well-to-do *tom* in her mid-forties, enjoyed a life of relative leisure, with frequent golf weekends and trips upcountry with groups of *tom* friends. Phorn looked masculine in her men's trousers and short-cropped hair and had held a *tom* identity and a strong sense of being masculine since she was young. She had been involved with a professional woman, also in her forties, for several years, yet still maintained a sense of individual identity and space by accessing her "partial man" discourse: "I always tell them, 'Don't think that I am a man. I am not a man.' I can't give them [everything]. I have my own life. I enjoy my social life—my own. Sometimes they don't come with me, and maybe you think I am selfish, but it is true in life that they also need their own social life. . . . I can't give them anything like a married life. Maybe they want me to give them a house, a car, children, money, but I cannot. If we stay together like friends, it is possible to be together, but if not, she has to find [something else]."

It is tempting to label this resignation as fatalism. However, this discourse positions *tom*s as ethically and morally responsible. Ying, the *tom* tour-company owner introduced in chapter 2, explained that she planned to marry her girlfriend, with permission of her girlfriend's family. Ying clearly wanted to convey that she was a "good" person. She earnestly described her yearly charity donations and her regular good deeds. She was very insistent that she was not like some of those selfish, "bad" *tom*s who cling to *dee*s and refuse to let them go when the time comes for a *dee* to move on. To Ying it was obvious that *dee*s were "normal" women whose stay with *tom*s was a way station to their natural destiny—marriage to a man and having a family.

Statements that a *tom* would give up a feminine lover in order to allow her to lead a "normal" life emphasize distinctions between *tom*s and *dee*s. *Tom*s never suggested that they too could decide to marry and lead a "normal" life. The suggestion made most *tom*s I asked laugh. To try to force oneself to not be masculine and to disguise oneself as feminine were ludicrous and even insulting to many of the *tom*s I questioned. Nuu, like many others, positioned herself as morally good by making distinctions between herself as a *tom* and *dee*s as "normal women": "I am not selfish. If a woman says she can go on living a normal life with a man, I'll say please go—to go is better, because I probably can't give her very much." Nuu was a well-educated middle-class *tom* who enjoyed traveling abroad and playing sports—she could clearly provide some positive things for a partner. In fact, she had had many experiences supporting women, but now she said that would never support another *dee* in her life because all *dee*s were after money rather than true love. Nuu defined her lack of interest in long-term relationships with *dee*s in terms of being morally good and sacrificing to the natural order of things, while simultaneously looking out for herself. Furthermore, Nuu clearly positioned herself as "not woman" by categorically and emphatically rejecting any suggestion that she too, as a woman, could get married and have a family—that was only an option for *dee*s and other "real women."

This theme of "releasing" the gender-normative partner to lead a "normal" life is also found among some homosexual men who identify as feminine (either calling themselves gay or words associated with *kathoey*s, such as "second kind of woman"). The feminine partner may disassociate himself from his masculine partner by "releasing" him to lead a "normal life." This pattern is exemplified in an interview with Seri Wongmontha, a well-known Thai academic who is openly homosexual, during a debate about gay male rights held at Thammasat University in February 1983. Presenting male homosexuality as a kind of suffering, Seri said:

Those who aren't [gay/homosexual][5] don't become [gay/homosexual]. If you are born normal like that, you are lucky already. If somebody is at the crossroads, please don't become gay, because if you are gay already, it's a dead-end. [Question: So if you don't want others to be gay, why did you get involved with others, thereby making them gay?] The people I will mess around with have three characteristics. First, they must be full men who have had experience with women already, so it won't be like tasting sex with a man for the first sexual experience and then they get hooked. Second, they must be confident in their "sexuality" [English word used]. Third, they must continue to be with women too. If they stop seeing women and I can see they are becoming hooked on this kind of sex, I must "say goodbye" [English used, meaning "end the relationship"]. . . . But if you tell me you haven't been with a woman yet, I'll say, "Go and try," and [I'll] say, "Women are better for sure. Go and try. . . . But if after a while you still don't go, and if you are just with me, I don't want that—you must have a girlfriend." Almost all the men I've been with are married. I dumped three men for the same reason: they all were showing tendencies [to be gay]. . . . They fell for me more than I did for them, so I broke up with them and persuaded them to see prostitutes. After I persuaded them, they still didn't go. Four years later, they are more womanly than I am. You can't blame me. The truth is, I helped them step out of the closet . . . and stopped them from being a "closet queen" [English used] and to become a "screaming queen" [English used]. (Kirati, Aphirat, and Kittisak 1993, 138–139)

Seri's discourse is based on mainstream Thai understandings of male homosexual relationships in which feminine *kathoeys* are paired with gender-normative men. Thus the *kathoey*/man paradigm is patterned much like the *tom*/woman (i.e., *dee*) paradigm. Seri insisted that his partners were normative men and hence had to visit female prostitutes and have girlfriends to give evidence of this. He also asserted that all of his male partners had been married. If his masculine partners turned "gay" by showing evidence of femininity, he would reject them. If the partners turned out to be "womanly," he said that he was not to blame, because he gave them every chance of maintaining a normative masculine identity. If they became "screaming queens," it was because they were that way to begin with, according to Seri. He stated that he selflessly renounced his relationships with men so that they could pursue "normal" relationships with women. Interestingly, the pattern of his relationships fits hegemonic norms for Thai masculinity. It is permissible for "normal" men to engage in sexual activities outside of marriage, as long as such sexual adventures do not infringe on the man's duty to maintain his marriage. Men's extramarital relationships can be either homosexual or heterosexual, with lovers or prostitutes, as long as the man does not take on a feminine identity or abandon his wife and family.

*Tom*s also repeat and reinforce hegemonic gender norms for women, by asserting that women (not *tom*s) should marry and fulfill a woman's "natural" duty to be a wife and a mother. *Tom*s, on the other hand, by nature of their masculine status, are freed from these duties and responsibilities and thus are able to pursue personal goals and romances. Also, somewhat ironically, *tom*s who support hegemonic discourses that it is "natural" for women to marry men and to be mothers further isolated *dee*s and pressured them into relationships with men. Unlike *tom*s, who were pressured much less to marry than were *dee*s, *dee*s often felt keenly aware of social disapproval of their choice to be with a *tom* instead of a husband. Um had three *tom* lovers before deciding to marry a man. She said that the main reason for breaking up with the last *tom* was social disapproval of their relationship: "We split up because people around us didn't accept us. I felt awkward. I felt it was too strange, and for two years nothing changed—people around us still didn't accept it. I had friends who were *tom*s and *dee*s, and they are still *tom*s and *dee*s, and these friends accepted themselves as *tom*s and *dee*s, but I couldn't accept it. My *tom* didn't have a problem with it; she loved me very much. If you ask doctors, they will say to break up. Other friends didn't want me to be [a homosexual]. I myself didn't want to see any friends [because of their disapproval]." For Um, the uncomfortable mixture of feeling abnormal and being under pressure to have a "normal" married life led her to leave the *tom* and find a man with whom to start a family. What many *tom*s positioned as "natural" and "normal" for *dee*s was actually a painful choice for many *dee*s who never ceased in their romantic or sexual feelings for *tom*s. Um said she still felt attracted to *tom*s, and she seemed uncomfortably placed between the worlds of heterosexual hegemony and *tom-dee* society.

This discourse of suffering used by *tom*s forced me to recognize my own cultural attitudes that had been obscuring my understanding of *tom*s. The apparent contradiction between the relative freedom *tom*s had both sexually and in terms of lifestyle, and their discourse of suffering, nagged at me throughout the course of my research. Both working-class and middle-class *tom*s seemed to have more freedom of movement than normative-gender women experienced. Despite *tom*s' assertions that they were not like "ordinary women," I continued to think of them as "women" with relative sexual freedom. One day I voiced this opinion in response to a *tom* who was repeating these standard statements that she, as a *tom*, had to endure a life of hardship and suffering. In the anecdote above, Nuu was counseling Piin that she must accept this heartache as part of being a *tom*. I had heard Nuu say this so many times that I burst out with, "You don't seem like you are suffering so much." I said that she did not have a husband and children to run home to care for—she did not have to take care of anybody but herself. She used the money that she earned on new golf clubs and trips to the beach with various lovers. I asked her how she could think she was suffering, especially considering all the heterosexual women we knew with oppressive family situations and neglectful husbands. I said that being a *tom* seemed like a rather good deal in comparison, adding, "You know, everybody gets hurt in relationships, not just *tom*s." Nuu said calmly, "Why are you comparing me to a woman? Compare me to a man." Nuu concluded, "I lost something when I was born as a *tom*." Her response jolted me, and I clearly understood that I was interpreting her according to my own cultural paradigm in which individuals are exclusively categorized according to a system of binary sexes, so that one is understood as fundamentally either a male (man) or female (woman). Thai *tom*s simultaneously claimed an ambivalent gender identity that refused to accommodate itself to any category and claimed an unalterable masculine identity.

*Tom*s allowed *dee*s to fulfill the role of "ordinary women" through their resignation to the impossibility of finding lasting love as *tom*s— who, after all, would choose such a fate? Nuu and others felt uncomfortable with any suggestion of causality or choice that would imply possible change to "normal woman" status. Choice is a double-edged sword, proven so by the current Western debates over whether homosexuality is either inborn or a "lifestyle."[6] To postulate choice suggests that change is possible and perhaps desirable. To postulate "born-to-be" negates any suggestion of change and calls for acceptance of what cannot be altered; however, it also denies any personal agency or the "right" to make life choices concerning gender and sexuality.

Returning to Ting's critique of "*tom*s as men," discussed above, Ting further rankled at suggestions of "born-to-be" self-perceptions of many *tom*s. She said she did not know if homosexuality/*tom-dee*ism was inborn or not; there seemed to be so much research going on now, and she really could not say with certainty one way or the other. But she said that what she did know was that being in a relationship with a woman was a choice: "It cannot be anything but a choice." Ting sought to encourage *tom*s and *dee*s to rethink their own concept of self, so that they could feel that they had the right to be whatever gender they wished and to have whatever sexuality they wanted, and she hoped that I would convey this perspective in my work as a counter to the essentializing discourse of many masculine-identified *tom*s.

FANTASIZING THE MASCULINE

*Tom*s used imaginings of an ideal manhood that they could never fully achieve as a discursive device to position their manhood, life decisions, and relative independence as a kind of pathos. Fon explained that being born as a *tom* was a source of pain, and when asked if she would choose to be born as a *tom* or a man, she answered unequivocally that she would prefer to be a man: "[Being a man] would be better than being a *tom*, see? *Tom*s are, like, not fully equipped, right? My family would have more warmth, and my wife, whom I am with, would have everything, happiness for both the body and the mind." For Fon, manhood was an imagined category that bore little resemblance to the real world of heterosexual lives and the struggles, inadequacies, and disappointments that men actually faced—issues never raised by the *tom*s I interviewed. This idealization of maleness can lead to tragic consequences, as in a case of one young *tom* who said she had thought of killing herself in order to be reborn as a man and thereby be able to live with her lover in peace with social approval.[7] Tang, a middle-class *tom* in her mid-thirties, also expressed the thought that being reborn as a man would lead to the permanent satisfying love she wanted: "I would be a man if I could choose, and would have the same as a man and be with a woman like a man can, and then the woman wouldn't leave me." The vision of being the "correct" gender as an all-encompassing balm for life's travails engenders the *tom*s' utopian vision of the idealized man, to which no actual man need be compared (and none ever was in my research).

SEX AS SITE OF MEANINGS FOR TOMS AND DEES

Sexual activity was a key site for *tom*s in asserting their masculinity by appropriating dominant norms of Thai masculinity. *Tom*s persistently expressed the importance of penetrative sex for women's pleasure, despite their own partners' rejection of it. *Tom*s asserted that a major source of their suffering was their inability to maintain relationships (in spite of evidence to the contrary) because of what they perceived as their partner's need for penetrative sex. Mainstream Thai attitudes supported the belief that sex was primarily defined as penis-vagina contact.[8] Fon believed that not having a penis meant incomplete sex for her partner: "I'm not a man; I'm a woman like she is. If she can accept being with me, I'm OK. Regarding pleasure for the body, maybe I can't do enough, only pleasure for the heart. I try my best. . . . I have to ask her first. I don't have the ability to do it for her. Is she still satisfied to be with me?"

Before one of my trips back to the United States, Fon insistently asked me to buy a dildo for her, because they are not widely available in Thailand.[9] Every time she saw me she would run up to me with a strained look of anticipation and insistence, asking me to please buy it for her and saying that if I did not bring it back, we need not consider ourselves friends anymore. I took her insistence seriously and bought for her a top-of-the-line silicon dildo and harness while in San Francisco. Fon laughed and hurriedly took them from me when I returned, thanking me repeatedly. A few weeks later I asked her how it was going with her new dildo—did her "wife" appreciate it? Fon had lost her earlier enthusiasm and said that her wife preferred not to use it, much to Fon's disappointment. The same scenario repeated itself with another *tom-dee* couple I knew, Ot and Aa. After they received the imported dildo, Ot, the *dee*, said she was tired of it and preferred sex (manual, oral) with Aa the way they had been doing for years before, but Aa, the *tom,* insisted on using it.

*Tom*s often insisted that women preferred real men to *tom*s in terms of sexual satisfaction, considering it to be a reason why women would not stay with a *tom* for a long-term relationship. However, the discourse of "sexual inadequacy" in comparison with men clashed with the statement made just as often (by the same people) that *dee*s "used" *tom*s for sex or as "sex toys," without having sincere feelings toward the *tom*. The two most frequently given explanations for *dee*s' attraction to *tom*s, according to *tom*s, were financial support and sexual pleasure.

The ability of *tom*s to penetrate their partners (symbolically perhaps, with a dildo) was important to *tom*s, even though most *dee*s did not need or even want penetration. The sex act that most *dee*s expressed gave them the most pleasure was oral sex. Most *tom*s agreed that their partners seemed most pleased with oral sex or with manual stimulation of their partner's clitoris. However, even though their sexual experience seemed to indicate that their feminine partners were not particularly interested in penetration, *tom*s often said that their inability to perform this act would ultimately lead their *dee*s to find "real men." Some *tom*s said they knew that penetration was not as important as many thought, and they tried to explain this to others. For example, one *tom* posted the question on the Lesla WebBoard:

> I am very curious about triple-X things. I still have not had sex with my girlfriend. Whoever knows the answers, please tell me.
>
> 1. My finger is very short, only three inches. If I use my finger will it reach it?
> 2. I am afraid my girlfriend will hurt, because we have talked about this before and she said she was afraid it would hurt (so I still don't want to do it for her). So I want to know, how much will it hurt? If it hurts, is there a way to make it hurt less?
> 3. If her hymen tears, will there be a lot of blood? (so I can prepare to wash the sheet)
>
> Whoever knows, please let me know.

A *tom* answered:

> Explaining isn't the same as demonstrating. How about this: the size or length isn't important. The point that receives the feeling is at the mouth of the lane *(paak soi)*, not at the end of it.[10]

This exchange demonstrates that many Thai women are inexperienced in sex and model their sexual expectations after what they understand of heterosexual sex. Inexperienced *tom*s often understood sex as some form of insertion, either with their fingers or a self-fashioned dildo, and they expected their girlfriend to feel satisfied from this penetration. With experience, many *tom*s learned to experiment with other sexual techniques, such as oral sex and using their fingers on their partners' outer genitals. However, I was surprised by the insistence of many older, sexually experienced *tom*s that "women" needed intercourse for sexual pleasure. The *tom*s' assertion that this act was necessary for *dee*s but not for themselves or other *tom*s accentuated the difference between *tom*s and *dee*s, rather than reflecting the reality of their sexual experience with women. The popularity of dildos with *tom*s and the corresponding disinterest in dildos by *dee*s can also be understood as a product of the identity formation of *tom*s. It was important for *tom*s to insist that *dee*s are unlike *tom*s, in that *dee*s are "real women" who need the feel of a penis inside them, whereas *tom*s, they said, did not have this sexual need. The lack of a penis was consistently presented by *tom*s as the main handicap in their perceived need to compete with men for women.

Although *tom*s insisted that sexual intercourse was important for *dee*s, *dee*s just as often stated that sex altogether was a minor consideration in their relationship with *tom*s. For example, Um, mentioned above, said that sex was never a main concern in the three relationships she had had with *tom*s. She had sex with a *tom* she was involved with for two years and said she loved this *tom* very much. She even acknowledged that the sex was satisfying on some level and that the *tom* was better at sexual performance than the men she has been with since. However, Um said she felt that sex between women was "unnatural" and that she preferred sex with men because she felt it was "normal," even if it was less physically satisfying: "As for sex with women, I felt that it wasn't natural. All the time we were lovers, I felt we weren't just friends that liked each other but that it was something abnormal. So I felt uncomfortable all the time. I have a friend who is a *tom,* and she has a *dee* girlfriend. She said they didn't have sex, but that it was okay and they can still stay together. She said just kissing and hugging is enough; it isn't necessary to have sex, according to the *tom.* Just understanding each other and hugging is enough. . . . If you ask men, they will say sex is important, but if you ask *tom*s, they will say it's not. I don't know if this is true or not." Um described her sexual relationship with her *tom* lover: "We had sex, but it wasn't that important. It was more about emotions. Sex is only ten to twenty percent of being *tom/dee*. It is mostly about taking care of each other, paying attention to each other, helping each other, good conversation, and liking the same things. When we were together, we were happy."

For Um, sex was not just an issue of physical pleasure but a dimension of a larger, socially determined dynamic. Um said that none of her married friends enjoyed sex with their husbands (a commonly heard complaint of married women I spoke to), but her friends claimed that it was important as part of the marriage bond. Um said that without sex she would be afraid her male partner would find someone new to have sex with: "It is a bigger deal when men and women stop having sex than when *tom-dee* couples stop having sex, because if he cannot have sex with you, the man will find sex elsewhere. But we don't have to worry about not having sex with *tom*s. *Tom*s aren't as worrisome as men are, because *tom*s won't have sex with just anyone, like men can easily do with women."

Chang, a *dee,* agreed that sex was not a central concern in her relationship with her *tom,* Mai. Expressing sexual desire was uncomfortable for Chang and other *dee*s, and they preferred to describe their relationship in terms of emotional caring and friendship. However, not having sex, or having it very infrequently, led Chang to feel that the relationship lacked an intensity she had experienced with other *tom*s: "All I care about is love and understanding. Sex is the very last issue for me. We are together as friends or sisters. My first *tom* was very into sex. Then my second *tom* told me from the beginning that she wasn't really into sex. But I was used to the first *tom,* so I felt like I was lacking sex with Mai when I compared her with my first *tom.* But as a *dee* I never asked for things, especially sex from a *tom,* so I didn't dare say anything. I felt so uncomfortable and thought maybe she didn't love me. At least I wanted her to kiss or hug me to show that she loves me, as the first *tom* usually did. Sometimes after having sex with Mai, she would fall asleep right away, even though I was still awake. But I don't want to argue about sex, so I just keep quiet and adjust myself and try to get used to it. We have had sex only once in five or six months." Although Chang was obviously disappointed in not having sex, she positioned sex as a *tom*'s prerogative, saying, "Actually I never expect anything from my lover. I just accept what I get. It's about love, and if she wants sex, I will give it to her. If not, that's fine." When I pressed Chang about what she wanted sexually, she conceded, "I love her just the way she is, but actually I want sex more consistently, not just once in a while like this."

Although many *dee*s disassociated themselves from sexual needs in order to emphasize the emotional aspects of their relationships, other *dee*s were more direct about the sexual pleasure they gained from their *tom*s. Bua, a *dee* in her thirties, fondly recalled her first love affair with a *tom* and said she was "impressed" with how wonderful the *tom* made her feel physically, a feeling that she missed when she later had boyfriends. Other *dee*s who had frank personalities were able to laugh and joke about the good sex they enjoyed with their *tom*s, such as describing their "magic tongues." One significant feature of these pleasurable sex acts for *dee*s is that they were almost always described as being "one-way" *(thaang-diao),* meaning that *tom*s sexually perform (oral or manual stimulation) for *dee*s, whereas *dee*s are not expected, or are forbidden, to reciprocate. A *dee*'s sexual pleasure is typically considered by *tom*s and *dee*s the duty of a *tom*, whereas the reverse is not necessarily true. In any case, it is important to contextualize the comments about the unimportance of sex within the larger framework of Thai hegemonic constructions of proper femininity, in which women's sexual needs are associated with dirty or impure women.

CONCLUSION

The *tom*s and *dee*s I interviewed thought of themselves as being quite different from each other. *Tom* masculinity was variably positioned between idealized categories of manhood and feminine qualities. The dominant discourse of *tom*ness held that it was a product of unalterable karmic fate rather than a chosen lifestyle or sexual identity. Although not all *tom*s positioned themselves thusly, the hegemonic premise held that *tom*ness was a product of inborn gender. Through this hegemonic discourse, *tom*s made variable assertions about their obligations and social roles. Some *tom*s said they would prefer to be men, but given that they were not men, their partners had to understand that they could not provide what men could supposedly provide, nor were *tom*s obligated to do so.

Tom identity tends to draw greater attention than does *dee* identity, because *tom*s more obviously reject feminine norms and are thus both objects of criticism and visual indicators of a female same-sex eroticism. However, the emergence of the *dee* is arguably the more radical innovation in the Thai sex/gender order. Masculine women were present in the past, and many of them had feminine partners, but those partners were not categorized as a special kind of woman. *Dee*s are often marginalized as peripheral members of *tom-dee* society because they are understood as "normal" women and essentially unlike *tom*s.

The enactment of *tom* and *dee* "identities" simultaneously accesses heteronormative discourses and revalues those discourses to support and frame portrayals of self. For example, *tom*s appropriate dominant discourses of karmic suffering of supposed "misgendered" people and reposition those discourses in a way that supports their claims to masculinity. It is important to recognize that *tom*s and *dee*s are thoroughly embedded in their cultural context.

Thai Norms of Gender and Sexuality 4

*T*OM-DEE RELATIONSHIPS and identities are constructed within Thai hegemonic gender norms that deter female (heterosexual) promiscuity and simultaneously deny the possibility of female sexual agency. To understand why these new identities and subcultures are not radically disruptive of Thai mainstream discourses of proper female behavior, it is necessary to place female same-sex relations within the context of social anxiety over female heterosexuality. Within Thai society there is considerable space for women to engage in same-sex relationships, because these relationships are considered to be asexual and aspects of female friendship. These spaces for female homoeroticism uneasily coexist with relatively new narratives of "sexual deviance," and narratives of normative female sexuality within the larger social landscape affect and structure the lives of both *tom*s and *dee*s.

THE DANGERS OF HETEROSEXUALITY

For Thai women, heterosexuality is a morally dangerous and risky endeavor. Everyday conversations among village women and urban working-class women are replete with anxiety over daughters' sexual behavior, fear of daughters being seduced or raped, and negative comments about other women's perceived promiscuity. One discussion I had with several villagers in a rural area of Chonburi Province on the problems of drug abuse in Thailand quickly became focused on the special dangers of moral misbehavior that drug use had for women, because it made them sexually vulnerable. I had a difficult time pinning the women down on whether they meant that drugs would make women easier targets for rape or whether the women would feel sexually excited and then pursue sex with someone while under the influence—the distinction did not appear relevant to the villagers. Unmarried women, in particular, were moral minefields, easily suspected of plotting to steal husbands or attracting morally threatening male attention.[1]

The recollections of Nam, a twenty-seven-year-old *dee*, illustrate that *tom-dee*ism is sometimes seen as preferable to the perceived dangers of heterosexuality for Thai women:

> When I was seeing my boyfriend, I had to sneak around because I was still young, just in eighth grade [Mathayom 2]. I dated him until twelfth grade [Mathayom 6]. Once, my mother caught me and scolded me for having a boyfriend. My mother cried. She begged me to break up with this friend. I felt very uncomfortable *(lambaak-cai)*. I felt guilty too, but I kept seeing him until we broke up in college. After that, a *tom* flirted with me. After we were lovers *(faen)*, there was one time when she got into an argument with her family. She came to find me at my home and asked if she could stay with me. So I have to let her stay with me, because she is my girlfriend *(faen)*, right? I was afraid my parents would scold me the same as before, but I had to risk taking her into my home. I introduced her and said my friend has asked to stay with me for a little while. After a while she became close to my family. My mother, father, grandmother, and aunts—she got along with them all. I never thought about whether or not my mother would know what kind of relationship we had until one day my mother asked me if we were lovers *(faen)*. If we really loved each other[, she said], we should take care of each other well and help each other out. She didn't mind. Ever since then I have never been afraid of having a *tom* as a lover *(faen)*. (Manitta 2003, 81)

Phloi, a twenty-seven-year-old *dee,* described her parents' negative reaction to the boyfriend she had as a teenager, and their relatively relaxed response to her recent *tom* lover:

> I think my parents are strange. I asked them casually, if my younger brother was *tut* [feminine male homosexual], would they accept it? They said they couldn't accept it, [because] he is their only son. I went on and asked them, if I was a *tom* or had a lover who was a *tom*, could they accept it? They said they could accept it and would be happy too. I was confused and asked them what they meant. Didn't they want me to get married? They said they were worried, afraid that I would meet someone who wasn't good. To find a good man is difficult. And when I studied, they didn't let me hang out with

(khop) men. They were afraid I would be "ruined" *(sia-khon,* to lose one's future, to degenerate). Even when boys who were friends called my house, that wasn't allowed. We [my parents and I] fought a lot over it. They probably were afraid because around my house there are lots of "ruined" *(sia-khon)* girls. Before [these girls] could finish school, they got pregnant.[2] Also, my parents probably don't know really what *tom*s and *dee*s are. They probably think it's like kids who like each other [juvenile infatuation]. They know one of my *tom* friends. They saw her since first or second grade. They're used to [*tom*s], so they don't think anything much about their daughter being with a *tom*. But it's good for me. I don't have to worry what my family will think if I'm dating a *tom*, because they can accept it more than if I have a boyfriend.

According to Nicola Tannenbaum (1999), much of the discussion of Thai gender has used elite discourses of ideal models and Buddhist texts to represent Thai sexuality. Thus researchers have asserted that conservative ideas of female virginity, for example, characterize Thai gender structure. Tannenbaum states that her own ethnographic study among a Thai-related group, the Shan, contradicted this elitist discourse—female virginity was not highly prized. Her point is well taken: elite discourses and normative ideals need to be distinguished from the lived practices of real people. However, my own research and observations indicate that conservative ideas about sexual propriety of women were widespread among Thais of all class backgrounds. For example, I was surprised when I heard sex workers positioning themselves among one another as relatively sexually pure or defiled. The history of this conservative discourse needs to be studied, and Tannenbaum may well be right that this discourse is not as indigenous to Thai peoples as many researchers seem to believe. Nevertheless, prohibitions of female heterosexuality were ubiquitous in my ethnographic study.

Both *tom/dee* and heterosexual women have explained that an advantage of having sex with *tom*s is that one does not risk scorn for *sia*[3] (adultery, or promiscuous behavior), which a woman most certainly would face if engaged in sexual relationships with men. An eighty-five-year-old woman in Bangkok described a *tom-dee* couple she knew in her neighborhood: "The mother of the *dee* trusts the *tom*. She thinks women being with women is just a playful thing. There is no *sia*. They probably just hug and kiss, that's all. She probably thinks it is better than going out with a man. You don't *sia* at all this way. They stay together like normal. When they come home from work, they kiss each other."

Several women I met were married to men but were openly involved with *tom*s. Ot, a wealthy married mother of two, was in a relationship with a *tom* named Aa for around fifteen years. Aa lived with Ot and Ot's husband and helped raise Ot's youngest child. When I asked Ot how her husband reacted to her long-term relationship with her *tom* lover, she said he accepted it and showed no interest or jealousy in their private lives. He even expressed sympathy for Ot when she went through periodic depressions over troubles with her and Aa's relationship. Before she was married, Ot had relationships with several men, and her husband (then boyfriend) at that time was indeed jealous. But because Ot was no longer involved with other men and had Aa to look after her, they had all reached an agreement. Ot's sexual relationship with Aa was not perceived as adulterous by friends or by Ot's husband and family and was perhaps even seen as a guard against unacceptable adulterous behavior with other men.

Women are continually subject to evaluations of their moral worth, based on culturally embedded definitions of proper femininity, such as that embodied in the notion of *kunlasatri*. The term means be a properly reared woman, "to be ladylike," implying that women should be patient, subservient, and docile. In an essay entitled "Kunlasatri yuu nai?" (Where has proper femininity gone?), a columnist wrote: "Equality of the sexes and rights and freedoms are good things, but one should not forget that there are limits to them. No matter what, there will never be a day when men and women can do all the same things. . . . Women letting themselves go and following men's behavior and not preserving their proper femininity—society will look down on them and despise them, and they will be ashamed wherever they go. Wait until you are born a man before you do what men do, and while you are a woman, take care of your proper femininity, and you will then be praised by whoever sees you" (*Daily News,* August 26, 1998, 7).

Models of proper femininity pervade Thai social discourse, and a woman's sexual behavior is the most significant factor in determining her respectability. Maew, a twenty-nine-year-old married middle-class woman sitting in the lobby of her clean and spacious cosmetics shop, told me how much simpler it was to raise a boy than a girl. With a boy, she explained, you do not need to worry about whether he is having sex or not. I asked why she was not worried about her boy having sex, and she said, "Who would know? Nobody can tell if a man loses his virginity." I asked if she thought it would be dangerous for a woman to marry a man who might have been having sex and possibly have contracted a disease, and she said, "No, they could have a blood test first." Women's sexual behavior outside of marriage was highly stigmatized and frequently discussed with abhorrence and disgust by both men and women. Almost every informant questioned perceived the separate standards for male and female sexuality as natural. A study of women's attitudes toward male extramarital sex provides normative definitions of proper, or normal, sexuality (Chanphen et al. n.d.). Women thought that male premarital sex was normal and that men naturally needed sexual release and sexual variety. Women expressed distrust in men, saying that sex before marriage would leave them vulnerable to abandonment. Having the status of an abandoned woman was shameful.[4]

There is plethora of imagery of improperly (hetero)sexual women in the Thai public domain. A short story from a Thai magazine demonstrates the theme of women and improper heterosexuality. In the story, a male desk clerk at a women's dormitory in Bangkok bemoans the degraded and besmirched womanhood he encounters in his work. The women living in the dorm are often sex workers and come home drunk and with men. One day he meets a pure girl in the dormitory, who revives his faith in the possibility of good femininity. In the end he finds that she is a "kept wife" of a Japanese man. Where once he compared her to the lone rose in the decrepit garden, in the end he compares her to the fetid water and slime congealing in the garden's unused fountain: "He sank down on the bench, sighing deeply, the weak sunlight fading away and the building's gloomy shadow weighing down on the building's wall. The rose blossom had been picked and strewn on the ground, and the clean white petals were pulled off by a gust of wind and had fluttered into the foul water of the basin. He sat staring at the stem of the flower, feeling bitterly disappointed. When another gust of wind passed him, he lifted his hand and plugged his nose, noticing that the stink that wafted by this time was stronger than before" (Prachakhom 1994).

FEMALE ASEXUALITY

In contrast to the moral dangers of heterosexuality, female same-sex activity is portrayed as innocent and harmless by the Thai discourses of female asexuality. Women are held to be devoid of sexual needs, and their moral integrity depends on proper distance from or relation to male sexuality, which is perceived as natural and in need of expression. A brochure promoting safe sex and AIDS prevention explains to female readers, "Women might want only to be close to their lover and just to look into [his] face or hold hands and will feel warm and contented already. But men want more and [to go] further than women" (Program for Appropriate Technology in Health 1994a). Women were warned to make sure the man really loves them before they agree to any sex. A parallel brochure for men, on the other hand, explains that sexual feelings are natural [for men], and it sensibly warns them of the possibility of sexually transmitted diseases. The brochure advises safe sex (with a condom) or masturbation for men, but no mention is made of the possibility of women's masturbation or of women wanting to have sex purely for pleasure (Program for Appropriate Technology in Health 1994b). The idea of women having natural and healthy sexual needs is rarely mentioned in public discourse of sex in Thailand. Thais often find it difficult even to perceive of the possibility of female-female sex.[5]

Discourses of sex used in Thai society consistently negate women as sexual agents.[6] For example, the perpetual debates in the media, as well as in private discussions, about the situation of commercial sex work in Thailand often include a commonly held assumption that prostitution is a necessary moral evil because men's sexual needs are natural and in need of fulfillment (see Ekachai 1991 and Prudthatorn 1991).[7] According to Kasem Adchasai, a well-known Thai journalist and editor of the Thai-language daily *Krungthep Thurakij,* the common Thai practice of men having a minor wife is derived from a biological need for males to have "harems" and can "ensure greater variety in [men's] sex lives."[8] The writer asserts that "real Thai[s]" see polygamy as heroic and natural, for love and lust cannot be regulated by morality. The love and lust the writer speaks of are unquestionably applied solely to men.

Academic interest in sexual attitudes among Thais has increased as a result of efforts to control AIDS. Such research has often demonstrated that both men and women in Thai society commonly believe that sexual desire and behavior are natural and important for men rather than for women. For example, one female participant in focus group research said that men need sexual experience before marriage: "He must have experience and knowledge about [sex] so when he has a family, he can know about it. Because most women, when they get married, do not dare speak of sexual matters, right? It is shameful. So men must be the initiators" (Chanphen et al. n.d., 6). The researchers concluded that their female informants believed that the male sexual drive was strong and natural and needed release, whereas women were thought to lose their value *(sia-haai)* if they had extramarital sex: "It happens where women are taken advantage of—if he gets sex before marriage and then he dumps me" (Chanphen et al. n.d., 5). Women in all the studies expressed fear of gossip that they were sexually promiscuous if they were to lose their virginity before marriage.[9]

Research also indicates that Thai women often are perceived as sexually passive, even by themselves.[10] For example, Warunee Fongkaew (1997) gives extensive examples of negative attitudes held by Thai girls and young women toward their own bodies and their own sexuality. Fongkaew recorded that young girls were taught from an early age not to display their bodies or be seen naked, whereas young boys were allowed to play naked and to display their genitals for several more years. Girls were taught by parents and teachers not to think about sex until they were married. The girls were ignorant about sex and felt shame toward their own bodies, including shame about the development of their breasts. For example, Fongkaew quoted a teenage girl as saying: "Women have things which are more shameful than anything men have. I think the most shameful thing that women have is female genitalia, and followed by breasts . . . I don't know why women's things are more shameful than men's. But I know that this is true" (p. 597). Fongkaew concluded: "Cultural norms based on gender inequality in sexual relations that expect women to be inexperienced and naïve in sexual matters, and to see themselves as passive receptacles of men's sexual passions, are widely held in this pre-urban Northern Thai society" (p. 582).[11]

Discussions of *tom-dee* relationships in academic and psychiatric literature repeat the essentially asexual nature of such relationships and the importance of friendship as explanation for women's choice of *tom*s as partners. For example, the high-profile psychologist Wanlop Piyamanotham explained the anomalous category *"dee"* by using the Thai cultural logic that a *tom-dee* relationship must be about emotion rather than sex: "Happiness for women naturally is not about sex but about caring, gentleness, and romance. Just to be close to a lover and to hug each other are the most excellent satisfaction, not like men think" (1992, 84).

The attitude that female same-sex sexuality is a harmless passing phase is exemplified in a column by journalist Plew Si-ngern about the relatively new phenomenon of *tom-dee* relationships: "It comes with the era and will pass away on its own. Like other things, it flows and will be replaced . . . why worry? It is a natural expression of teenagers and part of a chain of social factors. When they grow up and are twenty or twenty-five years old, that stage of thinking will pass away on its own. The students who fought on the streets in the past era—now several are members of Parliament. Do you see them as thugs, like you worried [they would become]?" (*Thai Rath*, June 21, 1984, 5).

"FRIENDSHIPS"

Given that female heterosexuality is perceived to be a morally dangerous affair and that female same-sex activity is negated as a likely possibility or is at least framed in terms of innocent friendship, Thai women, with proper discretion, can engage in homoerotic activity free of much public notice. Same-sex friendships and intimacy are the norm in Thailand, and close companionships between girls, including hand-holding and spending the night together, are not presumed to be sexual. Students told me of the common practice of schoolgirl crushes, calling each other *"phii"* and *"nong"* (kinship terms between older and younger siblings, which are also used intimately between couples). *Tom-dee* couples are common among schoolgirls, and parents view these relationships as passing phases, soon to be replaced with a "natural" heterosexual relationship and marriage, a view commonly supported by magazine articles warning parents of the new homosexual fashions. Ung told me, "Thais think that in a short while they will quit [being *tom-dee*] and get married. They think that it is the feelings of young kids for the most part. But if someone does something with the opposite sex, it is much more serious [forbidden]."

*Tom*s and *dee*s support and reiterate the common assumptions that women are motivated by emotions rather than sexual desire. *Tom-dee* couples frequently coded their relationships as essentially friendships. For example, Nuu said: "When we live together, they all think the same, that they will stay with me forever . . . they won't get married, something like this. But I never believe this; I never think about it. I know that someday she will leave, because we just are two friends living together." Many *tom*s, including Nuu, simultaneously explained *dee* interest in *tom*s as due to the sexual freedom their relationships provided. *Dee*s also used the term "friendship" to describe their relationships. Ung, who expressed ambivalence about identifying herself as a *dee* and was involved with a *tom*, described their relationship: "It started from being friends—we were close friends. It started from writing letters and talking. We talked about what we thought, about books, about society, like that. . . . I thought we could really get along together. She was a very special friend, more than an ordinary friend, a very special one, but I still didn't think about her being my lover. I knew her for about three years, and I came to Bangkok, and that is the reason we came to Bangkok together. And we became girlfriends after we came to Bangkok, after we had been friends for a long time."

The ability of Thai women to demonstrate their "friendships" with other women as a weapon against slander provides a contrast to Western patterns of homophobia in Hollywood.[12] Thai female celebrities have even made it known they were involved with women rather than face slander that they were promiscuous with men. One example is the case of Wiyada Umarin, a well-known movie star of the 1960s and 1970s. Her nickname "Morm Um" was derived from the term "Morm Cao"—the royal title of her husband, film producer Chatrichalerm Yukhol—and "Um," meaning "full and fleshy," referring to her sensual curves from her early days as a swimsuit model. Wiyada was a sex symbol and had faced the usual gossip that she had numerous male lovers. As a result, a movie star magazine published a story on her life, stating: "She was slandered and gossiped about mercilessly, until she was despondent and she could almost bear it no longer. Our readers want to know if Wiyada Umarin is a virtuous Thai woman *(kunlasatri thai)* or an oversexed female star" ("Lao chiwit mai khorng 'morm um' wiyada umarin," 1982). She granted an interview to the magazine in order to show her normal life. According to the story, she lived with a female companion whom she calls her "friend," Phii Kaew, along with her own child by a previous relationship. The photos in the magazine showed Wiyada with her arm around her child and Phii Kaew. In an obviously intimate and sensual photo, Wiyada is looking into the eyes of Phii Kaew, with her hand under Phii Kaew's chin. The message was clear and direct—Wiyada was not promiscuous like people say. On the contrary, she had an intimate female friend with whom she shared a life.

Lee, a *dee* in her forties, said she felt more comfortable having a *tom* lover as a stepparent to her ten-year-old boy than having a man as a stepfather. Her *tom* partner was proud of being able to support the family financially and to care for them in many other ways, such as taking the *dee* to work everyday (on her motorcycle) and paying for the child's schooling. Many women have reiterated this stereotype to me and expressed the feeling that stepfathers almost never accept or care for their stepchildren. These women, like Lee, believed that it would be irresponsible of them to put their child at risk by taking a man as a new husband or lover. *Tom*s, however, were considered "safe" for their children and were expected to care for their family diligently and lovingly. The point here is how the cultural dictum that men are inherently dangerous to women may serve to justify and support female relationships, not that loving Thai stepfathers do not exist.

COMPARISONS WITH MALE HOMOSEXUAL/TRANSGENDER SUBCULTURES IN THAILAND

Tom-dee relationships must be understood within the cultural context of being female in Thai society. Likewise, *kathoey*s, or gay men, have certain social prerogatives as males. For example, there is a thriving commercial scene for male homosexual or transgender men in Bangkok. Nightclubs, go-go bars, and restaurants, as well as an extensive commercial sex industry, cater to homosexual men.

As men, gays and *kathoey*s have mobility and freedom to engage in commercial and/or nighttime entertainment that are not available to Thai women. It is considered inappropriate for a woman to go out alone for recreation or to go out frequently at night. Of course, in contemporary Bangkok, women do socialize and go to entertainment venues, but they participate in such activities as groups at local or well-known establishments. Schools, local vending booths, markets, and shopping centers are all popular sites for *tom*s and *dee*s to meet and spend time together, because these spaces are culturally appropriate sites for Thai women to socialize in general. *Tom*s and *dee*s consistently told me that they preferred meeting at friends' homes or at local restaurants. They did not want to go alone to a bar or club to meet other *tom*s or *dee*s. Recently, Internet social clubs for *tom*s and *dee*s have become popular in Bangkok. These clubs hold regular parties at private homes or restaurants that are almost always well attended. This type of forum provides a way for women to socialize in a commercial setting and meet new people, but in a way that does not require interaction of anonymous individuals. *Tom*s and *dee*s still usually attend these events in groups, with people well known to each other or known to friends of theirs.

Another distinction between male and female subcultures is the importance of sex in defining oneself. *Tom*s and *dee*s rarely, if ever, define their relationships or identities in terms of sexual desire. Associations with sexuality are highly taboo for Thai women. Thai men, on the other hand, are granted considerable freedom in sexual behavior. However, associations of men with femininity are more serious social transgressions. Peter Jackson (1997b) argues that *kathoey*s are a stereotypical model of "unmasculinity," against which Thai males can measure their masculine selves. *Kathoey*s are a regular source of amusement and a target of ridicule in the Thai media, particularly in television shows and movies. In contrast, many Thais whom I interviewed expressed the idea that *tom*s were "cute" *(naa-rak)* or "impressively capable" *(keng)*. The appropriation of masculinity by *tom*s does not have the same component of parody that the appropriation of femininity by *kathoey*s has.[13]

Most Thai academic material focuses on male homosexuals, and most of the patients studied in their research were males, indicating that more men than women are brought to psychiatric clinics for treatment for homosexuality. Male homosexuals have had greater exposure in the media in general, and the *kathoey* figure, very popular in drag shows and TV dramas, is male. However, several research studies indicate that female homosexual experiences are more common than male homosexual experiences and are more openly discussed among women than among men. A Mahidol research team conducting research on sexual attitudes noted: "In the men's discussions homosexuality was only mentioned in passing to tease individuals who claimed not to go to prostitutes. However, in the women's discussion there was a much more open and detailed description of lesbianism within the factory and dormitory setting" (Ford and Kittisuksathit 1996, 35). Health research has generally supported the view that female homosexuality is generally less stigmatized than male homosexuality in Thai society. For example, Ford and Kittisuksathit (1996) also found that stigmatization of male homosexuals, especially in the beginning of the AIDS epidemic.

Tom and *dee* relationships in factories and dormitories were described in detail by women interviewed by the Mahidol team (Ford and Kittisuksathit 1996). A reporter for the *Daily News* commented: "I think that society sees women in this group [homosexuals] in a better way than male homosexuals. Because when we see men walking together, close together, we feel weird. It doesn't look good. But if we see women together, we sometimes cannot tell. They might be walking together as friends."[14] The idea that women might be seen in a less threatening light was supported by Professor Chalidaporn Songsamphan of Thammasat University: "I think Thai people look at female homosexuals with a more positive attitude, as kind of cute, and as very fashionable by dressing up as men. But people tend to look at male homosexuals as something dirty." Sit, a seventy-four-year-old man from Bangkok, held a similar position: "I think it is easier to accept women who are *tom*s [than to accept feminine homosexual men, or *kathoey*s]. Guys who are girly are offensive. But when women act like men, they don't act in any disgusting way. Some look normal and act in a more proper way. A female couple I saw here in Bangkok, they looked normal. They lived together like husband and wife. At first I thought she was a man. When I asked her child where her father was going, she answered, 'That is not my father; that is my mother.' *[Laughs.]* Both of them worked and helped each other out."

Research on female sexual attitudes confirm that female homosexuality is not considered wildly deviant by young women. Amara Soonthorndhada (1996) quotes factory workers and students in Bangkok about their attitudes toward female homosexuality. For example: "I think close relationships between women are much better than between men and women. You will never get pregnant or contract a disease. You are safe and secure" (p. 28) and "I think women liking women is OK. They look lovely" (p. 28). The women who were interviewed also supported the idea that men have a strong, natural sex drive and that women have the duty to satisfy those needs of men.

CLASS AND THE MYTH OF URBAN TOLERANCE

In general, *dee*s, both rural and urban, were more susceptible than *tom*s to family pressure to abandon relationships with women in order to marry and start a family. This concern was linked to the status of *dee*s as essentially "ordinary" women who may have harmless fun with a *tom* at a certain point in life but should take steps to assure a secure future through marriage to a man. In addition to pressure to find stability, women are also subject to relatively new discourses that female same-sex relationships are a kind of mental illness.

Associations of rural areas with "backwards" or, alternatively, "authentic" Thai culture have produced a middle-class discourse that rural and lower-class people are less accepting of *tom-dee* relationships than urban and upper-class people are. Linking rural areas to the past also implies that Thais were less accepting of homosexuality in the past than now, given that contemporary Thailand—that is, urban Thailand —is aligned with imagery of the West, which many Thais assume to be accepting of homosexuality. The main sources of antihomosexual campaigns and discourses are the Thai state bureaucracy, academia, and the medical professions, all urban-based institutions staffed by people with a relatively high degree of education. Rural women, who may have less mobility than urban women and are more dependent on the judgment of their family and community, are also less exposed to these negative urban discourses.

Opposition to female same-sex relationships is usually based on the belief that these relationships are temporary and unstable and will not provide the security of marriage. Marjorie Muecke (1984) demonstrates that, in rural Thailand, women's social position and economic security depended on children. Unlike the situation of middle-class and well-educated women, being married and having children were often perceived as a source of security for rural women with little education or few employment options. Rural or working-class people usually based opposition to female same-sex relations on the belief that women need to marry and have children. Middle-class urbanites, on the other hand, were more likely to oppose homosexuality, believing that it was a form of sexual/gender deviance and psychologically abnormal. The nationalistic academic discourses had more of an impact on educated people than on rural people. For example, Ing, the seventy-eight-year-old woman from Ayuthaya Province mentioned in chapter 2, described her opposition to the relationship between her granddaughters, Pum and Jay, who were cousins: [15]

Pum was an ordinary woman, and the other one, Jay, acted like a man. When Pum was asleep, the one who was like a man came and kissed her and touched her breast. When I saw it, I yelled at Jay, "Don't do bullshit *(tor-lae)*. I don't like it. My granddaughter likes dick *(khway)*. She doesn't like cunt *(hii)*. And you don't like dick, huh?" *[Laughs.]* Jay answered, "I like dick and I like cunt." I chased her out of my house. She said she wanted to be together (with Pum) like husband and wife. Later my granddaughter got married, and the one like a man came to the wedding. The wedding couple were sitting together, and the one like a man asked Pum, "Why did you get married!?" I answered for her, "My granddaughter likes dick. When-ever she sees dick, her eyes grow big." *[Laughs.]* I said this in front of my grandson-in-law too, because I wanted to make fun of the one like a man. Women can get married once or twice, but like that [two women together] is bullshit. I don't like it. I am a normal per-son: if you are a man or a woman, just be clear about it. I know there isn't any loss [loss of virginity, loss of reputation, damage to feminine purity] in women being with women, and it is better than getting pregnant [before marriage]. But I want my granddaughter to get married and have a husband so I won't worry about her. I want to have great-grandchildren.

I have kept Ing's original speech, full of slang and bawdy expressions, to demonstrate her frank attitudes toward sexuality that form the con-text for her understanding of female same-sex relationships. Ing insisted that she was not against her granddaughter's being with a *tom,* but she wanted to make sure her granddaughter was safe and not vulnerable to being deceived or taken advantage of by men. Ing claimed that being married would provide such protection.

For Ing, being married to a man meant safety for a woman, both morally and financially. Ing was a wealth of stories, and she obviously enjoyed teasing and having fun with people she met. She did not describe these incidents as particularly surprising or indicative of any moral order. In a local market a couple of years before, she had seen a couple selling snacks at a roadside food stall: "At first I thought one of them was a man. I went up to talk to him and put my hand on his back and felt a brassiere. I laughed and thought, 'Hey, this is a woman.' So one day I asked the wife, 'Really, is your husband a man or a woman?' She said, 'A woman, but she does everything like a man. She does all the heavy work, including driving the car.' I have seen them sitting together at their stall, and I saw the one like a man grab the woman's breast. I teased them, 'If you touch it too much, she will get in the mood.' *[Laughs.]* The one like a man replied, 'They are mine already because I *(phom)* already bought them.'"

While this frank banter shows the level of everydayness of *tom*s and *dee*s in Thai society, it is important to avoid oversimplifying the seem-ing tolerance that Thai society has toward these relationships. Female same-sex relationships may be tolerated and even approved of in some contexts, but it is wrong to assume that these relationships are uniformly unproblematic. There are widespread discourses in which concepts of "gender/sexual deviance" *(biang-been-thaang-pheet)* and misgendering *(phit-pheet)* are deployed to express disapproval of these relationships. Also, as discussed earlier, marriage is a social and financial survival strategy for many families, and a woman's rejection of marriage may cause anxiety for her parents. Given the financial difficulties faced by rural people, it is possible for behaviors to be tolerated if they are seen to benefit the general well-being of the family. The high levels of reintegration of commercial sex workers into local villages are an example of normatively unacceptable behavior's being revalued, or at least tolerated, because of the benefits for local people.[16]

Upper-class people often had the strongest condemnation of same-sex behavior. Tooy, a seventy-five-year-old woman with an elite background, expressed strong disapproval and denial of female same-sex relations among elite circles.[17] Tooy's parents were music teachers for King Rama VII (1925–1935), and Tooy was part of palace life as a child. She reported: "I have seen newspaper stories about women with women, and men with men, killing each other. In the past there wasn't anything like this. I never heard of anything like this; it is a very shameful thing, people believed. In the palace there especially was no such thing. Children had to be under the watch of adults at all times. They could not go anywhere alone. They had to be escorted by an adult. In the past things were very strict. You could not act any old way." When asked about masculine women in the past, Tooy answered: "In the past, people like that would be berated as 'dirty bitch' *(nang nii sokaprok)* and *'lakkapheet'* to make them ashamed. In the past it was mostly men. Only recently have I seen newspapers about *tom*s and *dee*s murdering each other. . . . People in the past weren't like this, [weren't] people who like being bizarre. In the past, women didn't even wear pants. In the past, people were proper. They had more shame than people have now. They were afraid to ruin the reputation of their parents. Parents would teach their children not to act like this." Tooy's statement expressed elite moral authority and propriety. Tooy knew words used to shame people "like that," so they must have existed. Tooy also mentioned that parents taught their children not to be "like that," indicating that people who were *lakkapheet* existed.

Sit, mentioned above, came to Bangkok from Ayuthaya Province at the age of twenty-four. Now residing at a retirement home in Bangkok, he said he had heard of female same-sex couples when he was young living upcountry. He thought that women's being lovers with women was harmless if the women were younger, but it was inappropriate for older women, who should be starting families. Like Ing, Sit said that it was necessary for a woman to have children and a husband to ensure prosperity and security. Sit said he would not approve if his daughter had a *tom* partner: "It would not be *sia* [a loss of virginity], but it would be unnatural. It would not be good; it isn't correct. To have a husband is better, because women and men are a pair. You must have a family, to have kids and a home. To be like that [with a woman] would mean she would not prosper; she would be in the same position forever. If she doesn't have children and a home, what will she do when she is older? Maybe when she is young, she can stay with a woman, but when she is old, she will be ashamed because she won't have children and she is abnormal. I have never seen [such] a couple be together until they get old. I have just seen young people, and then when they get older, they split up."

Sit also mentioned stories he had read in the paper recounting how psychologists had tried to cure homosexuals and found that effeminacy was more difficult to cure than simple homosexuality. Familiar with the authoritative discourses that the media and academics had been spreading for some time, Sit said that rural people would not accept *tom-dee* relationships as much as urban people did: "I think that Bangkok people accept this more. Rural people won't accept it, won't sell things to them. Bangkok people don't care as much. But in rural areas they know everything about everyone. They will think of it as unnatural. They have a small society, and if people are like that, they will feel ashamed. They will have to hide and not let anybody know." Sit repeated the stereotypes of rural people as being narrow-minded and intolerant, ironically repeating his own beliefs as characteristic of rural people. He rightly recognized that people in urban areas had greater opportunity for privacy and that living in an urban environment might make it easier for some *tom*s and *dee*s.

Rural people said negative things about same-sex couples, but these attitudes were not embedded in a structured discourse of pathology and deviance, as were middle-class attitudes. There are clearly points of continuity and overlap among class discourses, given that class is far from being a hermetically sealed cultural category. I found that *tom-dee* relationships existed with the acceptance of parents, friends, and community within all strata of society—among villagers, factory workers, middle-class professionals, and elites.

Middle-class women often had the financial means to gain some independence from their families, were mobile, and had the means to go to restaurants and clubs where they could mix with *tom-dee* groups. On the other hand, they were the ones most aware of the pathologizing negative images of transgenderism and homosexuality produced by authoritative discourses. However, they were also exposed to the discourses of transnational gay and lesbian rights and pride.

At an annual Anjaree party, a mock beauty pageant was held to choose "Miss Anjaree" for the year, and *dee*s competed for the award. During the interview session, when asked what they would do if they won the contest and what prize would they want, most participants gave similar answers. Most said they would move away or go abroad to a place where they could lead their lives free of criticism and disapproval. One contestant said she would go to England, where people respected privacy and she could be left alone to lead her life with her lover. Others said they would go upcountry in Thailand, where they could be left alone to have a private life with their partners. One said she just wanted to be at home when her lover came back from work and to serve her dinner and eat together. Stereotypical domestic life, free of the society's scrutinized gaze, was the ideal for most contestants. The stories were strikingly similar and did not suggest that these women, largely middle class, felt that they were particularly accepted by society.

Women would often relate to me with ease their past experiences of being involved with *tom*s. Students in my university classes would freely offer to discuss their past experiences of being with *tom*s, often casually in front of classmates, without the oppressive shame that still characterizes lesbian experiences in the West. A well-dressed student, clearly well-off and with a professional job, cheerfully told me of her love affairs with *tom*s in her private girls' school. She has since married, but she said her parents did not object to these relationships.

Other middle-class *tom*s and *dee*s said that these experiences might be tolerated as harmless fun, but when these women grew older and continued their relationships, they felt alienated by social disapproval, especially in office environments. Stories of *tom*s and *dee*s being harassed and killing themselves periodically popped up in the print media. Two stories, for example, involved middle-class women whose families had condemned their *tom* identities.[18] *Tom*s and *dee*s who were college professors and media personalities or held other relatively high-status positions were often insecure about their openness or about how obvious their homosexuality/gender identity was to outsiders. I met *tom*s and *dee*s who were open in their professional positions, as well as others who were rigidly secretive. I met more working-class *tom*s and *dee*s who were open about their gender identity/sexuality, however.

White-collar and pink-collar employment opportunities for women have allowed them to pursue a life with greater independence and privacy, but office environments were also often sites of intolerance for *tom*s and *dee*s. Cot, a twenty-five-year-old *dee* who was an urban office worker, said that when she broke up with her girlfriend, she felt isolated, exacerbating her unhappiness. Unlike many *tom*s who have their own communities and groups of *tom* friends, many *dee*s have no group of their own apart for the *tom-dee* group of their *tom* partners. Cot said that on top of these problems the people in her office had always expressed disdain and disapproval of her homosexuality: "At first I wanted to talk and vent my feelings and have other people know, but nobody else could accept it. Nobody else accepts me. They would say things like 'playing cymbals,'[19] a very rude word, not good at all. Now everything's okay. I told my friends I had a boyfriend so they wouldn't bother me. Saying that just cuts off the problem. In my office there are two *tom*s, and everybody looks at them in a bad way."

Not only could office environments be difficult for *tom*s and *dee*s, but middle-class families could also be intolerant of *tom-dee* relationships. May, a twenty-six-year-old graduate from an American university, said she had to be secretive about her relationship with her *dee* lover. May said it was hard to find places for her to be alone with her *dee* girlfriend, but she enjoyed going to clubs and restaurants with her friends, and given that they were all women, her parents did not protest. However, May said she could not tell her parents she was a "lesbian," because it would hurt them. She insisted that she loved her parents, and this love prevented her from hurting them by letting them know she was a *tom*/lesbian (she used these terms interchangeably). May also worked as a graphic designer in her parents' company, and once again the issue of financial independence and the pursuit of an open life as a transgender/homosexual seemed to be relevant. For example, a middle-class woman wrote in a Lesla WebBoard discussion: "I still don't dare tell my parents I love women, because I remember several years ago, when I was in about tenth or eleventh grade, I heard my father say to his friend that he didn't need anything much in raising his children, just hoped they would not be addicted to drugs and or be mis-gendered/sexed (*phit-pheet*)."

Although I have found numerous cases of relative tolerance of *tom-dee* relationships in village/rural settings, I also found numerous cases of the opposite. Ung told of a woman from her village in Ayuthaya whom she knew as a child. This woman came home one day with a girl-friend, and her parents were very upset and beat her. She left home and never returned. Ung said that people are under more scrutiny in villages, and this is one reason she had chosen to live in Bangkok—to have the freedom to live her life the way she wants. We sat in her room as she talked. Surrounding us were her shelves of books and photos of her and her girlfriend—evidence of her own life. Ung said she never sent money home, but she never asked for money either. She totally supported herself. For Ung, Bangkok meant the ability to support herself, live in her own room, and make her own decisions about lovers and her life. This sounded remarkably similar to statements of many of the non-*tom-dee* factory workers I had spoken with. Independence and development of one's sexual and gender style are not unique provinces of *tom*s and *dee*s but part of the larger structure of sex and gender in Thai society.

The stories told by older people above make it clear that we should not assume that contemporary Thai middle-class discourses of homo-sexuality and sexual/gender deviance are representative of all Thai cul-tural discourses. These middle-class notions have had a tremendous impact on society, yet they are class specific and a product of recent social transformation. As a comparison to the harshly critical commen-tary of the academics and nationalists, a relatively relaxed attitude toward same-sex couples can be found in the popular press, such as the following advice column in a popular tabloid paper. A woman wrote asking for advice about her *tom* lover who had taken up with a minor wife. The columnist responded with stereotypical remarks that homo-sexual/transgender people are more emotionally unstable and prone to violence than others. However, the columnist also concluded that over-all the relationship could work. The columnist was aware of the pathol-ogizing analyses but did not expand on them. The columnist granted the *tom-dee* relationship the same normative interpretation as a hetero-sexual relationship: it is natural for men to wander, so do not worry about it too much. The columnist wrote:

Your life is loving the same sex, or what is called being a lesbian, which means loving the same sex. You are jealous and possessive like a husband and wife, where one side is a *tom,* or like a man, and the other side is a *dee*. Sometimes these people are more jealous than normal and have very strong emotions. They cannot stand it if one side goes off with someone else . . . which is what has happened to you. . . . You need to accept reality, that love is forgiveness. Your partner hasn't dumped you but just asked to be with another girl for three nights a month, but you are so jealous that you cannot bear it. If you love her, you will probably have to accept it. If you insist too much, she will probably go for good. It is normal behavior—everybody naturally wants to try something different and new, like men who like to have many lovers but just don't have the opportunity to do so because society does not accept that. She probably feels guilty that she has built up hopes in the new girl that she [the new girl] won't be able to fulfill. Don't rush to conclusions; it is really a very normal part of life. And don't get so upset that your health is affected over nothing. Sometime you may meet a real man who loves you, and you can change your situation to be a real woman and have much more happiness than loving the same sex. . . . Your partner probably cannot break up with you, because she doesn't want to lose you. Go and ask men who have minor wives if any of them wants to break up [with their wives]. . . . They don't want to because of the relationship and obligations that they have built, making a home. . . . You should accept the real situation. Whatever will happen will happen. If you cannot bear it, you must break it off with her. If you still depend on her, you must forgive her for having something with that girl. . . . If you can adjust yourself and not feel too jealous or possessive, everything will probably get better—the three of you as husband and wife, but there is one *tom* and two wives here. . . . [The *tom*] is somebody like this, liking to try something new, and cannot go without it, because it makes life exciting. I don't think you should get too confused. Work hard, take a vacation, and relax. To think of it as really a small thing is better.[20]

CONCLUSION

Thai women face the dual perceptions that women are moral minefields and are asexual except for their receiving role vis-à-vis men. The supposed openness that Thai society has toward female homosexuality must be understood within this context—this openness is not approval of an alternative form of female sexuality but rather a denial that women are naturally sexual. Within these everyday understandings of female asexuality and benign female homosexuality, *dee*s can position themselves as "normal" women, and *tom*s as unthreatening sexual partners for women. The ways of representing relationships, and the kinds of social activities in which *tom*s and *dee*s engage, are structured by social norms applied to females in Thai society. Being female is more significant to the construction of *tom* and *dee* identities than is being "homosexual." In other words, social discourses that define proper female behavior affect *tom*s and *dee*s more than discourses of homosexuality per se.

The struggles of both *tom*s and *dee*s over asserting their sexuality and identity demonstrate that the oversimplistic assumption that urban and middle-class people are more progressive or accepting of homosexuality than are rural and working-class people is more rhetoric than fact. The dynamic that structures the relative acceptance of *tom*s and *dee*s is not so much an acceptance of homosexuality as it is a rejection of a feminine sexuality independent of males and the strong prohibitions against active female heterosexuality.

Gender Dynamics between *Tom*s and *Dee*s 5

Subversion or Conformity?

*T*OMS AND *DEE*S ENGAGE in a kind of mobility and sexual freedom that is rarely seen in the lives of other Thai women. It is tempting to see *tom*s' claims to masculinity and to being sexual agents, and *dee*s' claim to sexual pleasure, as forms of empowering resistance to oppressive limits that society places on women. Although this is arguably true, the liberating aspect of *tom* and *dee* identities should not be overstated. *Tom*s and *dee*s have their own system of rules and restrictions. As Lila Abu-Lughod (1990) has pointed out, resistance to one hegemonic system often means inclusion in another. *Tom* and *dee* identities are not just isolated categories that women may pick and choose from but systems of meaning embedded in dynamics of power and social sanctions. Richard Parker and John Gagnon urge researchers of sexual identity to shift their understandings of sexuality from the individual, or individual identities, to systems of meaning and social networks: "[We need to] move from the isolated sexual individual to sexuality as existing not only within but between individuals. The attempt to understand sexuality through an understanding of the social networks in which people live sexual and non-sexual lives is a way to concretize this movement" (1995, 15).

The necessity of placing sexual identities within larger social patterns is demonstrated by Elizabeth Lapovsky Kennedy and Madeline Davis' work (1993) on butch-femme communities in the United States. The researchers found that, for American butches and femmes, the community was an active agent in forming butch and femme identities, and a dialectical relationship resulted in which butch and femme women structured their community, its norms, and its rules and in turn were structured by this community. Women were categorized as either butch or femme when they entered the community and were then taught how to be butch or femme. Strict rules segregating the categories were upheld within the community.

Toms and *dees*, too, can be understood as resisting social norms that restrict women. In challenging normative expectations of women, *toms* and *dees* have constructed their own system of hegemony with strict gender roles and rules that in themselves are experienced as oppressive at times. Women learn how to be *tom* and *dee* through their experiences in the community. The location of *tom* masculinity between normative understandings of both men and women leads to a particularly unstable and contentious gender identity. Although these creative manipulations of gender by *toms* and *dees* allow for pleasure and sexual expression in certain ways, they are continually emergent, contradictory, and subject to intense contention.

CRITIQUE OF GENDER ROLES AND THEORIES OF HEGEMONY

Feminists globally have often perceived gender roles within female same-sex couples as inherently oppressive. The presence of masculine-feminine pairings in same-sex relations has been critiqued as imitating oppressive heterosexual patterns, especially the role of the masculine partner, who is perceived as appropriating male prerogatives. The feminine partner has also been criticized for using her feminine identity as a way to blend in with mainstream society, thereby claiming heterosexual privilege while still engaging in relationships with other women. For example, Malu Marin (1996, 47) criticizes masculine-feminine lesbian couples in the Philippines, called *pars* and *mars:*[1]

Many non-feminist lesbians insist on perpetuating male/female dynamics in their relationships. The butch partner, or *pars,* acts out the male role, while the femme partner, or *mars,* acts out the female role. Thus, the dynamics of their relationship are derived from heterosexist patterns, with the *pars* functioning as the provider, in terms of economic and financial support. This role is even more pronounced in the sexual aspect of the relationship. The *pars* play out the male (dominant) role more pronouncedly in the sex act, priding themselves as the "doers" or "givers" in sexual intimacy. This means that they alone are responsible for the sexual pleasure experienced by the *mars,* and therein lies the power, that they can be as equipped as "real" men in making love to women. One of the most sacred tenets of this dynamic is that *pars* do not allow themselves even to be touched by their partner. To allow this would mean becoming "women" themselves, and as "women" they would be stripped of their power over the *mars* in the relationship. The *pars* provokes awe while posturing as a man, with male privilege and power extended to her as part of the illusion.

This criticism of "gender role playing" begs the question of what these "gender roles" mean to the women in any particular cultural setting, and it also neglects the process whereby these gender meanings are constructed within the couple themselves. Nevertheless, Marin's work is an important call for the recognition of the rights and dignity of Philippine lesbian women, and her work identifies the importance of gender within Philippine female same-sex relations.

Kennedy and Davis (1993) provide an alternative interpretation of female same-sex gendered identities. In Kennedy and Davis' account of the American butch-femme world of the 1950s, women's claiming of masculinity and valuing of feminine sexual pleasure were a significant challenge to the hegemonic gender system, not an imitation of it. Kennedy and Davis (1993, 6) describe the basic quality of confrontation that defined butch and femme existence in the American context: "Butches defied convention by usurping male privilege in appearance and sexuality, and with their fems, outraged society by creating a romantic and sexual unit within which women were not under male control. At a time when lesbian communities were developing solidarity and consciousness, but had not yet formed political groups, butch-fem roles were the key structure for organizing against heterosexual dominance. They were the central prepolitical form of resistance. . . . What does it mean to eroticize gender difference in the absence of institutionalized male power? Is it possible to adopt extremely masculine characteristics and yet not want to be male?" The authors conclude that the performance of butch masculinity and femme sexuality was a form of female empowerment in a repressive patriarchal setting.

Both repressive and liberating aspects of *tom* and *dee* identity are possible, and *tom*s and *dee*s participate in contentious debates among themselves over their identities and community rules. The meanings of their gendered identities may indeed be imbued with repressive norms, but these norms are not simple appropriations of dominant gender hegemonies; they are reworkings of these hegemonic codes in contradictory and novel ways. For *tom*s and *dee*s, *tom* masculinity is not simply a means to control or oppress *dee*s. *Tom* masculinity is as constructed by *dee*s as it is by *tom*s. *Dee*s patrol the boundaries of acceptable *tom*ness and are the ultimate judges and arbiters over *tom*s' claims to masculinity. *Tom*s also participate in critique and judgment over masculine claims by other *tom*s and define themselves as unlike *dee*s. So, we may ask, is *tom* masculinity liberating for either *tom*s or *dee*s? Are *dee*s subjugated as feminine women to masculine control?

SUBVERSION OR OPPRESSION?

A *dee* writes in a letter to *Anjareesaan:* "I can't accept it at all. I can't accept a *tom* who lets a *dee* do it for her. If it's like that, why are you a *tom?* Go and be a *dee* instead. Normally when I have sex with my partner *(faen),* she will do it for me always, which she says she enjoys. Just to see me enjoy myself makes her happy already, something like that. So I have never done anything for her. Another thing, like I have said, I cannot accept a *tom* who lets a *dee* do it for her" (quoted in Matthana 1996, 141–142).

Acting within the cultural system does not mean uncritically reproducing the dynamics of power. Thai *tom-dee* relationships demonstrate that gender role-playing relationships are not imitations of the structural dynamics of heterosexual relationships. Although the masculine status of *tom*s grants them certain masculine privileges, they do not fill the social roles occupied by men. One of the key areas in which men and *tom*s differ is in the widespread practice of *tom* untouchability.[2] "Untouchability" refers to the practice whereby *tom*s (or "stone butches" in the West) do not allow their partner, or cannot ask their partner, to touch them sexually. This practice is explained by saying that *tom*s, like men, are "active" and *dee*s, as is considered normal for women sexually, are "passive." Thus *tom*s are expected to perform sexually for *dee*s, using manual stimulation, friction, or oral sex to bring their partner to orgasm, while remaining physically untouched by their partners. "Untouchability" is not just a description of *tom-dee* sex but, more importantly, a hegemonic code that is enforced through gossip and criticism of *tom*s who are purported to need for or ask their partners to touch them sexually in return. *Tom* masculinity is not a simple repetition of oppressive heterosexual dynamics (which feminists correctly critique) but an attempt to distinguish *tom*s from their feminine partners. Untouchability is a reflection of what *dee*s expect and demand —that is, sexual pleasure and an affirmation of their own feminine status as passive.

The extreme irony of untouchability is that, rather than imitating sexual behaviors of men, it most fully demonstrates the femininity of *tom* identity. *Tom*s are expected to provide sexual satisfaction to their partners, while minimizing their own physical needs. The sexual satisfaction of *dee*s, on the other hand, is the primary aim of the sexual experience, and thus explicitly feminine sexual desire is acknowledged and granted importance. Ting, a *tom,* pointed out that *tom* untouchability could stem from insecurity and embarrassment over their female bodies and fear that their lovers do not want to be reminded that they are not with real men. Ting posed the question, "Do you think Thai men are that insecure about their body [that they would not allow it to be touched or shown to their partners]?"

Research has demonstrated that shame over one's physical body is a characteristic of Thai women. Cuk, a *tom,* explained that she would be uncomfortably reminded of her femaleness if she allowed her *dee* girlfriend to touch her body:

My partner *(faen)* has never touched my breasts. Mostly I will be the one who does it [to/for her]. At least I wear a bra and a shirt over it, and I wear pants. I have never taken it all off. I asked her if she wanted me to take it all off. If she wanted me to, I would have taken it all off because [otherwise] it was taking advantage of her too much, because she took all her clothes off and I didn't. But she said if I took all my clothes off, it wouldn't be the same; it [my body] would become a woman. I understand that she will feel like that. We have been together for a long time; I will get that feeling from her. If I take all my clothes off, I'll look like a woman, and I won't be confident in myself. I'll feel embarrassed, something like that. I've had orgasms without taking off my clothes. Everyone is different. I always ask my partner if it feels good there. If she says yes, I immediately will have the same feeling. Just this and I feel good—I don't need her to touch my body. . . . We hug, but once we hug, [my partner] will feel it, but at least there is a shirt covering me. I've asked her, and she thinks that I am a man; it's just that I can't have children with her. (Matthana 1996, 142–143)

Baimai, a *tom*, asserted that the untouchability practice is right and proper for *tom*s and *dee*s: "With my girlfriend *(faen)*, who is a *dee*, she is the one who goes along with my wishes always, so I have never asked her to do it [perform sex] for me. She is the one who takes off all her clothes. As for me, it depends on whether I feel like it or not. She never complains. She just lies there. I think that's good. I don't think anything of it. I don't want anything more than that. I just go ahead and do it for her; there's no time to notice if she does it for me or not. I just try to do my duty *(naa-thii)* the best I can. I just do it until I think she is satisfied —I estimate the time that I think is right" (Matthana 1996, 142).

The resultant cultural hegemony that subsumes *tom-dee* identities is a negotiated process, not a one-sided process with *tom*s appropriating masculine privilege.[3] *Dee*s have both resented and upheld the norm of *tom* untouchability and enforced norms of masculinity for *tom*s. *Tom*s have also upheld norms of appropriate femininity to critique *dee*s and have sought to distinguish themselves from *dee*s by excluding *dee*s from a sense of "we." The subversiveness of *tom-dee* identities or, alternatively, compliance to Thai hegemonic gender norms is articulated within the dynamics of *tom-dee* interactions and relationships.

Critical theory and its anthropological offshoots have developed the concept of hegemony in order to deal with this kind of ambiguity—the complex power relationship between members of particular identities and the larger social discursive context of which they are a part.[4] The concept of hegemony has largely replaced in social theory the rigid dichotomies of oppressed and oppressor forces. Hegemony, though once wedded to a strictly Marxist political agenda, has become popular within the social sciences to describe the often ambiguous and complex nature of power relations in society. Hegemony describes a process of control that is based not on brute force but on constructions of a dominant culture—a set of ideas that are taken as descriptions of the way things really are or should be. It is a process of continual reframing of competing discourses in society to encompass subversive voices within the dominant set of ideas, and as a process of inclusion of subversive messages, it cannot be an absolute totalizing system of all possible meanings (R. Williams 1977). According to William Roseberry, "[Hegemony can help] not to understand consent but to understand struggle, the ways in which the words, images, symbols, forms, organizations, institutions, and movements used by subordinate populations to talk about, understand, confront, accommodate themselves to, or resist domination are shaped by the process of domination itself. What hegemony constructs, then, is not a shared ideology but a common material and meaningful framework for living through, talking about, and acting upon social orders characterized by domination" (1994, 360–361).

The question of what constitutes resistance within a hegemonic system is taken up by Martha Kaplan and John Kelly (1994, 128), who state that Gramsci's separation of "resistance"—unconscious behavior of subaltern classes—from "revolutionary" action creates overstated divisions. Kaplan and Kelly urge transcendence of this rigid dichotomy and look for ways that people seek change within dominant structures. This focus on manipulation of meanings within dominant structures is echoed in media studies theory, especially studies of popular culture. John Fiske explains the fluid nature of power within cultural systems: "The same person can, at different moments, be hegemonically complicit or resistant, as he or she reforms his or her social allegiances" (1989, 45).

*Tom*s are resistant to social control over their bodies as women—they openly express themselves as having sexual desire (they desire women and act on that desire). *Tom*s reject feminine codes of deportment, socialize at night, drink, and have a high degree of mobility seen as not appropriate for "good" women. Yet their embodiment of masculinity aligns them with the dominant power structure, which circumscribes female behavior—a point of much contention among feminists in the West and in Thailand. However, the masculinity of *tom*s is not a simplistic imitation of normative masculinity.

*Dee*s also conform to hegemonic notions of proper femininity—they are considered passive sexually, and they dress and speak as women are expected to. However, *dee*s are also understood (by many *tom*s as well as *dee*s) to enjoy sex, to demand satisfying sex, and to change partners frequently, while maintaining feminine status. Their position within *tom-dee* subcultures allows them to engage in a kind of femininity and sexual expression that is not isomorphic with hegemonic feminine sexuality and gender identity in Thai society.

Applying the concept of hegemony to gender systems has been systematically developed by Sherry Ortner (1990). The concept of gender hegemony proposed by Ortner resolves the problematic division between norms and practice that constantly plagues studies of gender. Ortner explains that many have argued with the idea of universal male dominance by noting that there are discrepancies between the norms or ideology in which men are said to have "prestige" and the lived reality in which women often hold more concrete power than the ideology would allow. Ortner notes that "although a given ideology and/or pattern of practices may be hegemonic, it is never total" (p. 78). In hegemonically male-dominated societies there may be instances of female power and prestige, and in hegemonically egalitarian societies there may be aspects of male dominance, which are contained. Ortner concludes that "one must always look at *both* the cultural ideology of 'prestige' and the on the ground practices of 'power'" (p. 79, emphasis in the original) and must look at the changing relationships between the two over time.[5]

In my study of *tom*s and *dee*s it has become clear that the ways they describe and define *tom*ness and *dee*ness may have complex and contradictory relationships to their lived practices and reality. For example, *tom*s are not supposed to be touched physically during sex, but in practice it is more likely to occur than most *tom*s will admit. Both *tom*s and *dee*s have admitted to me that they engage in sexual reciprocity, but they would not admit it to other *tom*s or *dee*s. Other rules are routinely broken as well, such as the rule that *tom*s should financially support *dee*s.

*Tom*s and *dee*s appropriate hegemonic discourses of masculinity and sexuality, such as the ideas that men are sexually active and have a "natural" need for sexual activity. However, *tom*s and *dee*s rework these ideological principles in ways that seem to convert their meanings to counterhegemonies. The ideas that men are sexually active and have powerful sexual desires reflect hegemonic notions of masculinity, yet when they are applied to the sole goal of feminine-female orgasm, the hegemony looks a little less familiar. *Tom*s also asserted that it was necessary to be of (sexual) service to women in order to gain love, producing a model of masculinity dissimilar to the Thai normative model of woman as (sexual) service provider and man as leader.

*Tom*s and *dee*s are operating within the larger Thai gender hegemony system, in which men are granted prestige as leaders (such as community leader or "head of the family") and are considered both spiritually superior and more emotionally stable. Within this hegemony are elements of a limited feminine prestige, such as the image of women as nurturers and emotional caretakers of others, as well as the ultimate image of the good woman as self-sacrificing. It is with considerable irony that, based on these well-known aspects of Thai ideology, the *tom*s most closely match the ideal feminine image of a suffering, self-sacrificing provider of comfort, sexual and otherwise, to others. Thus the *tom*s and *dee*s are not denying normative or hegemonic gender as much as reworking it in unique ways that grant women sexual license and sexual satisfaction.

If hegemony is understood as a struggle over meaning within a dominant culture, sexual and gender practices do not need to be exterior or rigidly opposed to dominant norms in order to be subversive. Such is the case with *tom-dee* gender/sexual practices. Judith Butler (1990) has argued against certain feminist assumptions, represented by Luce Irigaray (1985), that nonoppressive sexual and gender practices are exterior to the heterosexist and patriarchal social norms. Influenced by Foucauldian concepts of power, Butler rejects this rigid distinction between "oppressive" and "liberating" sexual practices. Butler states that feminist claims that women's sexuality is distinct from dominant patriarchal sexuality essentialize sexuality as a precultural entity that can be separated from the social and cultural matrix in which it emerges. Noting that all expressions of sexuality are constructed within the existing power and hegemonic structures, and following Foucault, Butler asserts that sexuality is coextensive with power itself; sexuality cannot exist devoid of socially determined power structures. Butler explains, "To operate within the matrix of power is not the same as to replicate uncritically relations of domination" (p. 30).

Butler (1990) argues that pure resistance to a dominant cultural system is therefore an illusion. Challenge and change to the system come from social activity within dominant meanings systems. Gender and sexual roles practiced by transgendered/homosexuals, such as butch/femme (or *tom/dee*), should not be seen as delusory imitations of a heterosexual or phallic power structure, says Butler. Both heterosexual and homosexual gender/sexual identities are performances of an assumed natural archetype, neither more natural than the other is. However, according to Butler, homosexual gender/sexual performances expose the constructed quality of this archetype, through parody, excess, and dissonance. The *tom*s and *dee*s of Thailand illustrate that nonconformist expressions of gender and sexuality are not outright rejections of dominant meanings. *Tom*s and *dee*s do not usually express themselves as resisting or opposing dominant sexual and gender models, and they pursue an ostensibly nonconfrontational expression of their gender/sexual identities.

SEEN BUT NOT HEARD: ABSENCE OF CONFRONTATION

*Tom*s and *dee*s do not hold a radically nonconforming position. They acknowledge that their identities and sexuality are not acceptable for society. Most *tom*s and *dee*s assert that although society misunderstands them, they agree that their relationships are not ideal, either for "normal women" or for children of *tom*s or *dee*s. Through its Web-Board the Lesla group discussed the issue of having children. One participant asked, "For couples of the same sex, what do you think about having babies with your partners? Would you find a way for artificial insemination or adopt?" Most members answered that it was not proper for homosexual couples to raise children:[6]

> MEMBER 1: I have thought about adopting and raising a child. It would be like making a life for a child, but when the kids grow up, would they call the *tom* "Dad" and the *dee* "Mom" or not? They would have to question whether they have one or two mothers, which would be a source of insecurity for them. In my opinion when the kids grew up, they would have to be part of society. Their friends would ask them questions.

> MEMBER 2: I have thought about having my own child, adopting or asking my sister-in-law to get pregnant—even to the extent that I took my sister-in-law to the doctor to get pregnant. But then I thought, no matter how warmly I would raise the child, the child would certainly have problems. If it is a family problem, it can be solved, but this would be a social problem if people around the children would not accept it. What would they do? So I stopped thinking about this project.

Many of the *tom*s and *dee*s I interviewed, and in the Lesla group, supported mainstream positions that negative imagery of *tom-dee* and other homosexual identities was due to the "bad behavior" of the group in question. Although most *tom*s and *dee*s felt they were misunderstood by society, they also, to a degree, repeated the ideas produced in the media that gays, *tom*s and *dee*s, and *kathoey*s are violent, emotionally unstable, and insecure. For example, a Lesla member wrote: "The society of those who love the same sex is so small, why don't we love each other and feel good about each other? The public looks at the society of same-sex love in a negative way, such as [thinking] we are violent and like to steal each other's lovers. We should stop doing bad things to each other and love each other so that society will see us in a better way, and society will not oppose the society of same-sex love as much." Another *tom* member added, "To tell bad people to stop being bad is difficult. People tell me *(phom)* to stop being such a flirt, but I can't stop. Some *tom*s are bad by nature—if they are born again, will they be better, I wonder?"

Many *tom*s also did not challenge the assumptions that heterosexuality, or "correct" gendering, was natural and that they were in some ways abnormal. I asked Kralok, a middle-aged *tom,* why she said she wanted to be a man. She replied, "Then I could give more warmth to my girlfriend." I said, "But it seems you already do that." Kralok replied, "Yes, but if I am a man, I won't be misgendered *(phit-pheet).* Actually I don't care that much about society, but it would be smoother for my girlfriend. Maybe I could do more for her than this."

*Tom*s and *dee*s did not position themselves as openly challenging society, and direct verbalizations of self as *tom/dee,* transgendered, or homosexual were uncommon. "Coming out," the verbal declaration of one's homosexuality, is not common in Thailand, even among women who are easily recognized as *tom*s. The Women's Day parade on March 8, 1995, is a case in point. Organized by a coalition of local women's organizations, a variety of groups were present for the parade and the panel discussions that followed at Thammasat University. The two largest groups, by my approximation, were sex workers and factory workers, who marched as identified groups and carried signs and chanted slogans. I estimated that several hundred women participated in the march. The lesbian organization Anjaree also participated, but only three or four members showed up for the march. The contrast was vivid; sex workers, a group most obviously despised and denigrated by society, openly organized themselves as a group and demanded their rights. Likewise, factory women, well experienced in protests and group organizing, were present in full force, making demands. Both of these two groups had developed a sense of group identity and a conceptual framework in which they could perceive themselves as being systematically exploited and therefore deserving of redress. Participation in union and NGO (nongovernmental organization) activity helped cultivate and structure these perceptions. Also, the vast majority of women in these two groups came from poor backgrounds (in many cases, desperately poor backgrounds): factory women and sex workers, mutually overlapping groups, were situated clearly within class boundaries. *Tom*s and *dees*, however, come from many class (and ethnic) backgrounds, and the empowered politics of representation evident in the factory women, sex workers, and other rural communities who have been mobilized in recent years are conspicuously absent from the *tom-dee* communities.

Empowered assertions of self do not occur only, or even most importantly, in banner-waving parades. Declarations of self and unapologetic claims of identity within intimate space and daily activities are important sites of resistance and subversion of social control. A sex worker's heavy gold jewelry expresses open declaration of impressive wealth certainly gained by means disdained by the viewers—I sense an "I do it, and I do very well at it—see for yourself" attitude in these displays. *Tom*s also openly enact their masculinity through their obviously masculine dress and hairstyles: *tom*s are easily identified in almost every venue imaginable—shopping centers, offices, factories, schools, and markets. *Dee*s are easily identifiable when they associate with *tom*s. Easy recognition of *tom*s in Thai society serves as a visual marker of a significant transgender/homosexual community in a society in which verbalizations and open declarations of female sexuality are taboo. However obvious *tom*s are visually, the act of verbal declaration of self is seen as too confrontational by many of the *tom*s and *dee*s I spoke with—an attitude in sharp contrast with the attitudes of the politicized sex workers and factory workers.

The contrast between visual explicitness and verbal silence concerning *tom* identity was obvious in the most intimate spaces—their families. Almost all the *tom*s interviewed said that their families knew that they were *tom*s, but very few *tom*s or *dee*s had actually had open discussions with their families about their identity or sexuality. Suay, a *tom* in her early thirties who lived in a provincial town, stated that her girlfriend, Bin, would complain that Suay would dress too much like a man and should not wear her hair so short. Bin claimed that if Suay looked too much like a man, people would disapprove of Suay, saying that she would drink and smoke. I interpreted this interaction to mean that Bin wanted to be less obvious about their relationship, veiling people's disapproval of *tom*s and homosexuality as general disapproval of stereotypical male behavior. Suay said she had not told her mother that she was a "lesbian," although her girlfriend lived with her and her family. She said her family knew, and there was no need to tell them directly. If she told her mother directly, Suay reasoned, her mother could forbid her. It is easy to hide sexual relationships between women,

Suay said, because nobody really thinks that two women together are lovers anyway.

As in Suay's case, open declarations about sexuality in general were not considered proper, and *tom*s and *dee*s rarely verbally declared their identity; they said it would appear inappropriately revealing. As Peter Jackson (1995) points out that there is very little open and frank discussion about the realities of sex, especially homosexual sex, in Thailand, because public revelations of what are perceived to be private and personal matters are disapproved of. The closest that the *tom*s and *dee*s I interviewed came to receiving any formal sex education in schools was having courses in morality in which the teachers warned the female students of the immoral nature of premarital sex or adulterous behavior. Members of Lesla discussed the issue of openly verbalizing their identity on their WebBoard:

MEMBER 1: I have never come out, but everyone else sees that I am [a *tom* or a *dee*] anyway.

MEMBER 2: Coming out to my family is the biggest deal, and there will never be a day when I do it, for sure. I am a *dee,* and so I don't have a problem with my family, because they can't figure it out. Even if I take my girlfriend to my house, I just warn my girlfriend to be careful of her behavior. I make my *tom* insist to my family that we aren't [girlfriends]. I am afraid that if my family knows, I will be left alone, because my family is old-fashioned. I am afraid they will be upset too, but as for my friends, I have totally come out. Whoever asks, I tell them that the one beside me is my girlfriend. I don't care if a friend can't accept it, just my family. I don't want them to be sad because they think that this is abnormal, like Thai society and many other societies think.

Another *dee* posed the question, "What is a good way to explain to your family if you love women? I feel awkward because there is a *tom* who comes to my house often." She received these answers:

MEMBER 1: You might have to tell your girlfriend *(faen)* that when she comes to your house, she must not be obvious, in either her behavior or dress.

MEMBER 2: Before, I thought if I had a lover who was a woman, I would let my family know. But after talking to people on this Web-

Board, I think it isn't necessary to let anybody know, but just let them find out on their own. I think that I can take responsibility for myself. I have never made my parents uncomfortable; I have been a good daughter. Most parents don't want their children to be like this, because they don't want society to look at their child as strange. I believe that what is important is to know correct behavior and not express too much, because our parents are still influenced by society.

The lack of explicit verbalization about female sexuality and the existing cultural norms of female friendship and intimacy, combined with a cultural logic that approves of female intimacy and friendship, allows *tom*s and *dee*s the maneuvering space to engage in transgender identity and homoerotic activities. However, the silent complicity in dominant gender sexual models has simultaneously hindered the formation of larger *tom-dee* communities. The Internet has provided an invaluable solution to this conundrum, because women can access Web sites, correspond with others, and learn about events and parties in relative privacy.

Social sanctions against homosexual behavior in Thailand do not usually take the official, legal forms found in the West (see Jackson 1995, 1999b; Kittisak 1993). *Tom*s and *dee*s have described feeling that people malign them behind their back. Likewise, this oblique criticism exacted grievous retribution from its targets. Gossip and innuendo can be brutalizing in a society in which social appearance and "face" are highly valued.[7] At the 1996 International Thai Studies Conference in Chiang Mai, a Thai lesbian activist spoke to the audience during a panel discussion of lesbians in Thailand: "Thai society looks like it is tolerant, but it is really an ignorant society more than a tolerant one. Deep down, behind the smiles, people talk about you, and that kills too. There is no pride in being gay; you are just abnormal."

Homosexuality, like most other supposed vices in Thai Buddhist discourse, is considered essentially a private affair and not subject to extreme repression, as long as the behavior is kept discreet and private. Not to speak of homosexuality or transgenderism can be considered a form of tolerance, as shown by the comments of a Thai Catholic priest who was on a panel on homosexuality in Thailand at the Foreign Correspondents Club in April 1997 in Bangkok. He said that, at the school where he worked, homosexuality was not considered a major issue and thus was never spoken of. *Tom*s, *dee*s, and gays are "tolerated" as long as they do not make their identity or behavior obvious through verbalization, which would require acknowledgment of a possibly confrontational misappropriation of gender and non-normative sexuality.[8] This attitude, coming from a Thai priest, sharply contrasts with the anti-homosexual stance of Western Catholicism. *Tom*s and *dee*s, by blending in with normative codes, such as passive acceptance of negative stereotypes, lack of verbal declarations of self, and low levels of political organizing, have bought for themselves a level of social maneuverability in which they can construct their own social world.

Although not explicitly political or confrontational, *tom*s and *dee*s challenged these normative models of female sexuality in important ways. As mentioned above, *tom*s and *dee*s positively valued female sexuality, and *tom*s were accorded the status of active sexual agents. This is a remarkable difference from normative heterosexuality described often in research studies. For example, Fongkaew (1997) interviewed middle-aged women about their sexual experiences. One woman said: "Most men are selfish. They just please themselves. They just get on top of the women while making love and do it until they are finished. They do not think about their wives' pleasure or if their wives reach orgasm. Sometimes she just let him get it done because she was fed up with it" (p. 584).

*Tom*s, by virtue of their masculine identity and their lack of participation in heterosexual sex, were granted freedom from the moral restrictions applied to other women. *Tom*s could positively value their own sexuality with enthusiasm, as could Thai men. *Tom*s talked openly about sex, even bragging about their ability and number of partners; this openness would not be possible for any Thai woman who was concerned about social opinion. Feminine women who bragged about sexual ability, experience, and sexual needs would be speedily condemned as prostitutes and slandered with one of the numerous Thai epithets for such a sexually experienced woman, such as harshly negative slang meaning "slut" or "prostitute" *(ee-tua, karii)* or "promiscuous" *(sam-sorn)*. *Tom*s talked with excitement among themselves about women to whom they were attracted, as well as sexual techniques and experiences. The lack of stigma of female same-sex behavior, and the freedom that women and girls have to pursue such relationships, have been described by a professor at Thammasat University: "I went to a Catholic school [all-girls school] when I was young, and homosexual relationships were quite common because in this country it might be better to have a relationship with a woman or a girl than to have sex with a man. [Female homosexual relationships] were very intimate and maybe not sexual. There wasn't the negative gossip. In fact some nuns and teachers encouraged this kind of relationship because they felt it was safer for girls to have sexual or intimate relations amongst themselves than to let them go off and have sex with men" (English used).

*Tom*s and *dee*s have found a way to express sexual desire, and to engage in sexual activity, that is not allowed for women in general. *Tom*s have also used masculinity to structure their lives with greater freedom and assertiveness than would be considered proper for other women. The price of such freedoms is inclusion in a *tom-dee* community with its own rules and limitations.

TOM-DEE HEGEMONY: UNTOUCHABILITY AND SEX

*Tom*s and *dee*s have constructed an alternative hegemonic structure with its own codes. Ting, a *tom*, described how good it felt to be masculine and to be the pursuer in sexual relationships rather than the passive recipient of a man's attention, as is expected of Thai women. The trade-off for gaining sexual agency as *tom*s, explained Ting, is that *tom*s are expected to adhere strictly to the ideas of *tom*s' untouchability. To break away from rigid feminine social roles and be the one who pursues is a good feeling, said Ting, but the role you must play as a *tom* has its own rules.

Jaat, a wealthy jet-setting *dee* in her forties, had a reputation among a circle of *tom*s for taking each of them to task for their lack of appropriate masculine qualities. One of her ex-lovers, Khiaw, bitterly complained to her close friend that Jaat would gossip about her to all Jaat's lovers, saying that Khiaw was not manly enough. Jaat would even call Khiaw's place of work and complain, trying to humiliate and intimidate Khiaw. Jaat would say that Khiaw was not a real *tom*, because she asked to have Jaat perform sex for her on occasion. Jaat also accused Khiaw of asking Jaat to support her financially. Jaat was an unusual case—her viciousness (along with her supposed wealth and beauty) was the subject of much discussion. Feeling upset and intimidated by *dee*s' demands that *tom*s be properly manly—that is, untouchable—affected many of the *tom*s I spoke with. Nuu, a *tom*, was talking with her friend Ot, a *dee*, about Ot's relationship with her *tom*, Aa. Ot was happy, having just made up with Aa after one of their many separations. Ot giggled about her sex life with Aa, saying that Aa had a "little dick." Nuu was visibly annoyed and said to me later, "Why can't [Ot] accept that [Aa] is a woman? Why does she have to say that? It's like she can't accept the truth that she's with a woman!"

Taaw, a *tom* in her late forties, had lived with a woman for four years. Taaw said she was always the one who initiated sex with her girlfriend and that her girlfriend never touched Taaw sexually in return. I asked her why and whether she wanted it that way. Taaw said they never spoke about it, and she did not dare bring up the subject. Taaw said that was why she liked Westerners *(farang)* now—they did not have the same rigid sexual codes that Thai *toms* and *dees* held. Other *toms* told me the same thing, that they were "bored with Thai *dees*" and the gender norms that *dees* upheld.

Dees, however, often felt that *toms* were the ones who set the sexual rules. *Dees* frequently said they never felt that it was permissible to touch the *toms* sexually, and they felt too intimidated to try. Chang, a *dee*, explained that *dees* were often shamed if they tried to touch their *tom* sexually: "I've heard that some *toms* never let their *dees* touch any part of their bodies. One of my *dee* friends said she accidentally touched her *tom*'s breasts while making love. Then the *tom* stopped and left furiously without saying anything. That *dee* never had sex with a *tom* before, so she thought she could touch her lover. After that, her *tom* said she could not touch her because she is a man. So I said maybe that *dee* should have her hands tied. *[Laughs.]*"

*Tom*s, on the other hand, often positioned *dees* as the main forces behind *tom* untouchability. Piin, a *tom* in her thirties, said she enjoyed the feeling of being a *tom* in many ways, but she disagreed with the idea that *toms* should be sexually "active" or the "doers" while *dees* were passive and never reciprocated sexually for *toms*. I asked her about *toms* she knew, and Piin answered, "I know some, and they are the hard-core ones who have never been touched by their girlfriends. I asked them if they feel anything sexually, and they said they feel neutral. It's fine for them. In my opinion I think they fool themselves—that they have sexual feelings through their fingers, that's impossible. *[Laughs.]*" (English and Thai used). Piin felt that *dees* enforce these standards and that this enforcement had become too rigid within the *tom-dee* community:

Some women say they can't tolerate it if *toms* ask them to be "doers" or take off the *tom*'s clothes. I say that is selfish. You want to have happiness, but the "doers" are tired too. Why can't you let them [*tom*s] feel happy too? I would say that that woman is selfish. I blame so many *dee*s in the WebBoard. Some *dee*s say, "No, I can't accept that." From my experience, I have had so many girlfriends when I was young. I met so many kinds of women. Some don't want me to do them, but they want to do me instead. [*Laughs.*] They are so *dee*, very womanly but still active. I met some *dee*s who do nothing, just lie down. Some love me so much, but if I ask them to do me, it will affect our relationship in a bad way. I met them all, so I have learned from that. And I also have gained some experience from talking to Lesla members on the Web. I have to accept the reality that I am physically a woman. I don't think the same as many Thai *tom*s—maybe I am a *dee*! [*Laughs.*]

Chang, a *dee* who was also somewhat critical of the untouchability rule, felt that *tom* untouchability was characteristic of "old-fashioned" *tom*s and *dee*s. She claimed that there is more flexibility with younger, more progressive *tom*s and *dee*s: "I usually meet that kind of conservative *tom* who is over thirty years old. But now I meet some couples who can take a shower happily together. I think *tom*s and *dee*s now are lovelier as a couple. They can kiss and play together like friends. They are not very strict, like the old *tom*s. Old-fashioned *tom*s—they have to be active, and *dee*s have to be passive only."

Despite Chang's comments, my interviews indicated that most younger *tom*s and *dee*s are actually like older ones, feeling uncomfortable with touching *tom*s sexually, and older *tom*s and *dee*s are about as likely to violate this rule as are younger ones. The Lesla group, composed of mostly younger *tom*s and *dee*s, used the WebBoard to express strong criticism of *tom*s who allow themselves to be touched. In any case, sexual exchange between *tom*s and *dee*s is labeled as progressive and modern. Chang elaborated:

I think that *tom*s think they must be active and *dee*s must be passive. *Tom*s think they have to start and manage almost everything and that *dee*s are happy with that. But now I've heard that there are some "two-way" [English word used] *tom*s, which means they allow *dee*s to "do" [perform sexually] for them. And *dee*s now can express that they want to take some action or make the first move. It's not the same as we've heard that *dee*s can't ask for sex or are not allowed to do this or that. Some older *dee*s still believe so, but the young *dee*s are more advanced. Some *dee*s said we are "husbands and wives," so we can switch. I have never asked or talked about sex with my friends. . . . I had never "done" my *tom* before, but now she has asked me to do her, so I do. I never thought that I could do this, but I love her so much that I can. I never thought that I could "do" anybody since my first *tom*. She never asked me, and I never thought about "doing" her. I was passive for nine years, although I sometimes touched her breasts and she never said anything.

Interviews with older *tom*s, however, demonstrated that many women in their forties and older were critical of strict sexual roles between *tom*s and *dee*s. For example, Kralok, a *tom* in her forties, disagreed with sexual role playing as definitive of *tom* identity: "I don't understand some *tom*s who sleep with women but are not willing to take off their clothes or let themselves be touched. And some *dee*s are not willing to do anything for the *tom* [sexually]. They sleep with the *tom* and let the *tom* do it all. I don't think that's right, because sex is giving the one we love pleasure. It is a happiness that both sides need. But in that I am a *tom,* I at first thought that I was a man. I did everything for the *dee* only. I thought that love was giving, so I thought I had to give sexual pleasure to her. My *dee* didn't know what to do, so I had to teach her how to kiss, how to touch me. It is natural for her to feel shy, as women do. I had to teach her that isn't a shameful thing, like the way Thais are taught that sex is a dirty thing." Thus, claiming that *tom* untouchability was "old-fashioned" was more of a rhetorical device than a description of older and younger women's attitudes toward sexual roles.

COMMUNITY LABELING

When entering a *tom-dee* community or relationship, women become well versed in the rules, and the repetition of these expectations has the effect of forcing women into the categories of *tom* and *dee*. Some *tom*s said that they never actually chose a *tom* identity for themselves, explaining that *dee*s pushed them toward being a *tom,* and the women they were involved with encouraged them to dress and act masculine. Piin said that she did not deliberately establish a *tom* identity, but her masculinity was something conferred on her by women who were interested in her: "I wasn't a tomboy when I was young. I went to an all-girls school, and some *dee*s flirted with me. I thought that was crazy: how can a woman love a woman? When I was in junior high school, a woman friend hugged me and tried to kiss me. I screamed, "You're crazy!" Then when I was in high school, a woman liked me and we had an affair. Nobody took roles. . . . I don't know why [I became a *tom*]. I didn't mean to change to be a butch. I don't know why [I did]. Maybe I have been forced by *dee*s to act like this or like that. Another reason is I have high self-confidence, so I can be anything I want to be" (English and Thai used).

For women who do not fit the normative model of femininity and have sexual interest in women, the label of *tom* can be inescapable and not particularly desired. Ngor, a woman known as a *tom* in her late twenties, was middle class and urban. She said that she had never labeled herself as a *tom*, but others had labeled her as one. Ngor said she had been attracted to women ever since she could remember. When she was in secondary school, there was an open atmosphere, with many couples in her all-girls school; "*tom*" was a relatively casual and stigma-free term, "like being called a basketball player." When Ngor moved to a mixed high school, friends began to ask if she was a *tom* in a new and stigmatizing way—"*tom*" was a means of separating her from others. Ngor said she didn't want to be thought of as a *tom*, because she did not want to be thought of as a man. Ngor described her identity as being forced on her. "Why do they have to separate people and label them?" she asked angrily. However, Ngor did claim a kind of masculinity, saying she had never liked to play with dolls as a child, nor did she like to hang out with groups of women and "talk about shopping." Ngor said that her family had long thought of her as ambiguously masculine, noting her strong distaste for skirts (not comfortable, explained Ngor) and the many girlfriends she brought home. Her parents wondered why she "was not a normal woman." Although Ngor held a masculine view of herself corresponding to others' perceptions of her as masculine, she said she did not like very masculine behavior. "Society doesn't accept women like that. I don't want to be thought of as a man," she explained. Nevertheless, Ngor's masculinity and homosexuality had led others to understand her as a *tom,* a label she begrudgingly tolerated.

Once labeled, some *tom*s grow into their identities through experience with lovers and friends who are *tom*s and *dee*s. Piin said that after she appropriated a *tom* identity, she enjoyed the feeling of being masculine. Piin described to me the way her younger *tom* friends felt: "They think like us when we were young. We wanted to be a man, to be active, to protect, be a leader, do cool things, be one who wins. This has to do with sex too. We don't want anyone [male] to touch us, because if we are women and have sex with someone, that means to be 'ruined' *(sia)*. We wanted to have many girlfriends, the more the better. That made us proud of ourselves. We had male values, like we have to flirt and then we will look cool" (English and Thai used). As Piin explained, some aspects of being a *tom* were experienced in a positive way, and untouchability, even if it meant not being touched sexually, was part of the package deal.

Points of contention over sexuality and identity arose not only between *tom*s and *dee*s but also between *tom*s, over the issue of being too feminine, such as allowing *dee*s to touch them sexually. *Tom*s, including younger ones, divided women sharply into *tom* and *dee* categories, depending on their sexual roles, such as in this Lesla Web-Board discussion:

MEMBER 1: Being done by my girlfriend makes me feel strange. I wonder if I am a *dee*.

MEMBER 2: Really? Why do you allow that? If you like it, you are a *dee*.

MEMBER 1: I allow it because I like it and want to try it.

MEMBER 2: Are you hooked? If you want to try it more, that means you are a *dee*. So you have to ask yourself [if you are a *dee*].

MEMBER 3: If you like it only in sex, you can't conclude you are a *dee* or not. You can't measure from sex alone. Maybe you are going to find something else that you are attracted to in that person.

*Tom*s were often especially embarrassed to talk about being touched by their partners in front of other *tom*s. Bang was a *tom* in her early thirties who struck me as particularly masculine. She was a police officer, drove a large motorcycle, had the short-cropped hair that identified *tom*s, and dressed in very masculine ways—jeans with a heavy belt, and a crisp white T-shirt under a button-down men's shirt. When the minister of the interior announced that pants would be an acceptable uniform for female police officers, Bang said she was so relieved. I asked her if she could ever be in a relationship with a *tom*, and she replied that she could, adding that she did not like the strict sexual *tom-dee* codes that dictated that only she could be the active one. Bang said she wanted a more mutual relationship sexually, but she hoped that nobody would know that she wanted this, because she would be embarrassed. When another *tom* came into the room, a close friend of mine who shared similar attitudes, Bang refused to speak about the issue anymore. *Tom*s were often shy about openly rejecting the *tom-dee* norm of *tom* untouchability.

Khaek, the tour company operator introduced in chapter 2, seemed to adhere rigidly to the notions of *tom* masculinity and clear distinctions between femininity and masculinity. We joked about how some *tom*s were ashamed to let themselves be touched, at which point Nuu declared loudly, "She [Khaek] is a woman, even though she is a *tom*. Why should she be ashamed of her body? She has breasts too!" Ying responded with peals of laughter, and Khaek seemed uncomfortable. I joked with Khaek about what sort of rules she played by, and Khaek, looking cross, replied, "I only do it—I don't let her do it," referring to sex. I said I was only joking, but Khaek did not seem satisfied and repeated that she was the active one.

GENDER AND FINANCES

Sexuality was not the only marker of distinction or source of tension between *tom*s and *dee*s; financial support of *dee*s was a particularly contentious aspect of the expectations of *tom*s. On the one hand, *tom*s often upheld notions that it was unmanly for *tom*s to depend on *dee*s financially. On the other hand, *tom*s, especially older ones, complained that they were victimized by *dee*s who used them for financial support.

One Lesla member asked on the WebBoard, "What do you think about a *tom* who lives off [financially depends on] a *dee?*" A *tom* answered, "Extremely bad. Like an old lady financially supporting some younger man in exchange for sex. I know that I *(phom)* love to flirt and fool around with many women, but I'm not so bad that I depend on a woman for support. I would lose my honor." Another member wrote, "If you use the word 'cling to,' I think of not loving each other but only taking advantage of each other. But if two people are in love, you have to call it 'support.'"

The first *tom* disagreed: "I *(phom)* don't agree with the point above. If a *tom* wants to support a *dee*, it is normal. But if a *dee* supports a *tom*, it is like a man living off his woman. I don't think it is any different from being a parasite." Another member agreed: "It is no different from being trash. We should depend on ourselves." However, some members tried to reframe the relationship in terms of mutual friendship. For example, one wrote: "If two people love each other, [and] one is rich and one is poor, the rich one supports the other financially, and the poor one takes care, protects, or helps the rich one. This is friendship—if we see a friend in a crisis, we will want to help." One *tom*'s response to this idea was "Do you know what a reptile is?"[9] Another *tom* answered, "I *(phom)* think it is a personal issue. Whoever is stupid enough to be ripped off, it can't be helped. This depends on individual satisfaction. But I do not agree with a *tom* being like a pimp." In this exchange, it was mostly *tom*s who upheld strict protocols for *tom* behavior.

As mentioned above, many *tom*s and *dee*s explained these attitudes toward "proper" *tom* masculinity in terms of age, claiming that young or modern *tom*s and *dee*s did not hold such restrictive beliefs. Curiously, the *tom*s who used the Lesla Web site were mostly young—early twenties or so, and this younger set seemed more firmly entrenched in *tom-dee* identity and strict roles than were older women I interviewed. Many of the older *tom*s said they had done so when they were younger, but now they felt exploited by *dee*s who expected financial support.

Kep's story exemplifies the resentment that many *tom*s expressed over the expectation that they be financially responsible for *dee*s. A sixty-year-old wealthy *tom,* Kep lived in a spacious home in a small town east of Bangkok on the coast of the gulf of Thailand. The marble floors and austere Chinese furniture indicated her obvious success as a businesswoman, but she did not share her home with anyone. Kep had a warm and honest style. We sat on the beach in front of her house while she told me her life story, including her experiences with *dee*s. When she was young, she had set up her business with her first girlfriend, to whom she was indebted, she says, for helping her start out. After they broke up, Kep had a series of relationships that all ended in ways she now says are predictable—the *dee*s left her to get married. She said that in the past she had occasionally visited go-go bars and paid female sex workers for sex, but she now discouraged *tom* friends from doing so, for fear that they would get involved with the wrong type of woman. Kep said she needs a proper woman, well dressed and well mannered, but she noted, "I don't want *dee*s. They just take advantage of me and make me pay all the time." Kep and one *dee* had made a mutual commitment that the *dee* would not marry. The girlfriend said she really loved Kep and that they would be together all their lives. At first Kep did not like her and felt she was not her type, but Kep explained that she felt sorry for her and soon became involved. They were "together like husband and wife," explained Kep. After seven years, however, the *dee* decided to marry a man from her village whom she had been seeing for only two months. Kep said that was the last time she would commit to a woman, and from then on she did not want a serious relationship—she would "just play around." She concluded, "Being with a woman is a burden. They will want me to care for them."

Most *dee*s did indeed expect *tom*s to care for them, although the financial reality was often different from the ideal. Chang complained that her *tom*, Mai, was not working. Chang said that Mai had been unemployed for too long and was not able to help Chang out with expenses other than just electricity and water bills. "I feel like it's my burden to take care of everything," concluded Chang. Chang ended her three-year relationship with Mai shortly afterward for this reason. Although many *tom*s, especially younger ones, express pride in being able to support a woman, most *dee*s felt that to support *tom*s was undesirable. Chang said she did not expect her *tom* to be like a man and completely support her, and money was not the most important thing in choosing a partner, but not having a partner help out financially would hinder her chance for a good future: "I have to work alone, and she doesn't do any work. Actually I had so many choices of rich *tom*s who flirted with me. But I think money is not as important as love and sincerity, and so I ignored them all. At first my *tom* was very nice to me, but she gradually changed. She stopped working after she was with me the first year." In reality, many of the *dee*s supported *tom*s, or both partners provided income, but *tom*s commonly criticized *dee*s, saying they used *tom*s for money. Likewise, a common criticism of *tom*s was that they were unmanly if they lived off *dee*s or were not able to provide adequately for them.

Another contentious aspect of *tom* performance of masculinity was the necessity to wear skirts or dresses to work. In Thailand, many office jobs for women, including private companies and government offices require that women wear skirts. One Lesla member asked what others thought about a *tom* who wore dresses and skirts to work. The response was sharply negative. For example, a *dee* wrote, "I totally can't accept it. If they don't want to be *tom*s, they shouldn't be *tom*s from the beginning." *Tom*s had to balance their status as *tom*s in their own communities with the demands of the larger society.

Most *tom*s and *dee*s combined ideas about sexual behavior, dress, and financial responsibility to describe their sense as masculine or feminine beings. For example, Kralok felt strongly about her own identity as a *tom* and said that being a *tom* and "misgendered" *(phit-pheet)* marked her as different from other people in society. Kralok dressed in obviously male clothing, such as male slacks and button-down shirts, had short-cropped hair, and used male-gendered pronouns when referring to herself. She was clearly identifiable as a *tom* to those around her and thought that people in her office at first kept her at a distance because of it. Even though she believed that being a *tom* was a distinct identity, she did not agree with strict sexual divisions between *toms* and *dees* or with the harsh criticism of Lesla members toward *toms* who wore feminine clothing at work: "In the situation where we see *toms* wearing skirts [and] wearing makeup and lipstick, we must understand whether that company is open-minded or not. Do they accept *toms* or not? If they don't, *toms* need to dress up like that for work. They must be willing to do it. But *dees* of the younger generation, they can't accept *toms* like this, because they don't know about real life yet. Younger *dees* should listen to the older generation. The new generation should listen to the older one." But Kralok did not deny that being a *tom* meant performing certain, culturally identifiable, masculine functions: "I have to be more mature than she is. For example, I have to protect her while crossing a street. I walk behind her to make sure that she is in my sight. I have to protect her all the time. I will do anything I can to be a leader or adviser. But in bed we are equal. I don't have to be a leader then. But when it comes to intelligence and thinking, I have to be a leader. Being a *tom,* you have to take good care of her feelings. I call her several times a day. Sometimes when I am on a public phone talking to her and somebody is waiting for the phone, I give them my phone card to use another phone so that I don't have to stop our conversation. This is a small sample of how I have to be good at taking care of her feelings."

Both older and younger women agreed that there were distinctions between *toms* and *dees* in terms of social roles, but there was widespread variance in how these distinctions were interpreted. The belief that *toms* and *dees* have different sexual and social roles resulted in marginalizing *dees* as temporary members of the community. Many women thought it was likely that many *dees* were only temporarily seeking sexual and financial comfort from *toms* and would soon return to men. *Toms* tended to classify all *dees* as heterosexual at heart, whereas some *dees* made distinctions between real *dees* and temporary *dees*. One *tom* Lesla member wrote: "Why does society like to see us as a substitute [for a man]? I don't like it when people ask *dee*s why they like *tom*s, and they answer they are heartbroken from a man. When I hear this, I feel bad. How many women are born for us?" A *tom* answered, "There are some, but it is easier to find a needle in a haystack." A *dee* disagreed, though: "I don't think that women born to be *dee* are that few. I know many people who are *dee*s, including myself, who are born to be *dee*, who like to look at *tom*s and are disgusted with men." Another *dee* said, "I am one, a born-to-be *dee*. Many of my friends are too. I can't see a *tom* without wanting to run up and hug her." Chang said she too was "born to be a *dee*." The common *tom* assertion that *dee*s were fundamentally unlike *tom*s created tensions in *tom-dee* communities by labeling *dee*s as outsiders to the core community, which usually centered around groups of *tom* friends.

TOMS' EXCLUSION OF *DEE*S

Although *tom*s complained that *dee*s did not take them seriously, *tom*s also tended to exclude *dee*s from their networks by saying that *dee*s were not like them. Nuu and I chatted with several *dee*s whom Nuu had known for some time as friends. Jaeng told us about her recent heartbreak over a *tom* whom she said she dearly loved. In telling us about her past, she said she had never been attracted to men and had only wanted *tom*s. Jaeng even said she was "born this way," which is how many *tom*s described themselves. Jaeng had been married for a short time to please her parents but said that she just could not bear her husband, because she had never had any sexual or romantic feelings for men, and so she soon divorced. Nuu, in order to comfort Jaeng, said, "You should look for somebody good. You don't have to think whether they are a man or a woman." I was struck by that comment, as I had never heard Nuu say something like that to a *tom*. She usually said that being a *tom* is suffering, the price one must pay for being born a *tom*. Jaeng had clearly told us that she was exclusively interested in women, but Nuu would not see her as being like a *tom*. Nuu consistently made the distinction between *tom*s and *dee*s, seeing all *dee*s as essentially bisexual and most likely to choose a man.

A *TOM* WHO BROKE THE RULES

Kung knew that other *tom*s, especially Fon, disapproved of her and criticized her behind her back. Kung and I sat at a table in the restaurant in front of the rows of one-room row houses that she and most of her fellow bar workers rented in North Pattaya. Kung's light makeup and long, silky hair, which reached her waist, clashed with what *tom*s, as I knew by now, were supposed to look like. Sitting a few tables away was Fon, who would occasionally glance our way and roll her eyes just as I looked her way. Fon had earlier told me that she disapproved of Kung, describing herself as not like "these other *tom*s" (glancing in Kung's direction) who claimed to be *tom* one day and slept with a man the next day. Fon's disapproval lay in the fact that Kung was a sex worker and therefore had sexual relationships with men. Fon's longtime girlfriend was also was a sex worker, and so Fon was not particularly scandalized by sex for money—rather, she was upset that somebody who claimed to be a *tom* would have sex with a man. Fon believed that economic necessity was not a reason for a *tom* to sleep with a man. When Fon compared her masculine self with Kung, Fon claimed that her own stable and incontrovertible gender identity had led to the acceptance of her masculinity in her village: "All my male friends in the village accept me. They have known me since I was a child. It wasn't like I got married and then all of a sudden I turn around and am a *tom*. This is very strange, to fool around with men and then turn around and be a *tom*—very strange."

Fon had said to me just the day before that she was not an "amphib-ian," referring to a woman who goes from men to women as partners, like some other "so-called *tom*s" around, such as Kung. Fon said some *tom*s are both male and female—that is, they have both femininity and masculinity within them, but that she was not that way. "Some people have the appearance of being a *tom* but say 'I can't give men up, even though I have a wife.' There are lots like this, who say 'I am a *tom*, and I work [a euphemism referring to sex work] and my wife works.' No way—that is not my way. I am a *tom*, and right away I accept all the burdens and take responsibility. OK, if you want to work, go ahead, but if I work at the bar and at night we are husband and wife, I think that is disgusting. I am speaking frankly; I think it is disgusting. Do you understand?"

Kung fidgeted and seemed agitated, and she suggested we go to her room to talk, away from the sidelong glances of Fon and other bar workers. We walked several yards behind the bar to the narrow lanes between the rows of poured-concrete rooms. The occupants had tried their best to decorate their cramped space, with rows of potted plants and benches lining the gravel path. Gas stoves, kitchen pots, vegetables soaking in buckets, and clothes drying in the sun clogged the already narrow lane. Kung's room was comfortable, with a bed, a dresser, a few fading posters, and a television. We both sat down on her bed, and she told me why she had decided to get married to a Western man she had met at the bar. "I have to think about my future," she explained. Kung said she planned to go to Germany with him and to study German for three years while her husband supported her. Kung said that if the marriage did not work out, she would still have a chance for a better future with the extra education and German language skills. "I could come back and work at a tour company," she explained. She spoke seriously and seemed tense as she described her plans to make a more secure future for herself. Kung is from a rural village in the northeast. Unlike many of the other bar workers, she could read, but she had only finished primary school. Bar work was the best means to find a way out of tedious, strenuous, low-income work that faced Kung and all the other young rural women like her, she reasoned.

I asked Kung about her relationships with women, and she seemed to relax a bit. She laughed as she told me of her relationship with a European woman who had come to the bar a year or so before. They had spent some time together, going to beaches and traveling around Thailand. After the European had gone home, Kung said she still missed her. Kung had had many girlfriends before, though, and she told me of her first love when she was a teenager. Kung said her own family accepted that she was a *tom* and liked women, not men. The girlfriend, Jip, came to live with Kung and her family. Jip's family was not so accepting, however. Kung explained: "You have to understand, Thai people don't accept things easily; they say things are perverse *(wiparit)* and deviant. Her parents couldn't accept it. Her parents made a big deal and came looking for trouble [when they] came to my house to take their daughter back. They brought the police, but when the police saw I was a woman, they said they couldn't arrest me, because there was no law concerning women.[10] [Jip's] parents then forced her to marry a man, but they couldn't get along well, and anyway she got pregnant. My girlfriend was twenty-one years old then. She wrote me, but I never wrote her back, because I didn't want to cause problems in her family. Even though I loved her, I didn't want to bother her, because her parents had hurt me."

Kung did not see much tolerance from either the world outside or her own *tom-dee* community. But being thin-skinned was not an option for bar workers, given that they face disdain and harassment daily. Being excluded from the large *tom-dee* community in Pattaya surely did not help matters. Nevertheless Kung saw her sexuality and *tom* identity as a means to freedom: "I think of myself as a *tom* because when I don't have a boyfriend, I feel comfortable. I feel the best when I am my own person and I can do whatever I want. I don't have to put on makeup. OK, sometimes I like to dress sexy and I dress as myself, but if I stay with him, I can't be casual. It's a pain, you know. I've said to him, "You —go back to Germany!" and when he does, I feel so happy! Because then I am my own person; I can do whatever I want. It's like when the man comes back, the same old situation comes back too. I don't want to be like a bird in a cage, you understand?" Kung's story traces the limitations of possibility for *tom* identity, as well as the conflicts that arise from various life choices that clash with notions of appropriate femininity or masculinity.

Clearly, many *tom*s and *dee*s were not satisfied with the sexual rules and roles that the community upholds, and as Ortner (1990) notes, lived reality is often at odds with hegemonic codes. The rules, though not uniformly practiced by any means, structured the ways *tom*s and *dee*s interacted and presented themselves. Although there is considerable pressure in the *tom-dee* community to uphold ideas of untouchability in *tom*s, some *tom*s, like Kung, are less wedded to full appropriation of *tom* masculinity and the difference between *tom*s and *dee*s, acknowledging mutual satisfaction in *tom-dee* sex. Kung said she had no illusions about heterosexual sex: "Men are men. As for *tom*s, their heart is a man's, but they have the body of a woman. But there are some people who observe that they are only women and can't do what a man can, but they can actually please women more." Kung said she and her partners did not have rules about untouchability, and although she was "like a man" and called herself a *tom*, she did not extend these distinctions to her sexuality.

CONCLUSION

*Tom*s and *dee*s have resisted cultural/social expectations and limitations of women, and their identity and actions can be seen as oppositional. However, some *tom*s align themselves with men and have described themselves as being like men rather than like women, and one must ask if it makes sense to understand them as women who are resisting. Furthermore, do *dee*s conform to gender stereotypes that women are passive, or do they challenge these stereotypes by actively enforcing a kind of female masculinity in which feminine women's sexual pleasure is prioritized?

Few *tom*s or *dee*s expressed pleasure in resistance, but rather framed their sexuality and gender in terms of normative social expectations of men and women. The concept of hegemony is based on the observation that "resistance" is never as absolute as it may seem. Hegemony and its resistance are complex processes whereby cultural rules are enforced, transgressed, and reinscribed, with social actors never completely outside or free from the system they resist. *Tom*s and *dee*s did not directly challenge social restrictions on women but found space within the social norms to express sexuality, assertiveness, and dimensions of masculinity that were liberating. These transgressive practices were partial and were largely structured by their own alternative hegemonic order. As Anthony Giddens (1992, 30) explains, "The self is a reflexive project, a more or less continuous interrogation of past, present and future." The example of Kung, a *tom* who visibly refused to participate in *tom-dee* norms, demonstrates that *tom* and *dee* identities are not simple reflections either of mainstream gender norms or of the norms constructed by *tom*s and *dee*s themselves. *Tom*s and *dee*s selectively pull from hegemonic codes that define *tom*s as simultaneously masculine individuals and feminine caretakers, active sexual agents yet secretive and embarrassed about their physical bodies. *Dee*s are "normal" women who reject social expectations that they have heterosexual relationships, yet they insist on masculine partners. They are properly feminine yet seek out sexual relationships with partners whose main duty is to give them pleasure.

Anjaree and Lesla　6

Tom and *Dee* Communities
and Organizations

THE NEWSLETTER *Anjareesaan* ran a story about an Anjaree representative who attended an international gay parade in New York City. A reader responded to the story:

> Dear Anjaree,
> I would like to ask for your comments. . . . In the Stonewall parade in New York, why was there a sign saying "Thailand" in the picture? And I also want to know about *tom*s—why do they have such small breasts? How can they make them so small? And do *tom*s also menstruate?
>   KUNG

Anjaree replied,

> Dear Kung,
> There was a Thailand sign because a Thai person joined the parade. . . . If you follow the news, you will see that people from every corner of the world joined in. There were a million people in this event. . . . They were women who love women and men who love men from all over the world.
>   People who are *tom*s are women. Sometimes they have small breasts, sometimes they have large breasts, but each one menstruates. This fact all the editors can confirm, but please don't ask for proof! (*Anjareesaan,* March 1995, vol. 2, no. 10)

Anjaree's letter sums up the main thrust of Anjaree's message: *tom*s and *dee*s are women who are united by their love for other women. As such, they are part of a global community of women (and men) with the same sexual orientation. Anjaree's message of a nongendered sexual orientation, with political and social aspirations, is a tentative challenge to entrenched beliefs held by *tom* and *dee*s and by society at large.

Two formal organizations for *tom*s and *dee*s exist in Thailand: Anjaree and Lesla. *Tom* and *dee* identities are increasingly popular, as is indicated by both the growth of their visibility and the growth of *tom-dee* communities in recent years. As these identities have grown in popularity, new challenges to *tom* and *dee* identities have emerged from within the communities themselves. Anjaree has also openly challenged the authoritative state-supported discourses of homosexual pathology that have dominated public discourse for several decades.

ANJAREE

Established in 1986, Anjaree is the oldest lesbian organization in Thailand. As of 1996 it had approximately seven hundred members on its mailing list and five hundred newsletter subscribers. After changes in leadership and organization, its membership dropped to two hundred and had since risen to four hundred as of mid-2003. Membership, which costs 200 baht (about US$4) per year, includes six newsletters, but activities are open to anyone interested. Anjaree operates an office and a Web site (http://www.anjaree.org), usually has a paid staff member, and has received grants from international funding agencies (such as Astria) and national funding sources (such as the Hotline Project of the AIDS Project in the Ministry of Health). Activities include monthly meetings for members to get to know each other and to discuss relevant issues; occasional trips to tourist sites; and workshops. Anjaree is also actively involved in a public awareness campaign and has given interviews to TV and radio programs, newspapers, and magazines. Run by a small committee of advisers and a staff facilitator, the organization has generally maintained consistent positions and policies over the years.

Anjaree has advocated the position that sexuality is a right and a choice. Feminism and human rights are philosophical underpinnings for Anjaree, and many of its leaders are veteran women's rights activists who have worked for other Thai women's organizations. Anjaree's staff and members have participated in international conferences on women's rights such as the 1995 World Conference on Women in Beijing. Anjaree organizers have also attended meetings of the Asian Lesbian Network, which they helped found. Anjaree has developed connections with various human rights organizations in Thailand and abroad, as well as with sympathetic academics. The Philip da Souza award, an international human rights award for gay and lesbian groups, went to Anjaree in 1995, and a representative traveled to Brazil to receive it. Through these connections, Anjaree has organized workshops and seminars to educate academics and the public on issues related to sexual rights and homosexuality. The staff of Anjaree has a clear activist agenda to correct negative stereotypes and to assist homosexual women in Thailand. The staff and organizers of Anjaree are well versed in transnational discourses of human rights, feminism, lesbian identity, and activism. According to Anjaree staff, the majority of the group's mem-

A member of Anjaree accepts a public service award on behalf of Anjaree.

Photo courtesy of Utopia Tours, www.utopia-tours.com (See http://www.utopia-asia.com/awards00.htm).

bers live outside of Bangkok, but most of the participants in Anjaree's activities are urban because the activities are mostly in the Bangkok area. Anjaree also has a regular activity called Anjaree *san-corn,* in which the organizers travel upcountry to visit members in rural areas and provincial towns to help them set up local groups. Anjaree's activities in Bangkok tend to be class specific. Its gatherings at clubs and restaurants are attended by mostly middle-class women, and its informal group discussions, held at Anjaree's office or members' houses, are attended by working-class women.

Most of the members identify as *tom*s or *dee*s, but Anjaree promotes a gender-neutral image of lesbians. Anjaree introduced the term *"ying-rak-ying"* (women who love women) as an alternative to *"tom"* and *"dee,"* focusing on the sameness of women rather than on gender differences in *tom-dee* couples. Anjaree and others have also started using the term "same-sex love" *(rak-pheet-diaw-kan)* instead of the pathological-sounding term "homosexuality." By redefining its target group in terms of sexual orientation, Anjaree has made links with both lesbian and gay activists and organizations. A few male-centered organizations emerged during 2002 and 2003 that focus on homosexual rights and issues. Whether these organizations will have the staying power or the public relations success of Anjaree remains to be seen. Anjaree has been the leader in protesting antihomosexual policies, such as a ban on homosexual students at Ratchabhat Institute.

LESLA

In 2000 a new *tom-dee* organization, Lesla, appeared on the Bangkok scene with sensational success. Lesla was founded as an Internet club, and almost all of its members are urban middle-class women. Lesla is not a political activist organization but a dynamic social group. The Lesla Web site has a WebBoard with hundreds of postings. The club also organizes parties approximately monthly at Bangkok pubs and discos, with consistently high turnouts of four hundred to five hundred women. In October 2000, Lesla published its first monthly magazine, which was distributed with a new paid membership system (400 baht, or approximately US$10, for a membership card and four newsletters per year). However, anyone can access its Web site (http://www.lesla .com) and discussion board and attend its functions.

Unlike Anjaree, Lesla is not involved in political/lesbian activism or academics. Lesla's membership skyrocketed to more than six hundred within the first year of its existence, surpassing Anjaree's membership. Although Anjaree has attempted to bring a sense of politics to sexual identities, Lesla is unapologetically a social organization for *tom*s and *dee*s. However, Lesla, like Anjaree, has provided a forum for the open discussion of the strict gender roles of *tom*s and *dee*s. Lesla has not rejected *tom* and *dee* roles or the possibility of female masculinity but, through Internet discussions, has given its members an opportunity to reflect on their beliefs that *tom*s and *dee*s are fundamentally different. In particular, the founder of Lesla has critiqued the idea that *tom*s and *dee*s should have separate sexual roles.

Many Lesla members are also Anjaree members, and the two groups often cooperate in setting up activities. Anjaree has tried to accommodate less affluent members by having monthly get-togethers at a designated house. Lesla is accessible only to women who can afford its glitzy nightlife activities and who use the Internet. Both Lesla and Anjaree have a predominantly middle-class membership, but Anjaree is more accessible to lower-income women than is Lesla.

ANJAREE'S MEDIA AND PUBLIC EDUCATION CAMPAIGN

Anjaree's public information campaign is significant in that it is the only direct, organized, and systematic effort to counter dominant narratives of homosexuality in Thai society by a group identified as lesbian, gay, or *tom-dee*. Anjaree has requested interviews by sympathetic reporters at Thai magazines and newspapers to address the persistent problem of negative reporting. Reporters who want to write sensationalized stories about sex and deviance are screened out by the Anjaree staff. The content of Anjaree interviews stresses that homosexuality is no longer considered a disease or an abnormality, according to leading health organizations, including the American Psychiatric Association and the World Health Organization. The Anjaree political agenda includes challenging the ubiquitous discourses of homosexuality as a national threat.

Anjaree has recognized the dual significance of the symbolic construction of "the West" in Thai nationalist discourses of sexuality. "The West" can imply either progressive modernization or decadence and anti-Thai-ness. Anjaree has been able to use these dual meanings as they function in Thai nationalist discourse by positioning homosexuality as both an internationally recognized right and a traditional Thai practice.

Anjaree has positioned same-sex love in Thailand as legitimate in terms of the prestigious transnational discourses of rights. The tactic of accessing transnational discourses of human rights was successful in challenging the Ratchabhat Institute's ban on gay students (see chapter 7). Anjaree's knowledge of current social and political theory helped ridicule Ratchabhat's pretense of holding a scientific and current position on sexuality and deviance. Anjaree has linked acceptance of homosexuality with international standards, a highly prestigious concept within the Thai bureaucracy. The content of Anjaree's dozens of interviews is largely the same: homosexuality is not an illness, according to contemporary Western psychology and international health organizations; sexual choice is a right, not a social or psychological abnormality caused by poor parental role modeling; and homosexuality is not pathological, as theories promoted by many Thai academics, and even some Anjaree members themselves, suggest. Anjaree has emphasized that homosexuality is not only a Western phenomenon but also part of human sexuality found cross-culturally: "Up until now, relationships of women who love women are usually seen and understood by most [Thai] people as coming from foreign places, especially the West, and [Thai people think] that in the past there were no relationships like this in Thailand. This perspective makes people question the legitimacy of the relationships of women who love women. These kinds of relationships are seen negatively, and women who love women lose self-confidence to express their life needs and their own feelings even though [women loving women] is a human right. Therefore, Anjaree aims to create better understanding and perspective for the majority of people in Thai society" (Anjaree 1995).

Anjaree has also positioned women who love women as part of the Thai tradition by accessing historical records of female same-sex love, in particular records of homosexual behavior, or *len pheuan,* among concubines in the palace. Anjaree has provided images of the temple mural that illustrate concubines in sexual poses with each other and in cages as punishment for *len pheuan.* This evidence is used to reject the assertion that homosexuality and *tom*s and *dee*s are products of Western infiltration.

REACTIONS TO ANJAREE'S PUBLIC INFORMATION CAMPAIGN

Anjaree's position that same-sex love is a right and is compatible with Thai identity is not widely accepted by mainstream Thai society. Although Anjaree has acquired the support of sympathetic academics, including some psychologists and social scientists, many academics and psychologists are hostile to Anjaree's attempts to challenge their pathologizing discourse. Attitudes toward Anjaree's educational campaign are summarized in the coverage given to a talk sponsored by Anjaree and the Thammasat Women's Studies Program, in which an American psychologist spoke of current understandings of homosexuality in the profession. The talk was covered by several newspapers and was included in later articles on the subject of *tom-dee*ism. *Matichon* in particular gave the talk extensive coverage and, as is typical for high-brow papers, included a section in which psychologists and leading authority figures commented. In that accompanying piece, "Perspectives of Psychologists," psychologist Kittikorn Miisap was quoted as agreeing that leading psychological organizations have changed their position on homosexuality, no longer classifying it as an illness. To "balance" Kittikorn's position the well-known anti-gay psychologist Wanlop Piyamanotham was interviewed. Wanlop said that it was very dangerous for the lesbian group Anjaree to reveal itself in public because people will learn that there are many lesbians in society:

> Anjaree has opened up to the public for the primary reason of making more lesbians, because Anjaree thinks it is a normal thing, and they are without shame. This will make our society be laughed at, as being all lesbians. . . . Whoever is lesbian should be quiet about it. It is not necessary to announce it. You do not have to make the whole country follow suit. You should not make it a bigger trend than it already is. I do not agree with activities that have Westerners come and explain about lesbians to Thai people. You do not need to have Westerners *(farang)* be behind-the-scene supporters for things that they do or say is the right thing. The media should be quiet. They do not need to talk about this and to make people think this is something they should be interested in. (*Matichon Weekly*, August 8, 1995, 76–78)

An example of the struggle between Anjaree and the authoritative discourses occurred during the 1996 International Thai Studies Conference. Anjaree's central figure, Anjana Suvarnananda, introduced the organization and its objectives in a panel discussion at the conference. She outlined the extensive misunderstandings, prejudices, and stereotypes that homosexual women in Thai society face. During the question-and-answer period at the end of her talk, a professor of psychology at Thammasat University asked her what to do to "help" *tom*s.

The professor said several had come to her and she had helped them to "become normal" so they would "not be forced to be *tom*s." The professor insisted it was "better of course to be normal" and that being a *tom* was just the result of "negative environmental factors." Anjana took a deep breath and answered respectfully, "Thank you for your contribution. This is a good example of a typical middle-class attitude."

As has been discussed, *tom*s and *dee*s avoid open confrontations or challenges to social norms. This tendency of Thai women in particular to avoid direct and open discussion about sexuality has hindered Anjaree's political effectiveness, because it lacks the broad-based support that other forms of political protest have depended on. Few members show up for public marches or demonstrations, and few members want to openly declare their sexuality or fight against society. Most members are interested in developing satisfying personal lives, which consist of having a lover and a group of understanding friends. Anjaree can help provide these things through its social activities and membership services, but its political activities have depended on the dedication and sophistication of a small group of women's activists. Although Anjaree has had moments of victory, in general its success in challenging authoritative discourses has been partial, for these discourses continue to be printed and spoken with regularity.

ANJAREE'S CHALLENGE TO GENDERED IDENTITIES

Anjaree has walked a delicate path between challenging *tom* and *dee* identities and providing a community for its membership, who predominantly identify themselves as *tom*s and *dee*s. Anjaree has introduced its membership to the concept of "lesbian," using the Thai expression "*ying-rak-ying*" (women who love women). *Ying-rak-ying* is a sexualized identity without a gendered component (i.e., the gender binary is elided). A nongendered sexual identity, a radical new concept in Thailand, is popular with a small group of educated urban middle-class women.

One member wrote to *Anjareesaan* that she and her lover did not seem different from each other like *tom* and *dee* and asked, "Can women who love women but who don't divide themselves into *tom* and *dee* be called lesbians? And are there women who love women who don't divide themselves into *tom* and *dee*?" Anjaree answered: "People who don't identify as *tom* or *dee* are one kind of lesbian, because "lesbian" means women who were born as women and love the same sex.

There are relationships that don't have gender roles, like the one you have between yourself and the one you love" (*Anjareesaan,* July–December 1996, vol. 3, no. 18, 32–33).

Anjaree's newsletter published another member's letter that asked, "Are there any women-who-love-women couples who love each other because they are both attracted to women and don't expect either partner to act like a man?" Anjaree replied, "Yes, there are. If you have been reading *Anjareesaan,* you probably have seen stories about couples who aren't strict about being *tom* and *dee.* In our group, we always try to emphasize this point, which is obvious in our choice of the most neutral term we can think of, which is 'women who love women'" (*Anjareesaan,* March–April 1998, vol. 3, no. 22). Thus Anjaree has provided an alternative vision of female homosexuality that is not limited to strict *tom* and *dee* identities.

ANJAREE PUTS ON A SHOW

The annual Anjaree party held in October 2000 was well attended, as had been all previous ones. It was held at a disco in the fashionable RCA (Royal City Avenue) area. Rainbow streamers and balloons, transnational symbols of gay pride, decorated the entrance, with Anjaree newsletters, booklets, and rainbow items sold by the door. As usual, the party focused on stage shows and performances by Anjaree members themselves. Of the several hundred people attended the party, most were in their twenties and thirties, but a small group of women in their forties and fifties sat around an outside table and chatted as the younger ones clapped and cheered for the performances indoors. One of the wildest shows was a bump-and-grind parody dance by Ning, a *tom* in her twenties who was well known in the Anjaree circles and had even been interviewed in a Lesla newsletter.

What made Ning's dance hilarious to onlookers was that she was a *tom* and yet she wore a sexy white sequined two-piece go-go outfit, with makeup and sparkles to complete the act. Previous Anjaree parties had also played with this device of gender-crossing by having particularly masculine *tom*s dress in drag, wearing flamboyant dresses and feather boas. I could not help thinking of the popularity of male drag shows and *kathoey* beauty contests in Thailand—the ability of males to cross or transform into the feminine gender is either hilarious in its failure (such as obvious leg hair and deep voice) or awesomely impressive in its success. *Tom*s and *dee*s also delighted in the drag performances of *tom*s, with hilarity in its failure the usual humor device. However, Ning's performance was slightly different. It was funny, in that she wore boots and was aggressively sexual in an unfeminine manner. However, more striking was her success at being sexy in a very non-*tom*like way—she really did look pretty, as the onlookers agreed. When asked what they thought of the performance and whether they would be interested in Ning, *tom*s laughed awkwardly. "No way! She is a *tom!*" was the usual answer. Ning herself seemed to enjoy her indeterminate status as a *tom* who could be very womanlike. I asked her whether she thought of herself as a *tom* or not, given that she seemed to be successful at being very sexy and attractive in her feminine outfit. She answered, "I guess I am a *tom* . . . a girly *tom*" (*tom kra-dae,* or a *tom* with affected mannerisms), making a playful wrist slap like *kathoey*s do on television shows to demonstrate affected feminine mannerisms.

Although Ning was performing to entertain the partygoers, her performance was also a radical expression of hyperfemininity mixed with masculinity (heavy boots) that both amused and shocked onlookers. Ning positioned herself as a *tom* but said she did not feel tied to any particular rules of masculinity. She had been romantically involved with a foreigner before, whom others had had trouble categorizing as either *tom* or *dee. Tom*s and *dee*s tended to be very concerned with identifying everyone's gender. Sometimes a newcomer would attend a party who was not obviously *tom* or *dee.* Gossip and whispering buzzed along, as the others tried to determine her gender. Likewise, *tom*s and *dee*s who did not know Ning tried to judge her by the status of her past partners, because she herself was hopelessly ambiguous. Ning, like Kung, the self-identified *tom* discussed in chapter 5, refused to be limited by hegemonic *tom* and *dee* definitions. Ning, considered by many *tom*s and *dee*s present at the party to be an anomaly, was perhaps most noteworthy in her public refusal to be a proper *tom.* Anjaree provided the space for women like Ning to express alternative forms of *tom* and *dee* identities.

REACTIONS TO ANJAREE'S VERSION OF "WOMEN WHO LOVE WOMEN"

The existence of an official organized group, Anjaree, has provided hundreds of women, both in Bangkok and upcountry, with the comfort of not being alone. Anjaree is one of the few voices in Thailand to assert unapologetically that it is OK to be homosexual. The experience of meeting a large group of *tom/dee*/lesbian women was a powerful one for many of the women I talked to. Num, a *tom* in her mid-thirties and a member of Anjaree, told me how important meeting the group had been for her and said that the group had helped her change the way she thought about being a *tom*/lesbian (she used both terms): "I don't think that being [a *tom* or homosexual] is about karma. I have chosen my own life. If we are like this, we just are like this. I choose it because I am this way. Before I used to think it was bad karma, because I didn't have my own group, my own friends like this. I would think, 'Why am I like this?' I thought it would be better to have a boyfriend so I wouldn't have to think of this bad karma. I hoped that someday I would have my own group, like I do now. At that time I didn't know Anjaree. I had to wait. [I know now that] being like this isn't a disease. People sometimes say it is a disease. I say, 'You're crazy. It isn't a disease! No matter how you try to treat it, it won't go away.'" Num blended Anjaree's discourse of "choice" with the popular understanding that being a *tom* or homosexual is a product of birth. For Num, her identity was both, and not something she needed to hide or apologize for.

Another member, Ung, said she learned to think of herself as a "lesbian" in a positive new way by Anjaree. Ung helped Anjaree in its activities and wrote for its newsletter. For Ung, being a *ying-rak-ying* was about escaping the social rules that structure women's lives: "I feel that I am a person who doesn't like life that is like, oh, you must get married, must have children. I like a life being with my partner more. It is not as restrictive as being married." Ung said that Anjaree had helped her understand who she was, and she believed that Anjaree had an important job to change society's thinking. Ung had incorporated concepts like "lesbian" and "rights" into her thoughts about her own identity: "I think the most important thing is to build the thinking of people in society that women who love women are not doing anything wrong. It isn't strange. It is a right, and anyone should have the right to decide."

Ung said that most of the members of Anjaree want to meet and talk with one another more than to get involved in political activism. Although fighting against public policy that is antihomosexual concerned the leadership of Anjaree, many members I talked to expressed a process of rethinking their family roles and social norms. When the group met, they would talk about how they felt about being female and lesbian/*tom*/*dee* in their family and community. During one monthly

Anjaree meeting (May 1996), a member, Ji, said she felt that she was always disregarded in her family because she was female. Another member, Ting, asked if Ji was Chinese, because Ting also felt poorly treated by her Sino-Chinese family. Ting said she was treated like "shit" by her family and that women were part of the family "just to clean" and to serve others. Ting explained that what it took to be a good husband and what it took to be a good wife were unequal. For a man, just to come home and be served was enough to be a good husband, but to be a good wife or mother, one had to work and serve others constantly. Ji agreed and said she wanted to be independent and had always been attracted to women. Ting had developed a *tom* identity and said she "wanted to be a leader," did not want to be neat and proper, and did not want to marry or have children. Ji said she did not even want to marry a woman but instead wanted to be friends with women. She said that marriage was never good for women, and they always gave up more than men did when they married.

Anjaree was a sympathetic site for expression of these sentiments and welcomed *tom, dee,* and gender-neutral *ying-rak-ying* into its social activities and discussion groups. One member wrote to *Anjareesaan:* "It's not that I look down on anybody, but I personally feel . . . why? Why, when some people probably don't like men, do they still have to act like men . . . the sex that they don't like? This is the point I don't understand. OK, you might have some part of you that is tough, but you should let it be your own kind of toughness, not an imitation of men's. For example, men's aggressive flirting. Damn, we have struggled to get away from men's aggressive flirting, but then we find it again in these kinds of *tom*s. Disgusting" (*Anjareesaan,* October 1994, vol. 2, no. 8, 33).

However, Anjaree's preference for gender-neutral categories at times alienated *tom*s in particular. Some *tom*s expressed discomfort at being labeled with the term "women who love women." I found this sentiment often expressed by older *tom*s who had participated in Anjaree's events. Anjaree did not uphold the popular notion that to be born as a *tom* was a tragic fate or that *tom*s were victims of *dee*s. Anjaree did not emphasize differences between *tom*s and *dee*s and spoke of them as a common group united by their shared attraction to women. For Anjaree, the negative experience of being either *tom* or *dee* was directly related to negative social attitudes and misunderstandings of same-sex love.

Some women, on the other hand, believed that Anjaree was too separatist. One woman, Cim, who was involved with a woman but did not claim any identity as *tom, dee,* or lesbian, asked, "Why do lesbians have to be separate?" Cim said she saw lesbian identity as limiting and had no desire for lesbian videos, movies, and books, unlike some members of Anjaree who craved representations and images that they could relate to.

Anjaree's campaign to introduce the concept of "lesbian" coded as *"ying-rak-ying"* has made an impression on many of the members I spoke with. Although few Thai women openly and exclusively identify as lesbian, some Anjaree members who identify as *tom* or *dee* also refer to themselves as "lesbian" (using the English word). Claiming a lesbian identity can be a way to challenge existing *tom-dee* norms and must be understood in the context of also having a *tom* or a *dee* identity. These identities were not mutually exclusive; women claimed lesbian identity in some situations and *tom* identity in others. For example, Nuu, a *tom,* had started to call herself a "lesbian" when talking to her *tom* friends of her generation—in their forties and fifties. Nuu said she felt frustrated over the self-hatred other *tom*s felt, including her friends. Nuu wondered why her friend Kep felt she had to be alone—"She is still handsome and charming; she doesn't have to be alone." Nuu thought that her *tom* friends Bee and Kep had self-fulfilling prophesies; they thought women would not really love them, and they ended up alone: "They don't think it's possible to have any more than this. They think that there is nothing in their life but drinking." Nuu complained that these *tom* friends did not think that they were worthy of having loving relationships; they either thought that all women want to be with *tom*s only for good sex or for their money. Nuu started to confront Kep, Bee, and other *tom*s in her social group by saying, "I am a lesbian!" She explained that, to her, being a "lesbian" meant being independent—not obligated to supporting anybody financially and not having strict rules about being sexually active or passive.

LESLA: A BOOMING MIDDLE-CLASS, YOUNG *TOM*-*DEE* COMMUNITY

Lesla's phenomenal popularity and growth in its first year demonstrate a new direction for *tom-dee* communities. Offering an array of social activities for both *tom*s and *dee*s, Lesla has been remarkably successful in creating a community that includes both *tom*s and *dee*s. Outside of Lesla, most community networks I witnessed were formed by groups of *tom*s who sensed sameness in other *tom*s—not in *dee*s. Lesla has demonstrated that younger, urban women are eager to be part of a large community of both *tom*s and *dee*s. Lesla—through the dynamic leadership of its founder, Manthana Adisayathepakul, and its stylish monthly magazine and popular Web site—has fostered a sense of being part of a common group.

Lesla's WebBoard has provided an arena for Thai *tom*s and *dee*s to communicate about a range of personal issues, including sex. Anjaree has attempted frank discussion groups among the members on the topic of sex, but these efforts have not been very successful. People generally felt awkward when they were in groups and asked to discuss sex. Even *tom*s who would make ribald jokes about their sex lives would be uncomfortable with frank discussions of sexuality. I had difficulty in talking to people in interviews about sex if others were present, even if they were close friends. People would be fairly frank to me in private but would rarely speak in a group of other *tom*s and *dee*s. There is a lot of playful teasing and sexual banter in groups at parties but little honest discussion of sexual issues. The Lesla Internet group has allowed for greater freedom of discussion of this sensitive subject. For example, one member asked, "Does anybody know the difference between lesbian and *tom-dee* couples?" The answers both reaffirmed and challenged sexual codes: "When lesbian couples have sex, they both take off their clothes. But when *tom-dee* couples have sex, the *tom* doesn't take off her clothes and takes care of the *dee* until she climaxes." A *tom* wrote, "Sometimes I take off my clothes when I sleep with my girlfriend, but she doesn't do anything to me. My main duty is to make her climax. Is anybody else like me *(phom)?*"

Lesla's founder, Manthana, has used the WebBoard as a forum for challenging the rigid gender hegemony of *tom* and *dee*. Manthana is a *tom,* has a clearly masculine appearance, and is very much part of the Bangkok *tom-dee* scene. However, she has criticized the rules that *tom*s and *dee*s uphold. In particular, Manthana has challenged the idea that *dee*s do not and should not perform sexually for *tom*s. Manthana has also tried to popularize the Western concept of "lesbian": "Lesbians are women who love women, and *tom*s are women. A *tom* who loves a woman or another *tom* is normal, but *tom*s in Thailand have been put under the control of rules that do not allow *tom*s to take off their clothes. *Dees* don't have to do anything in return, and *tom*s understand that they have to be like men. They are therefore ashamed to take off their clothes in front of anybody else. *Dees* who haven't done anything to their *tom,* ask yourself, if you really love your *tom,* why don't you like to make her have the pleasure that you get from her?"

The most popular topic for discussion on the WebBoard is the meaning of being *tom* or *dee.* Members ask for advice, express their opinions, and joke and flirt with each other. One member stated that *tom*s are "lesbians" too, but they are ashamed of their female body, since they would prefer to be men. Another member told of her sense of gender transformation as she switched from *dee* partners to a *tom* partner: "I used to think that I was the *tom* of the year because I am so manly. One day I fell in love with another *tom.* At first I was scared and felt strange. I was afraid that I was transforming *(klai-rang)* into a *dee* or slowly becoming a woman. The first time we had sex, I felt very shy, but I slowly learned that I was still a woman who loved women like before. I was still myself, still able to hit the punching bags as before. Why do I have to be categorized as *tom* or *dee* or lesbian? I am still a woman who loves women."

In an interview, Manthana said ideas of gender within the *tom-dee* community needed to be changed: "Actually I met some *tom*s and *dee*s in their early twenties. They believe in one way, but in their bed they take turns. *[Laughs.]* But they don't let anybody know, because they have been taught that if you are a *tom,* you can't let anyone do you and you have to be active only. Once you let someone do you, you will become a *dee.* That's why I'm trying to work on this point to make people accept two-way [sex]. Even on the WebBoard I usually tell them that if you are a woman who loves a woman, you are a lesbian, no matter if you are a *tom* or a *dee,* because you are physically a woman, and you don't want people to tell you how to act or dress" (English and Thai used).

Both Lesla and Anjaree are supportive of *tom* and *dee* identities because most of their members are *tom* and *dee* identified. These organizations also provide emotional support to women who feel alienated and rejected by their families and communities. For example, Muu, a *dee* in her mid-twenties, told me that her family did not accept *tom*s and *dee*s at all and have called them "perverts" and "deviants" in front of her. Her mother is aware of her interest in women and, without addressing the topic directly, has made offhand comments about Muu's being "deviant." Muu said she felt depressed and alone at home. As a result, she spent more than an hour a day on the Lesla WebBoard and is now on the organizing committee for Lesla activities. Muu told me, "Lesla is more of a home for me than my real home is."

LESLA *TOMS* AND *DEES*

The basketball players raced up and down the court, as the cheerleaders danced to the deafening beat of four sets of bongo drums, placed in each corner of the gym. Four hundred *tom-dee* spectators roared in support of their color-coded teams. The cheerleaders for the red team led a cheer: "Pick up the soap. Rub it left! Rub it right! Rub it on the kootchie![1] Rub it on the kootchie!"—with accompanying explicit gestures and hip thrusts. All of the other cheers had silly sexual lyrics too, such as "The chicken is roasting, the chicken is roasting! It's inserted with a stick, whoa! Inserted with a stick, whoa! Stuck in the ass, stuck in the ass, so damn hot!" How the content related to basketball was not clear, but the crowd loved it and roared their approval. The cheerleaders for the red team, two *tom*s and two *dee*s, each had short hennaed red hair, spiked with hair gel so that it was vertical or jutting out at wild angles. The two *tom*s wore matching white button-down shirts, red ties, red shorts, and red sneakers. The two *dee*s, dancing in pairs with the *tom*s, wore red spaghetti-strap tops, with tight white slacks reaching to midcalf. The cheerleaders wiggled their hips and belted out, "Pick up a purple one [of the opposing purple team]! Lift up their clothing! Lift to the left! Lift to the right! Lift [and see] the kootchie!" The basketball players took the game seriously and dashed up and down the court, as their coaches yelled instructions from the sidelines. Lesla sports day, held at Kasetsart University indoor gym, was a well-organized and highly successful day of fun for Lesla members.

Lesla caters to young *tom*s and *dee*s, many of whom are in their late teens and early twenties. They are urban and have free time, Internet access, and money to spend on Lesla activities, which include parties at clubs, discos, and restaurants. The members at the Lesla sports day knew each other from the Internet, and some wore their Internet names on their name tags. Lesla events are always well attended, with hundreds of *tom*s and *dee*s crowding into the selected restaurants and discos. The young crowd have fun with bawdy sexual jokes, and most are clearly defined as *tom*s or *dee*s. *Tom* and *dee* are not outdated or subsiding identities in Thai society, certainly not for Lesla members. On sports day the yellow team's banner playfully welcomed *tom*s and *dee*s: "Buxom lads, voluptuous girls, yellow team, surprise, surprise!" *(Num-uap sao-eum sii-leuang ta-leung ta-leung)*. The word for "buxom" *(uap)* is usually used to refer to women and at times to poke fun at gay men. The Lesla *tom*s and *dee*s enjoyed playing with gender codes, relishing their chance to parody themselves as *tom-dee* cheerleaders.

Lesla has provided a forum for open discussion concerning strict role playing of *tom*s and *dee*s, but most members have embraced *tom* and *dee* identities. Manthana explained that being a *tom* or a *dee* can be a source of enjoyment and an empowering experience, but not if people rigidly follow rules that limit them.

CLASS AND COMMUNITY ORGANIZING

Lesla is an example of a class-specific *tom-dee* community. Although *tom-dee* communities comprise women of all social classes—factory workers, urban professionals, students, and media celebrities—these communities are strictly bounded by class and often by age or gender (as in being either *tom* or *dee*). Many *tom*s and *dee*s have their own social group, and most do not feel comfortable associating across class boundaries. Reluctance to associate with lower-class women and avoidance of predictably awkward interactions with upper-class women limits and structures the social worlds of *tom*s and *dee*s. Although class does circumscribe their social worlds or preclude the possibility of a transclass community, it does not obviously determine the degree of tolerance or acceptance of *tom*s and *dee*s. Lesla members have a large formal organization, which is a new form of *tom-dee* community that rural and working class *tom*s and *dee*s are largely without.

Although *tom-dee*ism is a transclass phenomenon, *tom-dee* communities are not transclass social groups. Social distinction and class are essential and unavoidable aspects of Thai social interaction. Thailand is like most other Southeast Asian nation states—one huge metropolis serves as the economic and political center of the nation, with the majority of the population living in rural villages and small provincial towns. This profound cleavage of rural and urban life mirrors sharp class distinctions that characterize Thai society. Village and rural life is as alien to many middle-class urban Thais as is the life of another culture entirely.

Elitism and class differentials make it difficult to form social or political groupings that include women from different social backgrounds. I learned that my own efforts to ignore or pretend ignorance of class difference only created awkward and hurtful situations. I invited women from different backgrounds to my house for get-togethers or to clubs and bars for evenings out, but the women quickly sized each other up and split into groups. One time I took Tum, a *dee* who had come from a poor village, with me to an academic talk on *tom*s and *dee*s. At the club where the talk was being held were about ten or so Anjaree members, Bangkok professional types with mobile phones and designer clothing, whom we both had met before in Anjaree settings. After the talk, I found Tum in tears, asking me angrily why I had brought her there; nobody had talked to her or asked her to sit with a group, even though they all saw her sitting alone and had met her before. Tum was marked to the others as a lower-class woman, and one woman, an upper-class *dee,* told Nuu that she "did not want to hang around with a woman of that sort." Ordinarily, women from different class backgrounds would not have many occasions to interact with each other socially—they simply would not be part of each other's social world. It is only through the efforts of political organizations like Anjaree—or the efforts of misguided anthropologists—that these women would find themselves in the same social gatherings.

The failure of *tom*s and *dee*s to organize, either politically or socially, across class lines is symptomatic of the class structure of organizing in general in Thailand. The strongest and most successful social organizing in Thailand falls along class lines, such as labor protests, democracy movements (middle class), and movements focusing on the environmental and land issues of poor villagers (e.g., the Assembly of the Poor). Anjaree does attract interest from women of all classes, because they are hungry for any information and acknowledgment that women like them exist. The newsletter *Anjareesaan* is sent to women in rural areas as well as in Bangkok, and those who write letters to the magazine are from a range of social classes. In social activities, however, where the members come face to face, class is an ever-present divisive factor. Perhaps this is one reason that Lesla has been so successful in social organizing—it has no pretense of being a political organization representing cross-class interests.

Even within class perimeters, *tom*s and *dee*s have had difficulty establishing more formal or larger communities. An important site for the development of gay male identity and (middle-class) community in Thailand has been the commercial establishments, such as bars, clubs, and restaurants that are specifically understood as being gay hangouts. Unlike the marketing aimed at the Thai gay male population, niche marketing for *tom*s/*dee*s/lesbians in the forms of bars or clubs has not been successful. Bars specifically aimed at *tom*s and *dee*s have had a short life. One obvious reason is the lack of commercial sex and "cruising" in the *tom-dee* communities that are often components of the male gay scene. However, several restaurants in Bangkok and outlying provinces are popular spots for middle- and upper-class *tom*s and *dee*s. These establishments are owned by *tom*s and *dee*s, and their *tom-dee* clientele is mostly friends and acquaintances. Unlike the highly popular gay male clubs in Bangkok, these venues depend on non-*tom-dee* clientele to succeed and do not market themselves as *tom-dee*/lesbian places.

Experiments with providing alternatives to the commercialized gay sex scene and setting up exclusively *tom-dee*/lesbian places have not been successful. Utopia was a bar/club opened by an American businessman, John Goss, to provide an alternative to the atmosphere of commercial sex characterizing gay Bangkok clubs and to provide a space for Thai *tom*s/*dee*s/lesbians to congregate. Utopia was unique in the Bangkok gay scene because it strove to provide a sense of gay/lesbian identity, with gay/lesbian-themed books and magazines for sale, as well as activities such as lesbian poetry reading and parties. Goss set Friday as "women's night," and the first women's night in 1994 was a resounding success. I was astounded at the high turnout, easily approaching one hundred. At that time, I and the others present had never seen so many *tom*s and *dee*s in one room. As the months rolled on, however, attendance at women's night dwindled, until Goss was forced to open Fridays to men as well. Goss eventually closed the club because attendance was too low. As Lesla activities demonstrate, Bangkok middle-class *tom*s and *dee*s do enjoy socializing and going to bars, discos, and restaurants, and they do have money to spend. They do not need specifically lesbian/homosexual-themed establishments, however. I recently heard of a nightclub on Royal City Avenue in Bangkok that had formed a *tom-dee* club and a *tom-dee* night as niche marketing. The club was popular with some Lesla members and might indicate a new trend in the exploitation of commercial potential of the *tom-dee* niche market.

Lesla and Anjaree are the only official organizations for *tom*s/*dee*s/lesbians in Thailand that I am aware of, but there are countless local communities formed around groups of friends. These groupings are structured around the poles of class and age. For example, the "*tom-dee* dormitory" on Sukhumwit Road in Bangkok is a community of *tom*s and *dee*s who are mostly lower middle-class and working-class women who are self-employed vendors and clerical workers or who work in clubs and bars, sometimes as sex workers. Most *tom-dee* residents are in their early twenties to thirties. In Chonburi, a province bordering

Bangkok to the east, I found a small group of working middle-class *tom*s who would meet after work at a local bar for drinks. One restaurant they enjoyed meeting at was recently opened and owned by *tom-dee* friends. A group of *tom*s formed the core of this group, and their girlfriends would come and go. They had been meeting for ten years, in some cases longer, and were now in their forties and fifties.

CONCLUSION

Lesla, through its widely used WebBoard, provides a public and anonymous means for discussing issues in which dominant hegemonic norms held by *tom*s and *dee*s are questioned. It is also a site for the institutionalization of these norms—it provides a way for women to become integrated into *tom-dee* communities and to form an overarching system of meanings and norms that define and structure these communities. Once again, neat lines between hegemonic forms and acts of resistance are difficult to draw. *Tom*s and *dee*s are challenging mainstream heterosexist imperatives by building a large and active *tom-dee* community, which has assisted *tom*s and *dee*s in finding friends and lovers and in formulating their own identities as *tom*s or *dee*s. However, they are simultaneously reinforcing *tom-dee* hegemonic norms that constrain *tom* masculinity and *dee* femininity.

Anjaree is making a deliberate effort to challenge dominant norms and discourses in both mainstream society and among *tom*s and *dee*s themselves. The organization has challenged entrenched Thai middle-class notions that same-sex relationships are signs of psychological disturbance. Anjaree has also deployed middle-class discourses of human rights, attempting to translate transnational discourses of lesbian/gay rights into a culturally acceptable version. It promotes use of the Thai phrase *"ying-rak-ying"* instead of an English-based term, in order to assert an image of the cultural authenticity of female homosexuality. The discourses of sexual/gender deviance used against *tom*s, *dee*s, gays, and *kathoey*s are in themselves complex hybrids of local understandings of sex/gender and transnational discourses of sexual pathology. Anjaree has moved between discursive realms to challenge both mainstream society and its *tom* and *dee* members.

Discourses of "Homosexuality"

The State and the Media in Thailand

IN OCTOBER 1998, agents of the Thai state attempted to censor presumed immoral and "un-Thai" sexuality by banning an event called the Alternative Love Film Festival. Organized by a young professor in Chulalongkorn University's Department of Motion Pictures and Still Photography, the festival featured gay and lesbian films from abroad, as well as various international art films on the subject of sexuality and modernity in general. The festival was originally planned to be held at Chulalongkorn University under the sponsorship of the film department, but shortly before the festival the department head, Patamavadee Charuworn, publicly announced that the department would not sponsor the festival, because it had not been allowed to preview the films to assure appropriate content (*The Nation,* October 10, 1998). The university's ban generated a lot of free publicity for the festival, which was at a cultural center in Bangkok. The organizers decided to show the films "privately" to members of the newly established Film Lovers Association, with membership available at the door for the price of a movie ticket, thereby avoiding the jurisdiction of the censorship board. The head of Chulalongkorn's film department had a seat on the national film censorship board and exercised her authority by reporting to the police who had jurisdiction over the area that films of dubious moral and sexual qualities were to be shown there.

The atmosphere was tense on the opening night, as rumors abounded about a police raid and a showdown between the junior faculty member who had organized the festival and her department head. The police arrived shortly before the screening of the first film. The officer seemed somewhat embarrassed about being there. He meekly walked to the front of the theater, followed by boos and catcalls. He said he was sorry but there had been a report of immoral films being shown and he would have to watch a bit to see if that were true. The lights were dimmed, and *Bugis Street,* a film about a male transgendered community in Singapore, began. The opening happened to be a rather graphic and vivid scene of a drunken sailor having sex with a transvestite, and I was worried that this chance scene would bode ill for the struggle against censorship. However, after the scene, the policeman discreetly left the theater, saying quietly as he walked out that he did not see anything wrong in what he saw. The audience applauded, and the festival continued uninterrupted thereafter. Conversations between the organizers and the police officer indicated that the police were aware that the issue was really a power struggle between faculty members, and the censorship board and the police were not interested in being pawns in the game. The film faculty at Chulalongkorn University was bifurcated, with the more powerful faculty members presuming they had the moral duty and obligation to prevent Thais from viewing immoral sexual decadence, namely "homosexuality." The junior faculty member, with the support of other academics, persisted in bringing novel and creative art films to Thai audiences in spite of intimidation from various state agencies.

In recent years, Thai state officials, in collusion with educators and medical professionals, increasingly have harassed people with non-normative-gendered sexualities. These repressive actions depend upon discourses in which "homosexuality" is defined as a psychological abnormality that reflects social and national ills. State officials, the print media, and academics typically link "homosexuality" to problems in national development, national image, or imputed Thai traditional morality and culture. Thai academic theories of "homosexuality" are widely quoted in the press, and "homosexuality" is positioned as an indicator of social decay in Thai state and nationalist discourses.

"HOMOSEXUALITY" AS A THAI CATEGORY: ACADEMIC INTERPRETATIONS

The concept of "homosexuality," as it is used in Thai discourse, is typically linked to Western theories of sexual pathology and deviance.[1] These theories are repeatedly cited in Thai academic texts and in the Thai print media, which rely heavily on academic "experts" to lend legitimacy to their reporting, and are interpreted through Thai cultural paradigms of sex and gender. Thais in general make little distinction between the term "homosexuality" *(rak-ruam-pheet)* and transgenderism, which is usually referred to as "misgendering" *(phit-pheet)*. When asked in interviews to define these concepts, many Thais have defined "homosexuality" and transgenderism in terms of each other. Academics, the press, and public officials also use the terms "homosexual," "gay," and *"kathoey"* interchangeably. For example, Praphaphan Wongsaroot's study (1989) of "homosexual" men used all self-identified *kathoeys* as samples, leading Praphaphan to conclude that all "homosexual" men "like the role of the opposite sex/gender" and have "women's characteristics" (p. 63). Praphaphan also interviewed nonhomosexuals to sketch social attitudes toward "homosexuality" and received comments that revealed the popular equation of homosexuality with transgendered performances, such as, "Gays are irritating. They act so affected, like when they walk and toss their butt about, and they like to flounce about" (p. 46).

Jumphot Saisunthorn (1993) uses the terms "false men" *(chai-thiam)* and "false women" *(ying-thiam)* to refer to the "homosexuals" of her study. She ostensibly is supportive of "homosexuals," stating that because sex-change operations are now possible, legal restrictions against marriages between "false men" and "real men" and between "false women" and "real women" will soon be or at least should be nullified. Thus academics who were harshly condemning of "homosexuals," as well as academics who were generally sympathetic to "homosexuals," understood gender inversion as inextricably linked to "homosexuality."

Noticeably, the gender inversion model is not fully able to incorporate *dees*, male sex partners of *kathoeys*, or masculine gay men, because these individuals are gender-normative. The "sexual perversion" model of the West that is used in studies by Thai academics incorporates these gender-normative individuals into the category of "homosexuality" by asserting that they are products of dysfunctional families and fractured social norms—but exactly how that process occurs is left unclear in these studies. Gender-normative men and women, such as masculine gay men and *dees*, are not widely included in the public criticisms of homosexuality if they maintain normative gendered behaviors. Wanlop Piyamanotham (1992) is one of the few academics who has attempted an explanation of *dees*. He relies on stereotypes, however, saying that for *dees* the relationship with a *tom* is one of close female friendship: "Maybe they do not need sex directly but want a *tom* to take care of them, the understanding and sincerity. *Dees* can return to normal easier than other categories" (pp. 66–67); and "*Dees* are normal women, not noticeable from the outside. [However,] they are insecure, lacking love and understanding since childhood. *Dees* want somebody to look after them. They are well matched for *tom*s because *tom*s are still women inside, even though [they are] not willing to act like women. It is natural for women to be sensitive to other women's feelings. Happiness for women naturally isn't about sex, but about caring gentleness and romance. Just to be close to a lover, to hug each other, is the most excellent satisfaction, not like men think" (p. 84).

Psychologists and academics often add medical-sounding terms like "gender/sexual deviance" *(biang-been-thaang-pheet)* or "sexual/gender perversion" *(wipharit-thaang-pheet)* to descriptions of "homosexuality." These medical and academic authorities promote the belief that homosexuality is a kind of psychological abnormality often caused by poor parenting: "It is believed that homosexuals come from an abnormality in the way they developed emotionally, which stems from their not being raised with the amount of care from their parents that they should have had, making the girls and boys not confident in their own sex" (Wanthanee 1983, 4). Among the educated and middle-class people who use the discourses of sexual pathology, considerable slippage occurs among the terms "homosexuality," "misgendering," and "gender/sexual deviance," as well as specific identities such as gay, *tom*, *kathoey*, and *dee*, regardless of the actual differences among these communities and individuals.

GENDER AND SEXUALITY AND THE THAI STATE

The Thai state and its various agents (teachers, medical professionals, administrators) have produced vivid images of sexualized threats to the national moral order. "Homosexuality" and prostitution are the two most frequently cited indices of decline of Thai culture and morality. Geraldine Heng and Janadas Devan (1995) have described the process of "narratives of national crisis," in which the state or other power brokers identify and define threats to the nation. These threats usually entail the perceived loss of national autonomy or national identity. The source of these threats can be either external agents (neighboring countries, foreign powers) or internal agents that carry a dangerous or corrupting influence from external sources. In Thailand, perceived internal threats include leftists, radical students, feminists, homosexuals, and the mysterious "third hand," who is said to be behind most social movements by groups as varied as middle-class democracy activists and poor farmers. Heng and Devan explain that the nations that are most susceptible to narratives of national crisis are those that have recently emerged from a colonial status or threats of colonialism, and I would add nations that have experienced sustained conflict. Thailand, as a developing country and nation emerging in the context of imperialism, would fit this category. The narratives of national crisis focus on a sense of fragility. The Thai state bureaucracy and its academics have developed such narratives by exploiting images of prostitution and homosexuality as indices of cultural decay.

The Thai state is a sprawling, complex bureaucracy, with tentacles reaching into all realms of government, including regional and local governing bodies. It monitors religious organization and hierarchy, under the auspices of the Ministry of Education, as well as all levels of education, from kindergarten to university. The state's employees include street cleaners, bus drivers, doctors, nurses, teachers, university lecturers, police officers, forestry officials, military personnel, and local government officials. The military-style uniform of all state employees (worn on special days or formal occasions), from bus ticket collectors to university professors, is a visual reminder of the centralist and militaristic underpinning of the bureaucracy. Long-standing popular demands for "decentralization" of the state and its functions have been incorporated into the "People's Constitution" of 1997. Results of new decentralizing plans, however, remain uncertain.

In spite of the massive, sprawling nature of the Thai state and its personnel, it is not a homogenous unit: conflict, dissent, and factions are constant aspects of the Thai bureaucracy.[2] The issue of homosexuality has become an important medium through which state factions, such as liberal university lecturers and conservative bureaucrats, debate over conflicting visions of national progress and national identity. The state is not simply positioned on one side of these debates over homosexuality but is enmeshed within them. For example, liberal university professors capitalize on their authority as lecturers at prestigious state universities to make authoritative assertions about homosexuality that contrast with the statements of less educated bureaucrats who administer the Ministry of Education. State officials strategically deploy their authority in varying ways that both reinforce hegemonic notions of gender and sexuality and transform it. Although there has been a recent movement by some academics to promote the concept that homosexuality is a human rights issue, state discourses have been dominated by academics and medical professionals who have positioned homosexuality as a moral and psychological perversion.

Thai nationalist discourses are replete with references to gender and sexuality. Much of Thai nationalist history is concerned with efforts by the state to prove its level of civilization to Western powers. These efforts have focused on demonstrating that Thai women have high status, and are "modern." Rama VI (r. 1910–1925) wrote extensively on both the high status of Thai women and the need to eliminate "outmoded" practices such as polygyny and women's betel chewing. Rama VI's half-sister, Princess Walai, demonstrated how a "modern" Thai women should look, by wearing her hair long rather in the short-cropped style traditionally worn by Thai women. Rama VI ordered palace women to wear skirts, rather than the *congkrabeen*, the pantaloon-style garment worn by both men and women previously (Vella 1978, 160).

Military leaders repeatedly tried to modernize the nation by adopting Western styles of femininity over the following decades. Most infamous were the cultural mandates of Field Marshal Plaek Phibun Songkhram (referred to hereafter as "Phibun," following convention), who held political power intermittently from 1934 until 1957. Statism, or *rathaniyom*, was a series of cultural mandates (1939–1946) aimed at "civilizing" Thai social practices in the eyes of the Western powers. Perhaps the most notorious of these mandates was the one requiring men to kiss their wives before they left for work. Phibun, like Rama VI, stressed the need for women to wear their hair long, as in Western style; to wear skirts and dresses of plain color, rather than *congkrabeen*, or colorful prints; and not to chew betel, which discolored the teeth and was generally unladylike in the minds of Westerners. Phibun pleaded with his citizens: "If we dress like savages, foreigners would show contempt towards us. And they would try to help show us how we should dress. They would say that they wanted to introduce 'culture' to us. . . . This is evidence to show that to be well-dressed and to have decent houses are measures of national progress" (Chaloemtiarana 1978, 272).

Phibun presented "traditions" concerning gender as a stumbling block to national progress. However, the symbols of sex and gender have flexible meanings within nationalist discourses. In the project of creating images of the nation, gendered and sexual practices can be unseemly relics of a backward past, as in Phibun's examples above, or they can be declared unwanted intrusions of the Western other.

Within the Thai nationalist paradigm, "homosexuality" has become a discursive device used to represent or discuss the negative impact of westernization on Thai culture and identity. Within these nationalist discourses, images of the West are iconic, though semiotically unstable, representations of un-Thai-ness. The West has an ambivalent significance in Thai public discourse. The West can represent corruption of social values, vulgar consumerism, and sexual decadence, or it can evoke images of modernity, progress, and prosperity. In either case, "the West" is a common signifier of the non-self in Thai public discourse.[3]

THE PRESS AND DISCOURSES OF SOCIAL DECAY

The Thai print media is notorious for its sensational coverage of scandal and bizarreness. One of its favorite images is "sexual decadence," which is widely associated with "homosexuality." In addition to publishing *kathoey*/gay/homosexual stories, the newspapers began producing sensational stories of *tom*s and *dee*s about twenty-five years ago. The conflation of these terms by mainstream society ignores the distinctions made between individuals who self-identify as gay, *tom*, *dee,* lesbian, or transgendered male ("second kind of woman").

"Homosexuality," as an overarching reference to these varied identities, has been frequently linked by the press and its commentators to middle-class Thai youth—those most closely associated with the emblematic consumerism of Western society. In 1984 a monthly magazine published a fourteen-page article that detailed the supposed links between middle-class prosperity and the growing "danger" of homosexual youth: "Every day is the same. From morning to night there are thousands of youths in groups there to buy things they want . . . gathering in an atmosphere of continuous loud disco music. The image of hugging, kissing, and stroking between men and men, and between women and women, is easy to see in this place. . . . In brief, these days the customers who supply fashion retail places with money are youths who have altered sexual tastes" (*Pheuan Chiwit*, June 1984, 20). The article asserted that gay and lesbian bars were "popping up like mushrooms in the rainy season" and colorfully described the scene as a commodified free-for-all, noting that these new businesses were grabbing as much money as possible by selling expensive drinks and sex (p. 20). Images of decadent homosexual youth supposedly found in these establishments were explicitly associated with the new (largely Sino-Thai) middle class: "The dress, complexion, and abundant spending [of these homosexual youths] shows that most of them are the descendents of the well-to-do who have no time themselves to care for their children" (p. 19).

These themes are repeated in numerous other articles. The emergence of a profligate middle-class youth is linked to the perceived loss of Thai tradition at the expense of dominant Western culture. For example, a columnist for *Matichon* discussed an article that had appeared earlier on the subject of *tom-dee*ism: "[Kids] don't just walk around for fun. They buy clothes and expensive food, making for wasteful personalities. Kids don't think when they buy something expensive; they think the more expensive, the better. . . . [Parents] should teach their kids to know Thai culture too, or they will only know Western culture" (*Matichon*, October 16, 1984).

Links between Thai homosexual youth and the West are not usually claims that homosexuality, including the transgendered *kathoey*s, is directly derived from the West. Rather, the association with the West serves to denigrate some practices as culturally inappropriate and as violations of Thai culture. Middle-class youth, homosexuality, and the West are thus all linked, serving to mutually besmirch the image of all three. "Homosexuality exists in Thailand, but all the changes to society due to westernization have raised its visibility. Homosexuals are becoming more open. Homosexuals have low self-esteem because of their un-naturalness and have many psychological problems . . . 'sadness, anxiety, paranoia, loneliness.' They cannot form stable relationships," writes Nunthirat Kunakorn (1989, 1), who goes on to cite Western psychologists from the late seventies and early eighties.[4] Such social critiques are largely middle-class discourses, relying on Western psychological theory and other academic writings to promote an image of respectability and sexual morality.[5] This middle-class discourse in which homosexuality (implying transgenderism) is vilified does not necessarily reflect popular or non-middle-class attitudes, though its persistent presentation in the press disseminates these discourses across classes.

These statements that practices or beliefs are Western are rhetorical strategies rather than attempts to make factual claims. The West is an ambivalent figure, implying both the antithesis of an imputed Thai tradition and the epitome of modernity and power, against which Thai-

ness is negatively compared. Homosexuality and transgenderism, para-
doxically, have also been used in Thai discourse as a sign of the lack of
modernization. For example, commentators have associated homosexuality and transgenderism with the supposedly "traditional" practices
of sex segregation, such as same-sex schools, and social taboos on
teenage dating.[6] Politicians and journalists have asserted that Western-
style dating and mixing of the sexes are modern and will prevent homosexuality. In 1994 the minister of education argued that all state schools
should be transformed into coeducational facilities, claiming that allowing boys and girls to socialize would help prevent homosexuality. He
cited academics and psychologists and stated that single-sex schools
promoted homosexuality (*The Nation,* October 31, 1994). Concepts
from Western psychological discourses are routinely presented in the
Thai press as means to avoid homosexuality in children. For example,
"emotional health" and "modern" communication between parents
and children are promoted in one article as ways to prevent children
from becoming homosexual: "Raising children depends on the way you
talk to them. You must be modern, so they can take care of themselves.
But culture creates a lot of pressure, because old-fashioned beliefs are
enforced, leading to more negative results than positive" (*City Life,*
July 1994, 123–124).

This public avowal of the importance of mixing the sexes has little
resonance with mainstream attitudes toward daughters in Thailand. In
fact, Thai parents express much greater anxiety over their daughters'
possible heterosexual experiences than homosexual ones. Sex-segregated schools are still popular with many Thais interviewed, especially
for girls.

"Westernization" and "the West" are ambivalent categories used for
critiquing social change—the object of criticism can be portrayed as
either a negative imitation of the West or a lack of the modern qualities
associated with the West. This ambivalence is parodied in an article
entitled, "Homosexuality . . . in Developed Countries": "People always
say that in the developed countries there are so many gays that they are
a majority. So I can almost write a theory that homosexuality comes
from being a developed country. If [this means that] Thailand is developed because of its homosexuality, I ask to change my household registration to Karen" (Ophat 1984a). The writer sarcastically states that he
would rather live with the Karen—a minority ethnic group living in the
mountainous or rural areas of northern Thailand, which is perceived by

Thais as the antithesis of modernity—than live in a "Westernized" version of modernity linked to a perceived increase in homosexuality.

My interviews with media personnel and a review of media stories
reflected three common ideas: that homosexuality is increasing; that
this increase is caused by Western influences (vaguely defined); and that
"homosexuality" was consistent with Thai understandings of transgenderism *(phit-pheet).* A journalist for *Matichon,* the main "quality" Thai
newspaper, positioned homosexuality as non-Buddhist and alien to Thai
cultural values: "This is a problem that is being talking about a lot now;
in the past this was an issue that wasn't talked about. Personally, I don't
think homosexuality is right in Thai society. Thai society is Buddhist;
there is an answer for everything. [Homosexuality] is an abnormality
for Thai society. If you ask in general if Thai society accepts it, I would
say no, they don't. No matter what, there never will be a day when they
accept it. Thai society views it as an abnormality, something that should
not occur." A reporter for *The Nation* commented that Thais disapprove of homosexuality because they disapprove of both the "affected
mannerisms" of homosexuals and Western culture: "They see only this
image, so they think [all homosexuals] are like this. It starts from hat-
ing the mannerisms. And they don't know what homosexuality is, and
so they mix them both [affected mannerisms and homosexuality]
together and hate them both. But if they know someone who doesn't
have a personality like this, they accept them. Most Thais don't like
homosexuality because they think it is like Westerners, not nice. And
some people don't like anything American." The mannerisms to which
the reporter referred are the exaggerated feminine gestures used by
transgendered males and some gay men who have appropriated aspects
of femininity in their public personae. Thus the reporter states that what
annoys Thais is precisely the visual component of homosexuality, meaning the performance of transgenderism, particularly in males.

Many people have said that the West—and in particular the United
States—was open and tolerant toward homosexuality, unlike Thailand.
The United States and the West have also been positioned as indicators
of modern trends in Thailand. For example, in an interview in June
1998 a radio DJ commented that homosexuality was more accepted in
Thailand now than in the past. He doubted that homosexuals would be
fully integrated into society, though, because even in open and tolerant
societies like that of the United States, homosexuals remained segregated: "It's getting better, but if you think of [homosexuals in main-

stream society] as normal, it is probably not possible. Because even in societies that are very open, like America, there are homosexual neighborhoods because they want to mix with people like themselves." Of course, positioning the United States as a tolerant haven for homosexuals is ironic, considering the vociferous anti-gay/lesbian activities there at present, such as physical violence against gays and lesbians and efforts to legislate against gay/lesbian rights. "America" plays a special role in the Thai imagination as a site of excessively permissive freedom and social tolerance, regardless of facts to the contrary.

Almost all Thai academics claimed that homosexuality and transgenderism have become more acceptable in Thai society. M. L. Somchai Chakraphan, the director of Srithanya Hospital (in Nonthaburi Province, on the outskirts of Bangkok), was quoted in the newspapers as saying, "People nowadays accept homosexuality more than before. In the past, such behavior was viewed as a criminal act."[7] In fact, in spite of the brief law against it in the early twentieth century, homosexuality in Thailand has never been subject to the kind of legal repression that it has in the West. That brief law is little known, was never enforced, and was mainly an attempt to demonstrate modernity in legal reforms in the late nineteenth century (see Loos 1999). Acceptance of homosexuality has been positioned as both a negative sign of westernization and a positive sign of modernization, depending on the context and the discursive agenda of the speaker. Anjaree has portrayed acceptance of gay/lesbian people as a sign of modern and progressive social development. However, the much more common discourse has labeled acceptance of homosexuality as a sign of cultural pollution and decay. In an interview in May 1998, Chalidaporn Songsamphan, a professor of political science at Thammasat University, commented on the many statements that Thai society is open toward homosexuality: "I have had this discussion with many people. They say that Thai society is more open toward this issue, but I totally disagree. In this society we don't beat up homosexuals or openly say bad things about them; we just ignore them. This is a kind of violence to trivialize. This is not a positive attitude toward homosexuality" (English used). People do openly say bad things about homosexuals in Thailand, but Chalidaporn's point is that the popular belief that Thailand is now more open is inaccurate.

The position that homosexuality, including *tom-dee*ism, is more accepted now than in the past contains a presentist assumption. The sexual-gendered categories now existing and the present discourses of homosexuality are assumed to be natural and therefore to have existed in the past. In the same interview, Chalidaporn commented on these presentist assumptions about gender/sexuality and national image: "This is a very strange thing about attitudes in Thai society. Attitudes [about sex] have been influenced by Victorian thinking about sex, but people tend to believe that this is Thai. I think that this kind of Victorian thinking came with Westerners who came into [Thai] society about one hundred years ago, in the reign of Rama V. We had reform in this society, and we just adopted this sort of thinking, and we think it is Thai and that it has been Thai for so long. There is another issue about short skirts at Chulalongkorn.[8] People said that Thais usually dress properly, and we don't show this part of our bodies. But this is not true. In the Ayuthayan times women wore just a sash over their breasts. The way we believe Thai women should behave is actually very Western" (English used).[9] Chalidaporn suggested that these Western models were first adopted by elite classes and then later by the emerging middle class.

In a kind of reverse presentism, Thais have been introduced to the concept of "third sex/gender" in academic writing and the media as if it is a new concept. The history of the term "third sex/gender" is not clear. It probably was brought into Thai discourse through exposure to Western sexology, but it was easily absorbed into Thai vocabulary because it was consistent with preexisting understandings of intermediate gender/sexual categories such as *kathoey* (Peter Jackson, pers. comm.). I have been bemused by my Thai students' declarations that Westerners are more tolerant of "third sex/genders" than are Thais, assuming third sex/gender to be a universal category. Although the notion of third-sex/gender doubtlessly gained some official legitimacy with Thai academia through early twentieth-century Western inversion theories, it is clearly a local formulation resonating with the concept of *kathoey*.

THE STATE'S ANTIHOMOSEXUAL STANCE

Within the past several years the Thai state has begun to engage in periodic suppression of homosexuals, which has proven to be ephemeral and unproductive. This pattern is new and is unlike the control, surveillance, and suppression of commercial sex workers. There have been several recent attempts by government agencies to condemn homosexuality. In May 1998 the Public Relations Department, in response to complaints that Prime Minister Chuan Leekpai had received, announced a restriction on images of *kathoeys* in television programs. The order was essentially voluntary, requesting that producers of television programs screen their material to prevent images of sexual/gender deviance from harming children. The restriction provoked protests by various nongovernmental organizations and academics. The department claimed that the suggested ban was not on gays and lesbians, just on inappropriate images. In July 1999, in reaction to a news story claiming that there were many *kathoeys* on Ratchabhat campuses, the Ministry of Education announced that transgendered men would not be allowed to wear skirts on campus. The most controversial state interference with gender sexualities came in 1996–1997 when the system of teachers colleges announced a ban on homosexual students.

RATCHABHAT'S BAN ON GAY STUDENTS AND THE REACTION AGAINST STATE CONTROL

In December 1996, Ratchabhat Institute, the large system of government teacher training colleges, declared that it would not admit homosexual students. The ban prompted a massive protest against the "undemocratic" acts of the Ministry of Education (Ratchabhat's governing body) and Ratchabhat Institute. Academics, psychologists, journalists, and social activists publicly challenged Ratchabhat's position, arguing that the "rights" *(si-thi)* of students had been violated by Ratchabhat. The controversy was extensively covered in the Thai press, and the negative publicity generated by this public debate was instrumental in challenging Ratchabhat and the Ministry of Education. However, close inspection of the rhetoric used by commentators—primarily academics, medical professionals, and journalists—during the debate reveals that the concern over the rights of the homosexual students was inextricably enmeshed within competing political visions and struggles among an emergent civil society, the Thai press, and the ossified state bureaucracy. Throughout the debates, the understanding that homosexuality was abnormal and a result of failed social and family institutions was rarely challenged.

The critics of Ratchabhat were challenging the overcentralized, paternal Thai state and its autocratic and unresponsive bureaucracy. The debate over Ratchabhat's decision occurred during the contentious passage of the People's Constitution, and the media's challenge was framed in terms of the "undemocratic" and "unconstitutional" tendency of the bureaucracy, embodied in the Ministry of Education and its largest institution—Ratchabhat colleges.

Ratchabhat's actions had special significance in the politics of national development and democratization. Ratchabhat Institute, as a teacher's college, is associated with national development, producing the teachers that will go to the rural areas throughout the country to educate the people as Thai nationals. Teachers are the primary bearers of the state, teaching central Thai, standard nationalist history, and nationalist symbols to the rural majority. As the national symbol for teacher education, Ratchabhat had been the focus of persistent demands for educational reform, and it framed the ban in terms of responding to these demands. Protestors of the Ratchabhat ban found a largely willing ally in the Thai press.

Ironically, considering the vilification of Ratchabhat and the opposition to the ban expressed by the press, the newspapers' own negative and sensational representation of transgenderism and homosexuality was used as the initial justification of the ban. When Ratchabhat claimed that homosexual teachers were poor role models for students, it referred to the ubiquitous academic and media reports that asserted that transgendered sexuality/homosexuality was a perversion, an illness, and an abnormality, assertions that had been made by the media with stupefying repetition. For example, a particularly gruesome murder in Chiang Mai earlier that year involving a *kathoey* and a *tom* had been extensively covered in the media, replete with the usual psychological descriptions of sexual pathology.[10] This murder was cited by ministry officials as evidence of the need to protect society from "psychologically abnormal" people who should not become teachers.

A coalition of human rights organizations and academics charged that the Ministry of Education and Ratchabhat had violated the constitution and had acted undemocratically and against global trends. The press published commentaries by well-known academics who compared homosexuals to other oppressed minority groups in need of protection from the state. Chalidaporn Songsamphan wrote, "The new constitution gives importance to the needs of the people. For too long, people such as women, the handicapped, the poor, or people who deviate from the mainstream have been neglected. . . . Democracy is freedom from repression. . . . Ratchabhat goes against the democracy movement" (*Matichon,* January 25, 1997, 21). In an interview with the *Bangkok Post,* well-known academic Nithi Ieosriwong was described as expressing the following view: "Thailand's higher education institutions are already riddled with discrimination, especially against the poor, the disabled, and ethnic minorities, and the gay ban will only aggravate the situation" (Tansubhapol 1997). Sanitsuda Ekachai, a popular columnist for the *Bangkok Post,* expressed the widely held belief of Thais that the government was out of touch with modern standards and unaware of human rights: "It's frightening to learn that we are entrusting the ones whom we dearly love to the hands of those who probably haven't even heard the word 'human rights'" (*Bangkok Post,* January 2, 1997, 9).

The media provided the space for these academics to express their opinions and supported their critiques of the government. However, the press itself maintained consistently negative attitudes toward homosexuals themselves while simultaneously challenging the politics of the Ministry of Education.[11] The press charged that the Ministry of Education was unjustly denying an education to a group of citizens. However, the press also generally agreed that "homosexuals" were deviants and poor role models and therefore should not be teachers. For example, one article stated: "Just because people are gay, *tut,* or *tom* does not mean that they shouldn't study to be teachers. If there are obstacles put up because there is fear that kids will take them as models, then there should begin to be selection for teachers . . . not a hindering of people studying the field of education" (*Daily News,* January 28, 1997, 23).

Other academics criticized Ratchabhat for harming the national image by going against global trends. A prominent psychologist argued against the ban on the basis that globalization will not allow for such distinctions: "What I am really concerned about is not whether gays will be teachers or not, but that the professors of Ratchabhat have this way of thinking. It is hard to believe that all the teachers agree to split off humanity at the same time that the world is losing its boundaries over the past several decades. Geographical boundaries are losing their meaning in recent times, so you should not divide Thais. The national boundaries are slowly slipping away, and we are all humans who will have to live together and love each other. . . . We all have to learn to live together. . . . In summary, I am not worried about whether gays will be teachers or not, because the world has lost its borders surrounding Thailand. The worrisome thing is how Ratchabhat Institute has the idea of restricting the rights of other people."[12] The charge that Ratchabhat was acting against global trends and therefore harmful to the national image was the key weapon against Ratchabhat, eventually leading to its defeat.[13]

Many of the experts quoted in the press simultaneously challenged Ratchabhat and affirmed the negative image of homosexuality. For example, Seri Swanphanan, secretary of the Thai Law Association, said the ban violated the constitution, because all citizens had equal rights to protection by the law. The "problem of gender/sexual deviance" needed to be solved at its source, the home, not at the end point, Seri noted (*Daily News*, January 25, 1997, 12). The Ratchabhat case provided an opportunity for democracy activists, academics, and the press to express distrust and criticism of a government system that they felt was oppressive and dictatorial in nature. The concept of "rights" was a vehicle to frame such a critique.

Ratchabhat was clearly caught off guard by the barrage of criticism it received for its statements about homosexuals. In line with the common understandings of "gender deviance" and homosexuality, the ban was targeting visible images of social deviance, such as non-normative expressions of gender and other inappropriate behavior associated with it, not private erotic expressions (homosexuality). The primary image of homosexuality evoked by the officials was the television soap opera image of the *kathoey* as a flamboyant, screechy cross-dresser. However, through the all-embracing and technical-sounding terms used in the debate, such as "homosexuality" and "sexual deviants" *(khon biang-been-thaang-pheet)*, Ratchabhat found itself targeting all categories of transgenderism and homosexuality. This conflation of sexual behavior and transgenderism mirrored the lack of conceptual distinction within Thai discourse between sexual and gender categories, with both subsumed under the term *"pheet."* For example, a *Daily News* team editorial begins by linking all the popular Thai gender/sexual identities to transgenderism: *"Tuts,* closet cases, gay, *tom, dee, kathoey*—these are all names used to call the people who have the psychology or behavior that is deviant from one's true sex that nature has given one. Human beings have only two sexes, female and male, and also by nature women must be mates with men in order to propagate the species" (*Daily News*, January 27, 1997, 10–11). Ratchabhat unwittingly produced a discourse in which Thai concepts of "misgendering" became blended with transnational discourses of gay/lesbian/homosexual identities.

Protesters accessed the transnational discourse of "gay/lesbian" rights to oppose the ban. In conjuring up the ban, the educational officials were acting without awareness of the development of concepts of sexual rights and gay/lesbian identities in Thai society or awareness of the growing importance of the discourse of human rights. Ratchabhat's own confused use of homosexual/gender categories, indiscriminately referring to "sexual deviants," "homosexuals," the "third sex," "gays," and so on, allowed for the construction of an all-inclusive category of people, "homosexuals," who, according to international standards and transnational movements, had rights that needed to be protected.

Rosalind Morris (1997) has theorized that the discourse of homosexuality in the Ratchabhat case helped bring about the reality of "homosexuality" as a cultural category in Thailand. Indeed, the Ratchabhat discourse did vocalize and solidify a discourse of "homosexuality" in Thailand in which sexual behavior is given primacy in forming an identity, or social category. However, the general understanding in Thai discourse that "sex/gender deviance" and "homosexuality" are references to "misgendering" is still the dominant viewpoint. Also, Thais who hold a *tom-dee* or *kathoey* identity for the most part do not define themselves in terms of sexuality. Even among many psychologists and academics, homosexuality is an issue of gender deviance. The president of the Thai Psychiatric Institute described homosexuality as "losing one's sex/gender" and no longer being a "real man," referring to male homosexuals (*Matichon*, January 30, 1997, 9).

The Ministry of Education officials appeared to have been maneuvered into a debate about "gays and lesbians" and "homosexual rights," topics of which they were only the most vaguely aware. In a ludicrous attempt to fend off the intense criticism they had received, officials suggested providing separate educational facilities for "deviant students," an idea that was ridiculed and quickly withdrawn. Ratchabhat had hoped to promote an image of cultural conservatism and moral respectability by banning an assumed nonvocal and nonpolitical minority ("gender deviants") who had been routinely criticized and disparaged in both the popular press and academic writings for decades.

Government officials in defense of the ban combined the previously common media assertion that "gender/sexual deviance" was foreign and a threat to Thai identity, with the notion popular in psychiatric circles that homosexuals were violent. Deputy Minister of Education Suraphorn Danaitangtrakul stated that "this group has a high rate of violence in disciplining children," adding that "there is a big problem of gender/sexual deviance in Bangkok, so the Ministry of Education believes we should maintain the Thai way of life rather than the foreign one" (*Khao Sot,* January 22, 1997, 1–2). Despite its criticism of Ratchabhat, the media have repeatedly reasserted these themes of gender/

sexual deviance in various news stories, both before and after the Ratchabhat case; yet as long as Ratchabhat could be portrayed as an autocratic bureaucracy violating the rights of individuals, Ratchabhat could not win the argument.

The most likely reason for the ban was to counter a general criticism of the Thai educational system, including the Ministry of Education. Thailand had ranked poorly in a recent survey of Asian universities. There were scandals and disaffection with the system of entrance exams, teacher qualifications and salaries, and the general quality of education provided by the government school system. The ban seems to have been an attempt at public relations—homosexuals seemed to be an easy target to use in empty political rhetoric and posturing, without having to tackle the much more politically sensitive and contentious issues of educational reform. Sirot Phonphanthin, dean of Ratchabhat Dusit, was quoted in the Thai papers as having said: "We were criticized about the quality of teachers we produced. It was said they lacked moral principles, ethics, and a sense of responsibility. People did not come here to study as much anymore. So we raised the qualifications for student selection in 1993, focusing on elementary and junior high teachers and special teachers, by clearly considering the issue of people with sexual/gender deviance" (*Krungthep Thurakij*, January 25, 1997, 1–2).

Aimed at placating a dissatisfied public, the announcement of the ban on "deviants" from the teacher training program became a fiasco for Ratchabhat. Ratchabhat and the Ministry of Education officials who backed the ban were portrayed as backward, prejudiced, ignorant demagogues and typical representatives of an unpopular, overcentralized government bureaucracy. Ironically, considering Ratchabhat's efforts at public relations and image enhancement (albeit feeble), it was the charge that Ratchabhat was harming the nation's image by being "backward" and against the global trend of accepting homosexuality that led to the successful challenge of the institute's ban (*Matichon*, January 22, 1990, 1, 4; January 14, 1997, 32).

In September 1997, the month that the People's Constitution was passed, Ratchabhat, overwhelmed by criticism, backed down and rescinded the ban. Banning "homosexuals" was an unacceptable official act in the eyes of the middle-class public, who were frustrated and impatient with the imperious and out-of touch bureaucracy. Ratchabhat took a face-saving stance by claiming that the controversy occurred because of misunderstandings over terminology: "The Institute misunderstood and used the wrong word. That's why it seemed to violate human rights. What they meant to screen was 'sexually abnormal people,' not 'sexual deviants'" (*Bangkok Post*, September 11, 1997). The distinction that Ratchabhat attempted to make between the terms is not clear; both terms involve concepts derived from Western theories of sexual pathology and are technical-sounding references to "homosexuality" and "transgenderism."

Shortly after the Ratchabhat incident, I interviewed reporters and editors at most large newspapers to learn about the attitudes of the newspaper staff itself.[14] The media figures I interviewed consistently referred to homosexuality as a social problem and generally agreed with Ratchabhat's position that homosexual teachers were harmful to children. For example, the general news editor at the *Daily News* said, "The point that Thai society needs to think about is how to prevent homosexuals from creating problems for society." A DJ at Channel 5 Radio stated: "Many academics don't dare tell the truth that teachers who are homosexual influence children in primary school. Ratchabhat has the duty to produce teachers to teach children in the primary grades. So this is the point that Ratchabhat is making; it is afraid that homosexuality of teachers will make Thai children be homosexual. And there is research from foreign countries on provinces in the northeast of Thailand that found this to be true." The DJ mentioned several times in the course of the interview that he had read academic studies that support the theory that homosexual teachers "cause" children to be homosexual and are dangerous for children. However, the DJ simultaneously supported the protesters of the ban, saying, "I think that Ratchabhat should not restrict education, no matter who they are, if they are handicapped or homosexual."

Like Ratchabhat, most of the media staff focused on gendered behavior as objectionable. A reporter for the *Daily News* said she agreed that homosexuals who did not "express themselves" (that is, cross-dress or act like *kathoey*s) should be acceptable as teachers: "[Ratchabhat is right] because homosexuality might have an effect on the children. But if they don't express themselves, it is then a personal matter, because they are not harming the children." Speculating about Ratchabhat's reasons for the ban, the reporter added: "Their point is that they are scared the children will model themselves after the teacher. Another thing is, they are scared that the homosexual teachers have a mental illness

(rook-cit) and can harm the children. If you are in society and don't mis-
behave in a way that children will model themselves after [such as being
obviously transgender, such as *tom* or *kathoey*], and just have sex with
your partner in private, then nobody will blame you." Both the press
and Ratchabhat agreed that "homosexuality" meant inappropriate
behavior, such as excessively effeminate behavior in men or violence
commonly associated with *tom*s, *dee*s, and gays. These groups were
seen as a problem for society, causing crime, molesting children, and
acting in offensive ways. In spite of the general abuse heaped upon gays,
*tom*s, *dee*s, and *kathoey*s, many of the newspaper staff accused homosexuals of violating the rights of others. For example, the *Daily News*
general editor commented: "We need to figure out what to do so homosexuals stay in their own group and don't violate the rights of others.
It can create criminal cases. As far as I have seen, this group [homosex-
uals] violates the rights of others." The media staff said that their sensationalized reporting of homosexuality, which led to a gruesome gay
crime story being used as Ratchabhat's pretext for the ban, was necessary to "protect the public." The *Daily News* general editor, for example, stated: "Nobody can say if homosexuality is right or wrong, but
according to nature, it is not correct. I think that Thai families don't
want anyone in their family to be homosexual. When we present news
of a *tom* killing a *dee,* we want to show that sometimes hanging out
with homosexuals can make problems. We want society to be careful,
but we don't say if being homosexual is right or wrong. We just want
our readers to protect their lives and evaluate whether their lives will
end up like these news stories or not."

The consistently negative ideas about homosexuality and transgenderism held by the media staff were incongruously interspersed with
statements that "homosexuality" was more accepted at present. For
example, a reporter for the *Daily News* commented: "I think that society accepts homosexuality more and more, and there are more and
more opportunities to come out. But that means they [homosexuals]
should not harm others. In the past, Ratchabhat forbade homosexuality, but because society accepts it more and more, they changed the rules
[to accept gays]. Now you can test and enter in any field you want. But
it is implied that if you have affected mannerisms, you perhaps cannot
pass the entrance test. Ratchabhat probably changed this rule because
of the issue of human rights, so they must adjust their rules." When I
asked the reporter if she thought that her position that homosexuality

was a human right should be taught to the children in school, she replied no, adding, "You shouldn't teach the children that homosexuality is a personal right. You should not say that. But you should teach them that normally for people there must be reproduction. But if a child is homosexual, it must be something natural in him or her. Let them just develop according to their own hormones. But teachers absolutely should not teach that homosexuality is a human right. We have our Thai social norms." I then asked her, "But you think homosexuality is an issue of human rights?" She responded, "Yes, but teachers absolutely should not teach that."

The media staff were aware of Thai academic work that asserts that homosexuals are violent and unstable, and they cited these reports frequently. For example, the DJ at Channel 5 Radio said, "There was an academic study that said homosexuals who were teachers of primary school made the students have deviant sexual behavior. I think that all children, as they grow up, have heroes. Before, Thai children had their fathers and mothers, or people close to them like siblings and relatives, to be heroes. But now, when the media reaches more and more people, their heroes are no longer people in their homes but outsiders, like soccer players and celebrities. There is transmission of personality and ideas, and the ones who can stimulate this the most are teachers close to them."

The image of homosexuality became a vehicle through which both Ratchabhat and the protesters argued about the meaning of development, democracy, and nation building. Except for a small group of activists and academics who were pushing for greater recognition of sexual rights, the meaning of negative understanding of homosexuality held by state-controlled institutions was not directly challenged. The media and various activists promoted and used the debate over the Ratchabhat ban on homosexuals as a means for talking about changing visions of society. The People's Constitution set the tone for the debate, calling for an end to paternal and autocratic rule by an arrogant bureaucracy—symbolically captured in Ratchabhat's ban on gays.

CONCLUSION

Western psychological theories have been incorporated into Thai discourses of sex/gender *(pheet)*, producing moralizing discourses of sexual/gender abnormality embodied in the Thai term for "homosexuality" *(rak-ruam-pheet)*. These discourses are routinely portrayed in the press, by state officials, and in academic/medical statements to produce various social critiques.

Cultural iconography inherently contains contradictions and variation. John Fiske (1989, 5), in exploring the use of cultural symbols, explains, "This semiotic richness . . . means that they cannot have a single defined meaning, but they are a resource bank of potential meanings." Thai public discourse on homosexuality is particularly rich in semiotic manipulation and creation, and this chapter can serve as only an introduction to the myriad themes of homosexuality in Thai public discourse. However, the central theme of the discussions about "homosexuality" in Thai public debate concerns the nationalist assertions of the Thai self and social critiques.

Westerners often see Thailand as a kind of sexual paradise, or gay and lesbian utopia, because of its supposed openness toward sexuality. Although there is cultural space for the development of homosexual/ transgender identities and communities, the social context is complicated, as the recent state intrusions into homosexual/transgender practices demonstrate. Public pronouncements about homosexuality must be understood within the overriding concern of national progress that dominates almost all social debate in Thailand. The economic crisis of 1997 has increased nationalist sentiments of the populace in general and the urban middle class in particular, because the economic problems are portrayed as stemming from overreliance on the West and from exploitation by the West. Academics and medical professionals from a range of ministries and departments have situated their projects and goals in explicitly anti-Western and nationalist frameworks. Studies of *tom-dee*ism and homosexuality have been framed in these nationalist, anti-Western discourses. Thai academics include progressive social activists who challenge state power, but nationalism and anti-westernization are still important dynamics in their projects and perspectives. Nationalist discourses have dominated academic/professional imagery of homosexuality and *tom-dee*ism, whether the speakers are political liberals or conservatives.

Conclusion

GLOBALIZATION

The presence of masculine and feminine identities among women throughout East and Southeast Asia compel a greater focus on the very real possibility of regional connections. At a workshop on Southeast Asian sexualities at the Sexual Diversity and Human Rights Conference in Manchester in July 1999, the issue of regional borrowings was addressed. The use by female same-sex subcultures in East and Southeast Asia of terms derived from the English term "tomboy" to refer to masculine women was noted (such as the Indonesian *"tomboi"*). Whether these terms have been imported from British, Australian, or American English is not clear, but there appears to be regional circulation of these terms. For example, a member of Anjaree who attended an international lesbian conference in the Philippines in 2001 reported that some women in the Philippines used the terms *"tom"* and *"dee"* to identify themselves, in addition to terms in their local languages. Conference participants in Manchester questioned common assumptions that "tomboy" was adopted by Thais during the Vietnam War (through the presence of American GIs in Thailand), because the term is not commonly used in American English to refer to masculine lesbians.

In contrast to the popularity of the English word "tomboy," the term "butch" has not taken hold in any of these local languages. It is remarkable that the Philippines, with its historical connections to the United States, has not adopted the particularly American term "butch" or other American terms for masculine lesbians. Malu Marin (1996) claims that "tomboy" and its linguistic derivatives were popular identities in the Philippines from the 1970s until the 1990s, at which point the local language terms *"mars"* and *"pars"*—referring to feminine and masculine women, respectively—began to replace the earlier English term. Terms in local languages have not necessarily preceded English terms in identifying sexual and gender identities.

Rosalind Morris (1994) has argued that Thai *tom, dee,* and gay identities are the results of the introduction of Western discourses of sexual identity, which exist side by side with traditional gender categories consisting of man, woman, and *kathoey.* Morris asserts that there are diverging and contradictory discourses of gender and sexuality at play in Thai society, with one paradigm based on the primacy of gender in forming identities, and another paradigm influenced by Western notions of sexual orientation. Although it is clear that in Thai society hegemonic discourses of "sex/gender deviance" have been influenced by Western concepts, they have been transformed in the process of integrating them into a local meanings system in which sexual behavior in itself is not normatively a basis for the categorization of people. Thus gender-normative *dees* and masculine gay men are not accommodated in Thai discourses of "homosexuality." For many Thais, including *tom*s and *dee*s, *dee*s and masculine homosexual men are not clearly distinct "identities." *Tom*s, *dee*s, and Thais in general rarely classify *tom*s and *dee*s together as products of the same phenomenon and usually distinguish *tom*s, as "misgendered," from *dee*s, as "ordinary women."

The term "gay" has been widely adopted as both a positive self-referent among Thai men and a common term used by dominant Thai society to refer to homosexual men. In contrast, the term "lesbian" has much less appeal as a self-referent because it is associated with Western-style pornography.[1] The negative connotations of the word "lesbian" held by many *tom*s and *dee*s whom I interviewed stem precisely from the lack of gender division in pornographic images of female same-sex activity; the image of two feminine women having sex was described as obscene by *tom*s and *dee*s in that it was seen as an artificial act that only served viewers' prurience. Unlike many male gay communities cross-culturally, Thai *tom*s and *dee*s do not engage in the kinds of global imaginings that construct regional and local variants of "gayness" (see Johnson 1998).

There is an assumption in Thai discourse and in studies of sexuality cross-culturally that social change is inseparable from Western influence. In other words, all change is the result of Western intrusion into a supposedly "authentic" cultural order. Mark Johnson (1997) points out that cross-cultural studies of gender too often essentialize their target as timeless. Johnson believes that anthropologists need to move beyond the strictly comparative approach and to examine "the shifting historical contexts and spatial fields in which such categories and practices have emerged not as *sui generis* but as the specific product of political and cultural entanglements" (p. 233).

Tom and *dee* identities are products of a local history of female masculinity and female homoeroticism, combined with the dramatic socio-economic changes of the past three decades. There was no term used exclusively for transgendered females in the past—they were called "women/females *(phu-ying)* who are like men *(phu-chai)*." Both male and female individuals had been referred to as *kathoeys* before the 1970s, according to informants, but the women did not form the same visible and large subcultures as *tom*s and *dee*s currently do in Thai society.

It has been suggested that perhaps the Western "butch-femme" model is a likely source of influence for the emergence of gender-paired couples throughout East and Southeast Asia. Mere similarity, however, does not mean that one must have formed the other. This sort of conclusion privileges the West as the primary source of cultural change for the non-West, which then takes on an aura of timelessness and homogeneity. The proposal that the American/European model influenced the Thai sex/gender order must include a means of dissemination.

Western gay men have traveled as sex tourists or simply tourists to other regions of the world. Their presence in local bars and hangouts for homosexual men provides a point of direct interaction. Western literature and media have also been widely disseminated in Thailand and elsewhere in Asia. However, it seems unlikely that Western working-class women who were butch or femme did much traveling as sex tourists or otherwise to the degree that much of Southeast Asia followed these gendered models from their example. Even now, the amount of Western "lesbian" literature found in Thailand is minuscule in comparison with the abundant Western gay male literature widely available. Western butch-femme society was a fairly underground and hidden community, in fear of social condemnation and legal sanctions. Women in the 1950s and before did not have the financial basis to make the kind of personal connections with non-Westerners through tourism that Western men have had. Western men have also had military experience to bring them into contact, sexual and otherwise, with non-Western men. It seems unlikely that Western men, as soldiers or tourists, would have been a conduit for a relatively hidden, largely working-class sexual subculture of butch and femme women. Thai *tom*s and *dee*s emerged in the 1970s—after Western butch-femme communities became suppressed and had been largely replaced with "lesbian" communities and identity in the West.

Global discourses of sexual rights and gay liberation coexist with state-supported sexology theories in which *tom*s and *dee*s are condemned as evidence of Western influence and cultural decay. Within local nationalist discourses there is a polarization of the possible labels that a cultural form can take: either it can be "new" and therefore, by implication, not Thai, or it is "traditional" and, by implication, an unchanging reproduction of timeless tradition. These discourses of self (Thai) and other (West) are an important part of the social context of this study, but it must be remembered that these discourses themselves are products of a recent nationalist project. The notion of "hybridity" is useful for getting beyond the nationalist discourses, because it allows us to see the inclusive nature of cultural forms such as *tom* and *dee*: they are products of hegemonic notions of masculinity and femininity, labeled "traditionally Thai," but in themselves products of historical transformation.

Rather than positioning *tom*s and *dee*s as either Western or authentically Thai, however, a more fruitful approach to the phenomenon is to explore the ways in which these identities are creative hybrids constructed in the crossroads of various forces. *Tom*s are not passing as males. They have appropriated a form of masculinity that blends and selectively claims aspects of both normative masculinity and normative femininity. *Tom*s are caretakers, as is proper for Thai women, and they are independent, mobile, and granted recognition of sexual agency, like Thai men. Thais often view *dee*s as a nondisruptive category because *dee*s are normatively feminine, but *dee*s are perhaps the more truly novel category. They are women who are attracted to the masculinity of women rather than the masculinity of men and who do not reject their association with women in general, their femininity, or their desire for female partners. The reified categories of "Western" or "Thai" fail to usefully account for or describe these sexual and gendered identities of *tom* and *dee*.

ACCEPTANCE OF "HOMOSEXUALITY" AND TOM-DEEISM

Three main stereotypical assertions about *tom-dee*ism and homosexuality/transgenderism are found in Thai popular attitudes and the print media. First, people often state that homosexuality and *tom-dee* identities are more accepted now than in the past. However, these identities and the sexology discourses often used to interpret them are relatively recent developments.

The newer authoritative discourses of sex/gender pathology that have emerged within academics and the media, however, are usually negative and carry considerable weight among the educated classes. The images of homosexuality as dangerous and pathological have also penetrated rural areas among the working and rural classes. State institutions, such as the Ministry of Education and the Ministry of Health, and state employees throughout the vast bureaucracy are key players in the production of negative interpretations of *tom-dee*ism and homosexuality. The recent spate of prohibitions against homosexuals, such as the Ratchabhat ban on homosexual/transgendered students and the Public Relations Department's warning against *kathoey* characters on television, are examples of new state intrusion and prohibitions of homosexuality.

Thailand clearly does not have the same level of violence against or legal harassment of homosexuals as is present in the West. The West, on the other hand, has also developed powerful discourses of civil liberties and individual rights that have proven useful not only in defending gays and lesbians from harassment but also in building positive senses of self and community. Western countries also have a long tradition of anti-homosexual legislation that has led to harassment, imprisonment, and even death at times.[2] Although legislation has played a more direct role in the suppression of homosexuals in the West, legal means have been indirectly used to suppress and punish homosexuals in Thailand. Prosecution based solely on homosexual behavior—such as prosecution for sodomy among consenting adults, as is found in Western law—is almost totally absent in the Thai context. However, there are reasons to believe that homosexual sex crimes are more vigorously prosecuted than heterosexual crimes in Thailand. For example, a male member of Parliament, charged with buying the sexual services of underaged boys, was unequivocally reviled in the Thai press and unceremoniously arrested and removed from Parliament.[3] A male senator charged with buying the sexual services of schoolgirls was also removed from the Senate and eventually charged with crimes, but only after a protracted struggle in which his associates defended his honor, asserting that the sexual acts were "mutual" and perhaps only errors in judgment.[4] That the senator was eventually charged at all is evidence of the increasing power of civil society to assert itself as a counter to the traditional abuse of position and power among Thai politicians and bureaucrats. However, the unmitigated revilement meted out to those charged with homosexual crimes contrasts sharply with the more forgiving atmosphere that men charged with heterosexual crimes face.

RURAL VERSUS URBAN ACCEPTANCE

Following from this first dubious claim that "homosexuality" is increasingly accepted is the related claim that homosexuality/*tom-dee*-ism is more accepted in urban areas than in rural areas. Economic independence, regardless of class or rural/urban living, is certainly a crucial factor for women's sexual expression. Both middle-class women and factory women who lived away from family or had their own source of income had greater opportunities to engage in relationships with both men and women outside of the scrutinizing gaze of family. However, urban people were more affected by the pathologizing discourses and by bureaucratic control than were rural people. The notion that homosexuality and transgenderism, and therefore *tom-dee*ism as well, are forms of mental illness and harmful to national morality is of urban origin. Competing discourses of human rights and gay/lesbian rights are also of urban origin, and thus the urban context must be understood as both complex and contradictory in its reaction to *tom-dee* and gay identities.

CLASS

The third commonly made claim is that homosexuality/transgenderism is more restricted for high-status people than for lower-class people. This premise seems to contradict the previous assertion that urban people are more accepting. In any case, Peter Jackson (1995) concludes that homosexual behavior is more acceptable in lower-class men who do not have family standing to worry about. Jackson found that Sino-Thai men, who tended to be higher class, were especially discouraged from homosexuality. Although homosexuality and especially transgenderism may be seen as inappropriate for well-heeled men, there are plenty of examples of Thai men in powerful positions in politics and academics who are widely known to be homosexual, including at least two prime ministers of the past several decades. The homosexuality of such men is rarely mentioned in the press, and even then only in oblique reference.

Thai men in positions of power and authority have long been assumed to have the right to sexual access to others, whether these others are men, minor wives, or prostitutes. Enjoying sexual "flavor" and diversity is a perquisite of being a high-status male in Thai society. Suchada Thaweesit (2000, 143) reports, "The fusion of Hinduism and Buddhism . . . led to a particular manifestation of a male-dominated Buddhist society where sexuality is used to exhibit male potency."

Thai women, however, face a different moral paradigm. All heterosexuality outside of marriage is unacceptable for them, and even in marriage women should ideally be innocent and passive. In this context, it is more acceptable for a Thai woman to renounce marriage and to pursue female "friendships" with proper discretion. The case of the female movie star who openly displayed her female partner in order to deflect rumors abut her heterosexuality is illustrative of these Thai prohibitions on female heterosexuality. Upper-class Thai women have considerable cultural space to choose not to marry and to pursue private business or professional interests (Guest and Tan 1994).

The relatively subdued response to the homosexuality of high-status people means that they are not easily criticized for their sexual behavior, if this behavior is carried out with proper discretion. *Tom*s and *dee*s often mentioned their desire to improve their social and economic status because that was the best way to get society to accept them.

Through cultural praxis, *tom*s and *dee*s construct and manipulate the meanings of their gendered and sexual identities. The development of the formal organizations Anjaree and Lesla has provided additional stimulus for the growth of *tom-dee* identities, while simultaneously providing forums for more vocal debates over their meanings. *Tom-dee*ism is not a homogeneous or stable identity but rather a set of possible meanings that women can access as they position themselves within varying social contexts. Mainstream understandings of ideal masculinity and femininity, as well as popular Buddhism, are embedded in the discourses of self and identity for both *tom*s and *dee*s. For example, claiming to be a *tom* or a *dee*, or participating in a *tom-dee* community, can be a way to assert sexual agency, masculinity, and all the prerogatives they provide or to express a reluctance to be categorized according to cultural expectations of women. Young *tom*s and *dee*s who police the boundaries of proper masculinity and *tom*ness coexist with feminist organizations, such as Anjaree, that advocate identifying communally as women, free of gender-specific identities and roles. It would be wrong to see Anjaree's feminist agenda as the new interloper in an old rigid *tom-dee* code. Anjaree and other feminist organizations have been operating since the mid-1980s, near the beginning of the surge in popularity of *tom-dee*ism. New *tom-dee* organizations are blossoming, such as Lesla, and are increasingly popular with young women who embrace *tom* and *dee* identities. Watching how these groups interact and perhaps form hybridities of their own will be a fascinating topic for future studies.

APPENDIX

Toms and Dees Referred to in the Text

PSEUDONYM	AGE	STATUS/OCCUPATION	IDENTITY
Aa	45	Supported by *dee,* working class	*Tom*
Bang	34	Police officer, working class	*Tom*
Bee	37	Private business owner, wealthy family, Sino-Thai, Christian	*Tom*
Bua	33	Office worker, Sino-Thai, working-class family	*Dee*
Buu	30	Private business owner, middle class	*Tom*
Chang	26	Office worker	*Dee*
Cot	25	Office worker, Sino-Thai	*Dee*
Euy	46	Truck driver	*Dee*
Fon	39	Wage laborer, raising partner's daughter	*Tom*
Ging	47	Private teacher	*Tom*
Jaat	48	Wealthy wife of Sino-Thai businessman	*Dee*
Jaeng	32	Office worker	*Dee*
Jiap	28	Ex-factory worker, supported by *dee*	*Tom*
Kaew	35	Middle class	*Tom*
Kep	60	Private business owner, wealthy	*Tom*
Khaek	34	Private business owner	*Tom*
Khiaw	48	Teacher, middle class	*Tom*
Khwan	32	Office worker, middle class	*Dee*
Kot	35	Owner of small business	*Tom*
Kralok	45	Sales officer in private business, middle class	*Tom*
Kung	30	Sex worker, rural background	*Tom*
Lee	40	Divorced mother, working class	*Dee*
Luat	45	Teacher, middle class	*Tom*
Lung	40	Private business owner, middle class	*Tom*

Continued on next page

Appendix—*Continued*

PSEUDONYM	AGE	STATUS/OCCUPATION	IDENTITY
May	26	Graphics designer, middle class	*Tom*
Muu	25	Office worker	*Dee*
Nee	50	Sex worker	*Dee*
Ngor	27	Private business owner, middle class	*Tom* (ambivalent)
Ning	24	Office worker, advertising	*Tom*
Nit	28	Sex worker, wage laborer	*Dee*, "woman"
Nok	35	Married, mother, professional office worker	*Dee*, "woman"
Num	36	Office worker	*Tom*
Nuu	42	Sports teacher, middle class	*Tom*
Ot	30	Housewife, wealthy	*Dee*
Pek	30	Wage laborer	*Dee*, "woman"
Phorn	46	Professional	*Tom*
Piin	37	Private business owner, Sino-Thai	*Tom*
Pop	50	Private business owner, wealthy	*Tom*
Puu	34	Private business owner	*Dee*
Som	30	Wage laborer	*Dee*, "woman"
Suay	30	Office worker	*Tom*
Taaw	46	Teacher, athlete	*Tom*
Tang	34	Office worker	*Tom*
Tao	33	Private business owner, professional	*Tom*
Ting	30	NGO worker (social activist)	*Tom*
Um	34	Middle class, professional	*Dee*
Ung	25	Writer, working class, rural background	*Dee, ying-rak-ying*, lesbian
Ying	21	Wage work, agriculture	*Dee*

NOTE: Some of the ages listed here vary from the ages given in the text because the quotations and stories cited in the text were collected after the initial interview. The individuals listed are specifically quoted in the text; however, this is not a complete list of all *toms* and *dees* included in the research for this book. Most of the individuals were interviewed in Bangkok.

NOTES

INTRODUCTION

1. Although derived from English terms, *"tom"* and *"dee"* have uniquely Thai meanings and refer to a Thai cultural category of female transgender/homosexual identity. I thus have chosen to italicize these terms and other borrowed English terms to indicate their Thai meaning. Although I am using the Haas transcription system, in which the vowel sound of the long "e" as found in the word "see" is transcribed as double "i," I have chosen here to spell the word *"dee"* with a double "e" (rather than the Haas spelling as "dii"), which is the usual spelling of this Thai word in English. The word *"tom"* would be spelled as *"thom"* within the Haas system, leading to common mispronunciations by English readers, so I have chosen to use the common spelling, *"tom."*

2. Peter Jackson (1996b, 1997b) has reviewed the development of Thai vocabulary for sexual and gender categories. Many of these terms are derived from English words that are fit into the Thai context, such as "gay king" and "gay queen," reflecting binary gender distinctions within a couple.

3. The term "sex" in English also has a range of meanings and ambiguities. Originally, "sex," like *"pheet,"* referred to a distinction between men and women and only later came to refer to particular acts. See Raymond Williams (1976, 283–286) for a history of the term "sex" in English. "Gender" is a recent term brought into social sciences and feminism to make distinctions between biological and cultural factors that define the categories "man" and "woman."

4. My thanks to Peter Jackson for this interpretation of *"kathoey"* plants and animals.

5. At a talk at Thammasat University in November 2000, Peter Jackson said he could find no reference to males living cross-dressed lifestyles, or *kathoeys*, in the historical record of Siam before this century. Jackson suggested that although the notion of *kathoey* has a long history in Thailand, the lived identity of *kathoey* has perhaps been an unintended by-product of the efforts of the Thai state to develop a "modern" (meaning Western) gender system. Jackson tentatively postulated that exaggerated femininity and its expression through strictly segregated systems of dress are impositions of westernizing Thai governments and have allowed the expression of *kathoey* to be formed.

6. My thanks go to Peter Jackson for clarifying this point that the visibility of *kathoeys* does not mean that gay men are visible. On the contrary, gay men are perhaps the most invisible of the Thai sex/gender subcultures, because

of their normative gender and their rejection of the obvious masculine-feminine pairings that characterize *kathoey* and *tom-dee* subcultures.

7. See J. Bao (1998) for an analysis of gender dynamics in Sino-Thai families.

8. According to Keyes (1987), approximately 95 percent of the population practice Buddhism.

9. About 10 percent of the urban population is of Chinese descent (Keyes 1987, 16). Wyatt (1982, 292) notes that calculating exact numbers of Chinese or Sino-Thais is difficult because of the high rates of Chinese assimilation into Thai society; the descendants of Chinese immigrants increasingly have Thai citizenship, speak Thai as their first language, marry Thais, and have assimilated mainstream Thai cultural practices.

10. See Whittaker (1999) and Lyttleton (1999) for a discussion of the historical shifts in brideprice practices among northeastern villagers. In particular, they discuss the increasing commodification of sexual relations among villagers within the capitalist economy.

11. The high value of light skin tone is reinforced by the relative high status granted to European-looking people because of their association with prosperity, power, and modernity.

12. Possible references for this insight are too extensive to give a comprehensive list. Important works on the topic of cross-cultural gender and sexual variation include Blackwood (1984), Ginsburg and Rapp (1995), S. Murray and Roscoe (1998), Ortner and Whitehead (1981), Rapp (1975), and Rosaldo and Lamphere (1974).

13. For histories of sexual practices, see, for example, Duberman, Vicinus, and Chauncey (1989); Faderman (1981, 1991); Herdt (1993); and Miller (1995). The work of Jacques Lacan is popular with scholars concerned with the origins of gender identity; see Judith Butler (1990, 1993).

14. "Sambia" is a pseudonym given to the cultural group to preserve anonymity (Herdt and Stoller 1990, xvi).

15. See Curran (1994) and Muscat (1994) for discussion of migration in Thailand.

16. Classes in general, and middle classes in particular, are notoriously difficult to quantify, because they can encompass a range of contradictory features, such as high education, low income, self-employment, and wage work. Max Weber has added to Karl Marx's economic theory of class the concepts of status groups, prestige systems, lifestyles, and culturally embedded values. Weber also considered noneconomic sources of power, such as holding positions in the bureaucracy, to be important factors in determining social position. Pierre Bourdieu has further extended the concept of class to measure individuals' relation to social, symbolic, cultural, and economic capital in a kind of all-encompassing scheme of social categorization. In recognition of these complex ways of labeling class position, I have tried to form loose categories of working class, middle class, and upper class—

based on a general schema of education, profession and employment, and income—to label individuals, with the knowledge that these labels are not airtight absolute categories. See Coser (1977) and Bourdieu (1977, 1990) for analysis of status and class.

17. See Mary R. Haas' *Thai-English Student's Dictionary* (1964) for a complete explanation of the transcription of Thai into romanized letters, upon which the system used here is based. Because of Haas' use of linguistic symbols to represent some vowel sounds, it has been necessary to make some modifications to her system for the sake of publication.

1. GLOBAL SEX

1. It is awkward to refer to "Thai" culture in the premodern period, because the term stems from nation building in the twentieth century. See Winichakul (1994) for discussion of the construction of "Thai" identity. However, the term is used here as shorthand to refer to the ethnically mixed culture that provided a mythological and intellectual heritage evident, to a debatable degree, in present-day Thailand.

2. For a comparative attitude toward marriage by a gay African man, see Stephen O. Murray (1998). See also Donald Donham's work (1998) on the construction of gay identity in South Africa for another interesting study of the confluence of transnational and local meanings.

3. See also O. Lewis (1941) for an account of "manly-hearted women," or berdaches, in a native North American cultural group, the North Piegan.

4. These groups are too numerous to list here; see Blackwood (1984) for a complete list of cultural groups for which there are historical references to female berdaches.

5. See also Devereux (1937), Lang (1999), Roscoe (1988, 1991, 1993), Whitehead (1993), and W. Williams (1986a, 1986b) for further discussion of North American berdache traditions.

6. See Kendall (1999) for a similar point that sexuality is not necessarily indicative of an identity.

7. For examples of the use of the term "transgender" to refer to pre- or postoperative transsexuals, cross-dressers, and individuals with a transgender identity who do not desire surgical reassignment, browse Web sites of support groups for transgendered people (mostly extensions of American-based support groups and organizations). Some of these groups make a distinction between the categories of transsexual, transvestite, and transgender, for example, and others use the term "transgender" as an overarching category. Some groups deliberately reject subcategories, such as transsexual and transvestite, in order to avoid the divisive effects of these separate labels, and such groups may even include gays and lesbians as their target population. In general, the term "transgender" is widely used

in the West as a popular alternative to the more clinical-sounding terms of these subcategories. Explanations of psychological and medical terminology to define and describe different terms, such as "homosexual" and "transvestite," were once widely provided by Western homosexual activists and academics to fight common stereotypes about the supposed gender deviance of gays and lesbians. It seems that this trend is reversing itself in the sense that inclusiveness is currently being promoted by activists who believe that all these groups, however they are labeled, share common ground politically and experience common problems that are best addressed by a unified collective.

2. GENDER AND SEXUAL TRANSITIONS

1. *"Len"* means "to play," and *"pheuan"* means "friend." *"Kap,"* meaning "with," has been dropped from this expression, as is common in Thai phrasing, leaving just "play friends." As a result, the phrase *"len kap pheuan"* retains the meaning of "play with friends," whereas the phrase *"len pheuan"* has become a specific reference to lesbian sex. (My thanks to Peter Jackson for this clarification.) Wieringa (1999, 216) describes similar practices in the royal courts of what is now Indonesia (Surakarta and Yogyakarta), where female soldiers dressed as men, according to nineteenth-century accounts. Early twentieth-century accounts of Indonesian cultures describe the presence of both masculine women and feminine men. For additional discussion of *len pheuan,* see Anjaree (1995); Suphot (1989); and Thammakiat (1994).

2. Kittisak (1993) notes that in the Thai context the regulation of concubines has led to more historical references to female same-sex sexuality than to male same-sex sexuality, which was not regulated by law. Many Western countries, in contrast, have historical records of male same-sex sexuality because of legal prosecution of male homosexuality, while female homosexuality is largely absent from those historical sources.

3. The Department of Fine Arts published a version of the poem to commemorate the renovation of the temple Theepthidaram in 1964, entitled *Klorn pleeng yaaw reuang Morm Pet Sawan lae phra-akarn prachuan khorng Krom Meuan Apsornsudatheep* (The epic poem of Morm Pet Sawan and the symptoms of illness of Krom Meuan Apsornsudatheep). I gloss the title as simply *Morm Pet Sawan* in the text for simplicity. In a foreword to the publication, the Department of Fine Arts states that the temple was built by the princess. According to the temple's deputy abbot, Phra Sunthorn Kitkoson, who also wrote a foreword, the temple was built by Rama III and bestowed upon his daughter, the princess, when her royal title was conferred.

4. See Anake (1999, chapters 2–3) for a detailed description of the poem.

5. Page numbers in this paragraph refer to *The Epic Poem of Morm Pet Sawan,* cited in note 3.

6. The terms "female" and "male" refer to the biological classification of individuals, whereas "man" and "woman" refer to a socially ascribed identity based on classifications of masculinity and femininity. Thus, technically, it is contradictory to use the phrase "masculine women," and I have attempted to avoid such terminology throughout this work. However, referring to these individuals as "females" throughout the text seems to me disrespectful, as it rings of an almost zoological classification. Therefore, I refer to these individuals as "women," but it must be kept in mind that they have an ambiguous gender identity in which their masculinity and femaleness are both recognized. Also, the word used in Thai is *"phu-ying,"* which can be translated as either "woman" or "female."

7. See the chapter "Crisis in Wifedom" in Loos (n.d.b) for a study of the historical emergence of regulated marriage in Thailand.

8. Amory (1998, 71–72) includes a discussion of "rituals of inversion" in which men and women cross-dress in spirit-possession experiences and festivals in Africa.

9. *Phraratchakamnot laksana khomkhuen luangprawenii* (The royal enactment against rape and indecent assault) dates to 1898, or R.S. 118 in the Chakri dynastic dating system.

10. The first sodomy law in Siam was part of the 1898 provisional penal code, and the second law was part of the official Penal Code released in 1908. See Loos (1999) for a detailed discussion of these legal reforms and the politics of translation of legal terms. Also see Loos (1999, 124) for a discussion of the 1908 sodomy law as part of the section of the Penal Code entitled "Offenses against Public Morals."

11. Kittisak (1993) cites *Yut Saeng-uthai, Kotmaay ayaa phaak plai* (Final version of criminal law), 1947 [2490], p. 179, even though this work is dated seven years before the law was repealed.

12. See Barmé (2002), especially chapter 7, "Bourgeois Love and Morality: Gender Relations Redefined," which discusses the production of discourses of sexual morality that corresponded to the emergence of the Thai middle class.

13. See Mills (1993), appendix A, for a review of Thai migration studies.

14. See Phongpaichit and Baker's dramatic chart (1994, 114) on declining numbers of women in the upper echelons of the bureaucracy—a phenomenon the authors dub "the teak ceiling."

15. In the traditional practice of wealthy men, both Thai and Chinese, taking numerous wives, the first, primary wife is referred to as *mia-luang,* and other wives taken later are referred to as *mia-noi.* Laws against polygyny were enacted in the 1930s in Thailand, but Thai and Sino-Thai men still widely follow the practice of taking unofficial minor wives as demonstrations of wealth and status.

16. The expression "to wash the cock's face" *(lang naa kai)* refers to the belief that washing the face of a fighting cock in the morning will make it alert and ready to fight. The expression is sometimes used as a sexual joke to refer to early-morning sex, in which "cock" in Thai has the same double meaning that it does in English, referring to both a rooster and a man's penis. When Khaek used this expression, I interpreted her as saying that she had sex in the morning to feel awake and refreshed, and also poking fun of herself because she obviously does not have a "cock."

17. The data for women are an inversion of data for males, indicating that the lower the education of males, the greater the chance they will remain unmarried.

18. Comparative rates are from a seminar held by the Institute for Population and Social Research, Mahidol University, reported in *Thai Rath,* April 7, 1998, 1, 9.

19. See Rabibhadana (1984) and Tantiwiramanond and Pandey (1987) for reviews of kinship organization and marriage patterns in Thailand.

20. George Chauncey's study (1994) of the development of gay male society in New York City between 1890 and 1940 asserts that gay identity was a stable and vibrant entity before the social transformations of World War II. Chauncey also links the development of gay identity and communities to the urban environment and the space it provides for developing homosexual identities and relationships that are not possible in smaller communities. New York was a home of migrants in the early part of the century—men and women alone in an urban environment away from their home communities and families. Randolph Trumbach (1993) discusses communities of men and women who were transgendered and/or homosexual in the eighteenth century in London, supporting Chauncey's conclusion that the growth of urban areas is linked to the development of transgender/homosexual communities and identities.

3. GENDER AMBIVALENCE IN *TOM* AND *DEE* IDENTITIES

1. Jackson (1995, 54–56) cites a study of Thai attitudes toward sex, in which female homosexual acts were rarely considered to be "sex." Male-male sex acts were more often seen as "sex," but heterosexual intercourse was overwhelmingly the predominant concept of what constituted "sexual" acts.

2. The word *"sia"* here is pronounced with a low tone, rather than with the rising tone used in the term that means "losing virginity"—*"sia-tua."*

3. Ara Wilson (1997, 138) makes the same point about *kathoey* identity: "The role [of *kathoey*] is associated with women but not equated completely with born-female women. . . . To my observations, while *kathoey* perform Thai femininity, they do not typically adopt the social restrictions

and weightier familial obligations of those born-female women (including *tom*). Rather, the *kathoey* enjoy the social license for mobility and sexuality accorded to men."

4. The self-denial and sense of tragedy expressed by *tom*s bear close resemblance to a description in Radclyffe Hall's classic lesbian novel, *The Well of Loneliness* (1928). In this novel, the main character, Stephen, is a woman described as a gender "invert," or a man trapped in a woman's body. In the end, Stephen is resigned to giving up her lover, Mary, so that Mary can marry a man and lead a "normal" life. This novel has had a tremendous influence on Western lesbians, who for most of the twentieth century had little to read about a kind of lesbianism that they could relate to. See Newton (1984) for a description of the effect the book had on American lesbians.

5. Seri did not use the word "gay" here. He used the term "to be" *(pen)*, implying "homosexual." The word "gay" is used to refer to male homosexuals, whether they are feminine or masculine identified.

6. The debate over whether homosexuality is an inborn trait or a learned behavior can be dated to the work of sexologists Magnus Hirschfeld and Havelock Ellis. The idea that homosexuality is caused by a gene or other biological factors has gained a resurgence of interest in the past decade due to several scientific studies (such as the research of Simon LeVay, Michael Bailey and Richard Pillard, and Dean Hamer). The argument that homosexuality is an inborn trait has been used, both by the earlier sexologists and current gay rights activists, to suggest that homosexuality is a natural phenomenon and should be accepted as such. The position that homosexuality is a "choice" has led anti-gay/homosexual groups to argue that homosexuality is a failure of will and is a behavior that can and should be changed. The position that homosexuality is inborn has been used to challenge anti-gay/homosexual groups' assertions that homosexuals will be able to "corrupt" and "convert" others to being homosexual. Other gay and lesbian rights activists, particularly feminists, have argued against the idea that homosexuality is inborn, saying that sexuality is embedded in social relationships, politics, and personal experience and cannot be reduced to a gene. Choice, they argue, is the principle for which gay and lesbian groups should be fighting. For samples of this lively and heated debate, see Stein (1992) and http://www.pbs.org/wgbh/pages/frontline/shows/assault/genetics/.

7. My thanks to Matthana Chetamee for this information.

8. See note 1.

9. Dildos, like pornography, are illegal in Thailand. Pornography is widely available at vending booths and, like copied software and music cassettes or fake brand-name products, is subject to periodic crackdowns and confiscation by the police. Dildos are harder to find, and the quality is report-

edly poor. Shopping for dildos or other sex toys is embarrassing for most women. *Toms* prefer to construct their own dildos. The high-quality dildos available abroad are frequently sought after by local *toms*.

10. Streets in Thailand, rather than being arranged in grids, are arranged so that small lanes branch off of main streets, and the point where the lane meets the main street is called its mouth.

4. THAI NORMS OF GENDER AND SEXUALITY

1. See Mills (1995) for a discussion of the representations of female sexuality as threatening and dangerous, evident in popular beliefs in predatory and fierce female ghosts.

2. Pregnant girls or women are expelled from school, including universities.

3. Sex with a man is commonly referred to as *dai-sia*, where men "get" *(dai)* and women "lose" *(sia)*.

4. For example, see "Klua thuuk traa-naa pen phu-ying phua thing" (Fear of being labeled an abandoned wife), *Nation Weekly*, June 10–16, 1999, 57.

5. For example, one survey revealed that, of almost three thousand men and women questioned, only 7.4 percent of men and 7.0 percent of women considered caressing between females to be "sex," whereas 19.4 percent of men and 24.9 percent of women considered the same acts between men and women to be "sex" (Wiresit et al. 1991, cited in Jackson 1995, 55).

6. See Thaweesit (2000) for a review of dominant Thai discourses of female sexuality.

7. My Thai graduate students also repeated this platitude that commercial sex work was necessary to prevent "good" women from being raped.

8. Kasem Adchasai, "Of Love, Lust, and Human Nature," *The Nation*, April 21, 1997, C1.

9. See N. Ford and Kittisuksathit (1996) for summary of sexual and gender attitudes.

10. Esther Newton (1984) reports that Victorian sexual ideology promoted similar attitudes toward women's sexuality. Women were held to be properly asexual and passive recipients of male sexual energy, and those women who demonstrated otherwise were condemned.

11. See Bongkot (1990) for a description of Thai gender norms as represented in Thai films.

12. See Russo (1987) for a history of Hollywood attitudes toward homosexuality. See also Newton (2000, 34–62) for a history of gays in the theater.

13. Academic studies of transgendered males in other societies provide a similar interpretation. For example, Lancaster (1995, 139) describes the stigma attached to male homosexuality in Nicaraguan society, saying that this stigma reinforces the idea that men need to adhere to culturally prescribed "machismo," such as aggressiveness and domination of women, or else

these men would be denied masculine status. Lancaster argues that gender is structured not only as oppositions between men and women but also, and perhaps more importantly, within gender categories themselves, by using the image of the "queer" to condemn and threaten other men in competitive acquisitions of masculine status. Jackson (1995) also argues that masculinity in Thailand is defined more in terms of relationships between men than relationships between men and women. Likewise, Robert Levy's classic psychological study (1973) on Tahitian society gives a similar account of the "function" of transgendered males *(māhū)*; they define proper masculinity by performing its inversion.

14. This quotation and the remaining quotations in this paragraph are from interviews I conducted.

15. Ing distinguished between her "inside grandchild" *(laan nai)* and her "outside grandchild" *(laan nork)*. "Inside grandchild" means the child of her daughter, whereas "outside grandchild" refers to the child of her son. In rural kinship structure a child of a daughter is often seen as a closer relative than a child of a son.

16. See "Wattanatham thai? Luuk-sao-haa-ngern, luuk-chai-chai-ngern" (Thai culture? Daughters make money, sons spend money) (1994). See also Sobieszcyk (2000) for discussion of the reintegration of sex workers into village life.

17. My thanks to Sulaiporn Chonwilai for providing this interview.

18. "Thuuk saew pen thom sao sii 6 doot nam taai" (Taunted for being a *tom*: Level 6 bureaucrat drowns herself), *Thai Rath*, July 17, 1996, 1, 23; "Tom sao prinyaa thoo khaa tua taai prachoot yaat" (*Tom* master's degree student kills herself to spite relatives), *Thai Rath*, August 30, 1995, 1, 22.

19. "Playing cymbals" *(tii ching)* is Thai slang for the lesbian sex act of tribadism, or "friction," in which women rub their genitals together. Interestingly, in the Philippines, sex between two feminine-identified men is called "playing cymbals" *(pompyangan)* (M. Tan 1995, 92).

20. Dr. Nopphorn, "Seep-som bor mi' som" (Sex without satisfaction), *Daily News*, December 23, 1994.

5. GENDER DYNAMICS BETWEEN *TOM* AND *DEE*

1. Marin (1996, 54) explains that the term *"mars"* is derived from the Spanish word *"madre"* (mother), and the term *"pars"* from the Spanish word *"padre"* (father).

2. Masculine women's untouchability is a phenomenon found in many lesbian communities throughout the world that have established gender identities, including the United States in the middle part of the twentieth century and in other Southeast Asian societies (see, e.g., Faderman 1991; Kennedy and Davis 1993; and Reinfelder 1996).

3. When I say "negotiated," I am referring to Ginsburg and Tsing's definition of "negotiating gender" (1990, 2): "how gendered terms and social relations are debated and redefined by people pursuing particular and often conflicting interests—as in negotiating a deal; and, [how] women and men [struggle] with the ideas and institutions with which they live—as in negotiating a river."

4. See Laclau and Mouffe (1985) for a review of the development of Antonio Gramsci's concept of hegemony. For a review of critical theory and its origins in the Frankfurt School of cultural studies, see Calhoun (1995). For examples of cultural studies in which the concept of hegemony is explored, see Hebdige (1979), Nelson and Grossberg (1988), and R. Williams (1977).

5. The problematic contradictions between official discourses and actual behavior have been a central theme in recent work by scholars of homosexuality cross-culturally. For example, Deborah Amory (1998) and Rudolf Gaudio (1998) have analyzed the contradictions between official gender and sexual ideology and lived social practice of transgendered men in East Africa and West Africa, respectively.

6. I have numbered the members who responded, in order to distinguish between different respondents to any given question, but these numbers do not correspond to member numbers given for other questions.

7. The newspapers periodically carry stories of *tom*s and *kathoey*s who have killed themselves because of being "teased" over their sexuality/identity.

8. See the introduction for a discussion of tolerance regarding *tom*s and *dee*s in Thai society. Also see Peter Jackson's discussion (1999b) of the difference between "tolerance" and "acceptance" in consideration of Thai attitudes toward homosexuality. Jackson says that although Thai society is "tolerant," meaning there is room to be gay, *tom,* or *dee* without overt repression, these are still considered to be negative qualities, and most Thai parents would not want their children to be gay, *tom,* or *dee.*

9. In Thailand, a reptile is thought of as the lowest form of animal, and calling somebody a reptile implies that they are lowly and disgusting.

10. I assume the law in question concerned a man having sex with an under-aged woman, without her parents' permission.

6. *TOM* AND *DEE* COMMUNITIES AND ORGANIZATIONS

1. I searched for an English equivalent for the word used in the chant—"*cae,*" a cute term for female genitalia that can be used with children. The sexual connotation in this case is obvious, but the word is still silly and childlike.

7. DISCOURSES OF "HOMOSEXUALITY"

1. I have enclosed the word "homosexuality" in quotation marks when referring to its distinctly Thai meaning.

2. See Bowie (1997) for a discussion of the effects of state factions in recent Thai history.

3. See Thongchai Winichakul (1994, 2000) for discussions of the historical emergence of Thai national subjectivity and the use of negative identification (the "non-self") in the construction of Thai identity. For an enlightening discussion of this discursive process of construction of self through images of the non-self, see Toni Morrison (1993), who argues that images of the black other are an integral part of the classic American literary tradition, because the nonfree, nonempowered, and nonidentified figure is necessary in order to identify the "American" self as autonomous and individualistic. Morrison writes: "There was a resident population . . . upon which the imagination could play; through which historical, moral, metaphysical, and social fears, problems, and dichotomies could be articulated" (1993, 37). Like the image of homosexuality in Thai discourse, the black figure had no constant meaning but could be contorted to meet the changing needs of the discourse of self.

4. Although several of the Thai academics whose studies on homosexuality I reviewed were aware that Western academics and psychological associations no longer officially considered homosexuality to be a pathology, they interpreted the information so as to simply relabel homosexuality as another kind of illness. For example, Nunthirat (1989, 36) says that homosexuality was considered a "sexual perversion" but has since been relabeled as a "sexual orientation disturbance" and finally a "homosexual conflict disorder." The original intent of these categorizations in the Western psychological field was to indicate that a person's response to being homosexual could cause anxiety, not that homosexuality in itself was a disorder.

5. See Mosse (1985) for a discussion of the importance of sexual "respectability" for middle-class political aspirations in Europe.

6. For one example, among many possible, see *Matichon,* January 9, 1996, 69, which cites academic research that homosexuality is caused by poor family structure, the media, and lack of opportunity to meet and socialize with the opposite sex. Also, I placed quotation marks around the word "traditional" as it applies to segregated schooling, because separate schools for girls date from late nineteenth century and early twentieth century and were considered rather radical and progressive at the time (see Barmé 2002).

7. "N.ph m.l. somchai cakraphan naai-yok sa-maa-khom cit-ta-pheat morng pay nai look kwang rak-ruam-pheet mai chai rook" (Dr. Morm Luang Somchai Cakraphan takes a broad view that homosexuality is not a disease), *Matichon,* January 30, 1997, 9.

8. Chalidaporn was referring to a ban on short skirts for female students by Chulalongkorn University in January 1998. Interestingly, a poll conducted showed that many students agreed that women should not wear short

skirts to the university, but they also thought the ban was an infringement on individual rights (*Bangkok Post*, February 1, 1998). This common attitude that the behavior is wrong but should not be regulated by the government is strikingly similar to the ban on homosexual students by Ratchabhat Institute. Many people agreed that homosexuals should not be teachers but resented the ban on students as an infringement of rights.

9. See Loos (1999, chapter 2) for a discussion of the monarchial construction of a "traditional" Siamese order against which legal reforms could be justified.

10. In December 1996 a male student at Chiang Mai University killed and dismembered a female student. The male student was a *kathoey,* and the female student was a *tom.* Apparently they had argued over the *tom*'s returning money to the *kathoey,* who had killed the *tom* in a rage. The story was covered with sensational headlines, such as these rather wordy examples: "Faa-hua-cai n.s. 'tut tha-min' kha harn sop satharn meuang n.s. sao than-ta-phaet 'm.ch.' satheuan khwan thang mahalai" (Getting at the heart of how a vicious *tut* [derogatory term for feminine homosexual male] shocks the city by killing and chopping up the body of a female dentistry student at Chiang Mai University, shaking the morale of the whole university), *Matichon,* December 24, 1996, 88; and "'Tut tha-min' tham phaen kha chae nathi thup harn sop" (Vicious *tut* reenacts killing and dismemberment of body), *Khao Sot,* December 22, 1996.

11. There were notable exceptions to the general media homophobia, such as Pranee Srikamnert's articles for *Krungthep Thurakij.*

12. "Gay v.s. sathaban rachaphat: mum-morng cark cita-phaet" (Gay vs. Ratchabhat Institute: The perspective of a psychologist), *Matichon Daily,* January 31, 1997, 12.

13. Mark Johnson (1997, 229) notes the same argument made in the Philippine context.

14. The newspapers included *Khao Sot, Matichon, Daily News, Bangkok Post, The Nation, Siam Post, Krungthep Thurakij,* and *Chiwit Tongsu.* I also interviewed academics who had written about the case and DJs at a popular radio station that covered the Ratchabhat case.

CONCLUSION

1. Mark Johnson (1997, 183) explains the incorporation of gay identity into local Philippine meanings: "The appropriation of the term *gay* and the identification with an imagined *gay* universe signal their own transgenderal projects, projects which are informed less by contemporary Western homosocialities than by local sensibilities about love, kinship, gender and gifting relationships."

2. See van der Meer (1993) for a review of such cases in Europe.

3. See Sinnott (2000) for a review of the case of the member of Parliament and other cases like it.

4. For more information on the sex scandal involving Deputy Senate Speaker Chalerm Promlert, search the *Bangkok Post* archives (http://www .bangkokpost.com) for the following dates in 2001: January 24–28; February 1, 10, 16, and 22; March 12, 14, and 22; and April 29.

GLOSSARY

biang-been-thaang-pheet—sexual/gender deviance

kathoey—transgender (usually male); something in between or of an uniden-
tifiable category or mixed category; infertile plant or animal

khon rak-ruam-pheet—homosexual

kunlasatri—woman of good birth and breeding; ladylike, properly feminine

lakkapheet—transvestite/transgender; to steal another's *pheet* (sex/gender)

pheet—sex/gender

pheet-thii-saam—third sex/gender

phit-pheet—mis-gendered/sexed; sexually deviant; gender deviant

phom—masculine pronoun "I"

rak-ruam-pheet—homosexuality

wiparit—perverted, sexually perverse

ying-rak-ying—woman loving woman; women who love women

BIBLIOGRAPHY

Aarmo, Margrete. 1999. "How Homosexuality Became 'Un-African': The Case of Zimbabwe." In Blackwood and Wieringa 1999, 255–280.

Abelove, Henry, Michèle Aina Barale, and David Halperin, eds. 1993. *The Lesbian and Gay Studies Reader*. New York: Routledge.

Abu-Lughod, Lila. 1990. "The Romance of Resistance: Tracing Transformations of Power through Bedouin Women." *American Ethnologist* 17(1): 41–55.

———. 1991. "Writing against Culture." In Fox 1991, 137–162.

Adam, Barry D. 1986. "Age, Structure, and Sexuality: Reflections on the Anthropological Evidence on Homosexual Relations." In Blackwood 1986b, 19–33.

———. 1993. "In Nicaragua: Homosexuality without a Gay World." *Journal of Homosexuality* 24(3/4): 171–181.

Allyn, Eric. 1991. *Trees in the Same Forest: Thailand's Culture and Gay Subculture*. Bangkok: Bua Luang.

———. 1992. *The Dove Coos: Gay Experiences by the Men of Thailand*. Bangkok: Bua Luang.

Alter, Joseph S. 1993. "Celibacy, Sexuality, and the Transformation of Gender into Nationalism in North India." Paper presented at the Dimensions of Ethnic and Cultural Nationalism in Asia Conference, sponsored by the University of Wisconsin and Marquette University's Center for International Studies, February.

Altman, Dennis. 1996a. On "Global Queering." *Australian Humanities Review*, no. 2 (July–August). http://www.lib.latrobe.edu.au/AHR/archive/Issue-July-1996/altman.html.

———. 1996b. "Rupture or Continuity? The Internationalization of Gay Identities." *Social Text* 14(3): 77–94.

Amory, Deborah. 1998. "*Mashoga, Mabasha,* and *Magai*: 'Homosexuality' on the East African Coast." In Murray and Roscoe 1998, 67–87.

Amphorn Ratniwit. 1982. "Khwam-ma-hat-sa-caan khorng ror-chak phaap 3 nai homosexual" (The miracle of the Rorschach: The third picture of homosexuals). *Warasaan cit-tha-withaya khlinik* (Journal of clinical psychology) 13(1) (June): 37–44.

Anake Nawigamune. 1999. *Ying chao-siam* (Siamese women). Bangkok: Saengdaaw Publishers.

Anderson, Benedict. 1977. "Withdrawal Symptoms: Social and Cultural Aspects of the October 6 Coup." *Bulletin of Concerned Asian Scholars* 9(3): 13–30.

———. 1983. *Imagined Communities: Reflections on the Origin and Spread of Nationalism*. London: Verso.

———. 1998. *The Spectre of Comparisons: Nationalism, Southeast Asia, and the World*. New York: Verso.

Anjana Suvarnananda. 1984. "Rak prapheet sorng: Theu phit reu mai" (The second kind of love: Is she wrong?). *Satrithat* 2(1) (February–May): 33–41.

Anjaree. 1995. "Len pheuan." *Freestyles Magazine* 1(1) (June).

Araya Thongphew, M.D. 1978. "Krathoey-thae reu thiam" (*Kathoey*—real or fake). *Klai-mor* (April 2): 23–26.

Arnold, Fred, and Susan Cochrane. 1980. "Economic Motivation versus City Lights: Testing Hypotheses about Inter-Changwat Migration in Thailand." World Bank Staff Working Paper no. 416, Washington, D.C.

Atkinson, J. M., and S. Errington, eds. 1990. *Power and Difference: Gender in Island Southeast Asia*. Stanford, Calif.: Stanford University Press.

Bakhtin, Mikhail Mikhailovich. 1981. *The Dialogic Imagination: Four Essays*. Ed. Michael Holquist; trans. Caryl Emerson and Michael Holquist. Austin: University of Texas Press.

Bao, Daniel. 1993. "Invertidos Sexuales, Tortilleras, and Maricas Machos: The Construction of Homosexuality in Buenos Aires, Argentina, 1900–1950." *Journal of Homosexuality* 24(3/4): 183–219.

Bao, Jiemen. 1998. "Same Bed, Different Dreams: Intersections of Ethnicity, Gender, and Sexuality among Middle- and Upper-Class Chinese Immigrants in Bangkok." *Positions* 6(2): 476–502.

Barmé, Scot. 2002. *Woman, Man, Bangkok: Love, Sex, and Popular Culture in Thailand*. New York: Rowman and Littlefield.

Behar, Ruth, and Deborah A. Gordon, eds. 1995. *Women Writing Culture*. Berkeley and Los Angeles: University of California Press.

Benedict, Ruth. 1934. *Patterns of Culture*. Boston: Houghton Mifflin.

———. 1939. "Sex in Primitive Society." *American Journal of Orthopsychiatry* 9(3): 570–573.

Benstock, Shari. 1986. *Women of the Left Bank*. Austin: University of Texas Press.

Besnier, Niko. 1993. "Polynesian Gender Liminality through Space and Time." In Herdt 1993, 285–328.

———. 2002. "Transgenderism, Locality, and the Miss Galaxy Beauty Pageant in Tonga." *American Ethnologist* 29(3): 534–566.

Bhabha, Homi K. 1994. *The Location of Culture*. New York: Routledge.

Bishop, Ryan, and Lillian Robinson. 1998. *Night Market: Sexual Cultures and the Thai Economic Miracle*. New York: Routledge.

Blackwood, Evelyn. 1984. "Sexuality and Gender in Certain Native American Tribes: The Case of Cross-Gender Females." *Signs* 10(1): 27–42.

———. 1986a. "Breaking the Mirror: The Construction of Lesbianism and the Anthropological Discourse on Homosexuality." In Blackwood 1986b, 1–18.

———. 1995. "Falling in Love with An-Other Lesbian: Reflections on Identity in Fieldwork." In Kulick and Willson 1995, 51–75.

———. 1999. "*Tombois* in West Sumatra: Constructing Masculinity and Erotic Desire." In Blackwood and Wieringa 1999, 181–205.

————, ed. 1986b. *Anthropology and Homosexual Behavior*. New York: Haworth.

Blackwood, Evelyn, and Saskia E. Wieringa, eds. 1999. *Female Desires: Same-Sex Relations and Transgender Practices across Cultures*. New York: Columbia University Press.

Bleibtreu-Ehrenberg, Gisela. 1990. "Pederasty among Primitives: Institutionalized Initiation and Cultic Prostitution." *Journal of Homosexuality* 20(1/2): 13–30.

Boellstorff, Tom. 1999. "The Perfect Path: Gay Men, Marriage, Indonesia." *GLQ: Journal of Gay and Lesbian Studies* 5(4): 475–510.

Bolin, Anne. 1993. "Transcending and Transgendering: Male to Female Transsexuals, Dichotomy and Diversity." In Herdt 1993, 447–485.

Bongkot Sewatarmra. 1990. "Karn-sang khwam-pen-cing-thang-sangkhom khorng phaphayon thai: Koranii tua-lakhorn-ying thii mii laksana biang-been pii ph.s. 2538–3530" (Social construction of reality in Thai film: Unconventional female characters in 1985–1987). Master's thesis, Chulalongkorn University, Bangkok.

Bongkotmas Ekiam. 1989. "Gay: Krabuan-karn phathanaa lae thamrong ekalak rak-ruam-pheet" (Gay: The development and maintenance process of a homosexual identity). Master's thesis, Thammasat University, Thailand.

Boonchalaksi, Wathinee, and Philip Guest. 1994. *Prostitution in Thailand*. Salaya, Nakornpathom, Thailand: Institute for Population and Social Research, Mahidol University.

Boserup, Ester. 1970. *Women's Role in Economic Development*. New York: St. Martin's Press.

Bourdieu, Pierre. 1977. *Outline of a Theory of Practice*. Trans. R. Nice. Cambridge: Cambridge University Press.

————. 1990. *The Logic of Practice*. Stanford, Calif.: Stanford University Press.

Bowie, Katherine. 1997. *Rituals of National Loyalty: An Anthropology of the State and the Village Scout Movement in Thailand*. New York: Columbia University Press.

Bullough, Vern L. 1979. *Homosexuality: A History*. New York: New American Library.

Bumroongsook, Sumalee. 1995. *Love and Marriage: Mate Selection in Twentieth-Century Central Thailand*. Bangkok: Chulalongkorn University Press. *See also* Sumalee Bumroongsook.

Bunmee Metangkul. 1978. "Karn-baeng prapheet khorng krathoey taam thaam" (Categorizing *kathoey* according to the principles of dharma). *Klai-mor* (April 2): 36–38.

Burton, Richard Francis. n.d. *Anthropological Notes on the Sotadic Zone of Sexual Inversion throughout the World*. New York: Falstaff Press.

Butler, Judith. 1990. *Gender Trouble: Feminism and the Subversion of Identity*. New York: Routledge.

————. 1993. *Bodies That Matter: On the Discursive Limits of "Sex."* New York: Routledge.

Calhoun, Craig. 1995. *Critical Social Theory: Culture, History, and Challenge of Difference.* Oxford: Blackwell.

Caplan, Pat, ed. 1987. *The Cultural Construction of Sexuality.* London: Tavistock.

Carrier, Joseph M. 1980. "Homosexual Behavior in Cross-cultural Perspective." In J. Marmor, ed., *Homosexual Behavior: A Modern Reappraisal,* 100–122. New York: Basic Books.

————. 1985. "Mexican Male Bisexuality." *Journal of Homosexuality* 11(1/2): 75–85.

Carrier, Joseph M., and Stephen O. Murray. 1998. "Woman-Woman Marriage in Africa." In Murray and Roscoe 1998, 255–266.

Chaloemtiarana, Thak, ed. 1978. *Thai Politics: Extracts and Documents.* Bangkok: Social Science Association of Thailand.

Chamratrithirong, Aphichat. 1979. *Nuptiality in Thailand: A Cross-Sectional Analysis of the 1970 Census.* Salaya, Nakornpathom, Thailand: Institute for Population and Social Research, Mahidol University.

Chanphen Sængtienchai, Anthony Pramualratana, John Knodel, and Mark VanLandingham. n.d. "Pheet-samphan nork somrot khorng chai-thai nai thatsana khorng phanrayaa" (Extra-marital sex of Thai men from the perspective of their wives). Bangkok: Institute for Population Studies, Chulalongkorn University.

Chanya Sethaput. 1995. "Karn-wicai thii kiao-khorng kap phreuttikam-thaang-pheet nai pratheet thai" (Research concerning sexual behavior in Thailand). Salaya, Nakornpathom, Thailand: Institute for Population and Social Research, Mahidol University.

Chao, Antonia. 1999. "U.S. Space Shuttles Going to the Moon: Global Metaphors and Local Strategies in Building Up Taiwan's Lesbian Identities." Paper presented at the IASSCS Second International Conference, Manchester Metropolitan University, United Kingdom, July.

Chao, Yengning. 1996. "Embodying the Invisible: Body Politics in Constructing Contemporary Taiwanese Lesbian Identities." Ph.D. diss., Cornell University, Ithaca, N.Y.

Chauncey, George. 1994. *Gay New York: Gender, Urban Culture, and the Making of the Gay Male World, 1890–1940.* New York: Basic Books.

Chetamee, Matthana. 1995. "Concepts of the Family and Lesbian Lifestyles in Thailand." Paper presented at the Conference on Gender and Sexuality in Thailand, Canberra, Australia, July.

Chirawatkul, Siriporn. 1992. "The Meaning of Menopause and the Quality of Life of Older Rural Women in Northeast Thailand." In Van Esterik and Van Esterik 1992, 109–132.

Chonticha Salikhub. 1989. "Krabuan-karn phathanaa lae thamrong ekalak khorng ying-rak-ruam-pheet" (The development and maintenance process of lesbian identities). Master's thesis, Thammasat University, Thailand.

Chumsak Preuksaphong, M.D. 1975. "Karn-seuksaa-thaang-cit-tha-withaya nai khon-khai homosexual" (The study of the psychology of homosexual patients). *Warasaan cit-tha-withaya khlinik* (Journal of clinical psychology) 6(1) (May): 1–3.

———. 1978. "Rak-ruam-pheet: Phawa thii sangkhom reum yorm-rap" (Homosexuality: The condition that society is beginning to accept). *Klai-mor* (April 2): 16–18.

Clark, Jeffrey. 1997. "State of Desire: Transformations in Huli Sexuality." In Manderson and Jolly 1997, 191–211.

Cohen, Paul, and Gehan Wijeyewardene, eds. 1984. "Spirit Cults and the Position of Women in Northern Thailand." Special issue, *Mankind* 14(4) (August).

Conners, Michael K. 1997. "When the Dogs Howl: Thailand and the Politics of Democratization." In P. Darby, ed., *At the Edge of International Relations: Postcolonialism, Gender, and Dependency,* 125–147. New York: Pinter.

Copeland, Matthew Phillip. 1994. "Contested Nationalism and the 1932 Overthrow of the Absolute Monarchy in Siam." Ph.D. diss., Australian National University, Canberra.

Cory, D. W., ed. 1956. *Homosexuality: A Cross-cultural Approach.* New York: Julian Press.

Coser, Lewis A. 1977. *Masters of Sociological Thought: Ideas in Historical and Social Context.* New York: Harcourt Brace Jovanovich.

Curran, Sara R. 1994. "Household Resources and Opportunities: The Distribution of Education and Migration in Rural Thailand." Ph.D. diss., University of North Carolina, Chapel Hill.

Cushman, Jennifer W. 1991. *Family and the State: The Formation of a Sino-Thai Tin-Mining Dynasty 1707–1932.* Ed. Craig Reynolds. New York: Oxford University Press.

Dahlgren, Peter, and Colin Sparks, eds. 1992. *Journalism and Popular Culture.* London: Sage Publications.

Dararat Mettarikanond. 1984. "Kotmaai sophenii tii-thabian khrang raek nai pratheet thai" (Prostitution "registration" law: The first time in Thailand). *Sinlapa wattanatham* (Art and culture) 5(5) (March): 6–19.

Davis, D. L., and R. G. Whitten. 1987. "The Cross-Cultural Study of Human Sexuality." *Annual Review of Anthropology* 16: 69–98.

Dekker, Rudolf M. 1989. *The Tradition of Female Transvestism in Early Modern Europe.* New York: St. Martin's Press.

De Lind van Wijngaarden, Jan. 1999. "Between Money, Morality, and Masculinity: Bar-Based Male Sex Work in Chiang Mai." In Jackson and Sullivan 1999, 193–218.

D'Emilio, John. 1983. *Sexual Politics, Sexual Communities: The Making of a*

Homosexual Minority in the United States, 1940–1970. Chicago: University of Chicago Press.

———. 1993. "Capitalism and Gay Identity." In Abelove, Barale, and Halperin 1993, 467–476.

Denny, Dallas. 1998. *Current Concepts in Transgender Identity.* New York: Garland Publishing.

Devereux, George. 1937. "Institutionalized Homosexuality of the Mohave Indians." *Human Biology* 9: 498–527.

Dhiravegin, Likhit. 1986. "Nationalism and the State in Thailand." *Canadian Review of Studies in Nationalism* 13(2): 211–226.

di Leonardo, Micaela, ed. 1991. *Gender at the Crossroads of Knowledge: Feminist Anthropology in the Postmodern Era.* Berkeley and Los Angeles: University of California Press.

Docter, Richard F. 1988. *Transvestites and Transsexuals: Toward a Theory of Cross-Gender Behavior.* New York: Plenum Press.

Donham, Donald. 1998. "Freeing South Africa: The 'Modernization' of Male-Male Sexuality in Soweto." *Cultural Anthropology* 13(1): 3–21.

Donohue, Emma. 1993. *Passions between Women: British Lesbian Culture, 1668–1801.* New York: Harper Collins.

Douglas, Mary. 1969. *Purity and Danger.* London: Routledge and Kegan Paul.

Dowsett, Gary. 1996. "Response to Dennis Altman." *Australian Humanities Review,* no. 2 (July–August). http://www.lib.latrobe.edu.au/AHR/emuse/Globalqueering/dowsett.html.

Duberman, Martin, Martha Vaccines, and George Chauncey, Jr., eds. 1989. *Hidden from History: Reclaiming the Gay and Lesbian Past.* New York: Meridian.

Eberhardt, Nancy, ed. 1988. *Gender, Power, and the Construction of the Moral Order: Studies from the Thai Periphery.* Madison: Center for Southeast Asian Studies, University of Wisconsin.

Edelman, Lee. 1993. "Tearooms and Sympathy, or, The Epistemology of the Water Closet." In Abelove, Barale, and Halperin 1993, 553–574.

Ekachai, Sanitsuda. 1991. "How Did We Get to This State of Affairs?" *Friends of Women Newsletter* 2(1): 16–17.

Ellis, Havelock. 1933. *Psychology of Sex.* New York: Mentor Books.

Elliston, Deborah. 1995. "Erotic Anthropology: 'Ritualized Homosexuality' in Melanesia and Beyond." *American Ethnologist* 22(4): 848–867.

———. 1997. "En/Gendering Nationalism: Colonialism, Sex, and Independence in French Polynesia." Ph.D. diss., New York University.

———. 1999. "Negotiating Transnational Sexual Economies: Female Mahu and Same-Sex Sexuality in Tahiti and Her Islands." In Blackwood and Wieringa 1999, 230–252.

Engels, Frederick. 1972 [1891]. *The Origin of the Family, Private Property, and the State.* Ed. Eleanor Leacock. New York: International Publishers.

Enteen, Jillana. 2001. "Tom, Dii, and *Anjaree:* Women Who Follow Nonconformist Ways." In Hawley 2001, 99–122.

*The Epic Poem of Morm Pet Sawan and the Symptoms of Illness of Krom
Meuan Apsornsudatheep* (Klorn pleeng yaaw reuang Morm Pet Sawan lae
phra-akarn prachuan khorng Krom Meuan Apsornsudatheep). 1964. Published by Siwaphorn Partnership Limited, on the occasion of the Royal
Krathin for the Fine Arts Department, Theepthidaraam Temple, November
6, 1964.

Epps, Brad. 1995. "Proper Conduct: Reinaldo Arenas, Fidel Castro, and the Politics of Homosexuality." *Journal of the History of Sexuality* 6(2): 231–283.

Evans-Pritchard, E. E. 1970. "Sexual Inversion among the Azande." *American
Anthropologist* 72(6): 1428–1434.

Faderman, Lillian. 1981. *Surpassing the Love of Men: Romantic Friendship
and Love between Women from the Renaissance to the Present.* New York:
Quill.

———. 1991. *Odd Girls and Twilight Lovers: A History of Lesbian Life in
Twentieth-Century America.* New York: Penguin.

———. 1992. "The Return of Butch and Femme: A Phenomenon in Lesbian
Sexuality of the 1980s and 1990s." *Journal of the History of Sexuality* 2(4):
578–596.

Fausto-Sterling, Anne. 2000. *Sexing the Body: Gender Politics and the Construction of Sexuality.* New York: Basic Books.

Feinberg, Leslie. 1993. *Stone Butch Blues: A Novel.* Ithaca, N.Y.: Firebrand
Books.

Fiske, John. 1989. *Understanding Popular Culture.* Boston: Unwin Hyman.

———. 1992. "Popularity and the Politics of Information." In Dahlgren and
Sparks 1992, 45–63.

Fitzgerald, Thomas K. 1977. "A Critique of Anthropological Research on
Homosexuality." *Journal of Homosexuality* 2(4): 385–397.

Fongkaew, Warunee. 1997. "Female Sexuality and Reproductive Health in a
Northern Thai Suburb." In Somswasdi and Theobald 1997, 577–620.

Ford, C. S., and F. Beach. 1951. *Patterns of Sexual Behavior.* New York: Harper.

Ford, Nicholas, and Sirinan Kittisuksathit. 1996. *Youth Sexuality: The Sexual
Awareness, Lifestyles, and Related-Health Service Needs of Young, Single,
Factory Workers in Thailand.* Salaya, Nakornpathom, Thailand: Institute
for Population and Social Research, Mahidol University.

Foucault, Michel. 1978. *The History of Sexuality.* Vol. 1. London: Penguin.

———. 1980a. *Herculine Barbin: Being the Recently Discovered Memoirs of
a Nineteenth-Century French Hermaphrodite.* New York: Pantheon Books.

———. 1980b. *Power/Knowledge: Selected Interviews and Other Writings,
1972–1977.* Ed. Collin Gorden. Brighton: Harvester.

Fox, Richard G. 1990. *Nationalist Ideologies and the Production of National
Cultures.* Washington, D.C.: American Anthropological Association.

———, ed. 1991. *Recapturing Anthropology: Working in the Present*. Sante Fe, N.Mex.: School of American Research Press.

"From Gay to *Tom-Dee*: The Bizarre World of Youth" (Caak gay theung tom kap dii: Look phisadaan khorng wai-run). 1984. *Pheuan Chiwit* (Life companion) 2(6) (June): 18–31.

Furth, Charlotte. 1993. "Androgynous Males and Deficient Females: Biology and Gender Boundaries in Sixteenth- and Seventeenth-Century China." In Abelove, Barale, and Halperin 1993, 479–497.

Garber, Eric. 1989. "A Spectacle in Color: The Lesbian and Gay Subculture of Jazz Age Harlem." In Duberman, Vicinus, and Chauncey 1989, 318–331.

Garber, Marjorie. 1993. *Vested Interests: Cross-Dressing and Cultural Anxiety*. New York: Routledge.

———. 1995. *Vice Versa: Bisexuality and the Eroticism of Everyday Life*. New York: Simon and Schuster.

Garcia Canclini, Nestor. 1995. *Hybrid Cultures: Strategies for Entering and Leaving Modernity*. Trans. Christopher L. Chiappari and Silvia L. Lopez. Minneapolis: University of Minnesota Press.

Gaudio, Rudolf. 1998. "Male Lesbians and Other Queer Notions in Hausa." In Murray and Roscoe 1998, 115–128.

Gay, Judith. 1986. "'Mummies and Babies: Friends and Lovers in Lesotho." In Blackwood 1986b, 97–116.

Giddens, Anthony. 1992. *The Transformation of Intimacy: Sexuality, Love, and Eroticism in Modern Societies*. Stanford, Calif.: Stanford University Press.

Ginsburg, Faye D., and Rayna Rapp, eds. 1995. *Conceiving the New World Order: The Global Politics of Reproduction*. Berkeley and Los Angeles: University of California Press.

Ginsburg, Faye D., and Anna Lowenhaupt Tsing, eds. 1990. *Uncertain Terms: Negotiating Gender in American Culture*. Boston: Beacon Press.

Girling, John. 1996. *Interpreting Development: Capitalism, Democracy, and the Middle Class in Thailand*. Ithaca, N.Y.: Southeast Asia Program, Cornell University.

Godelier, Maurice. 1986. *The Making of Great Men: Male Domination and Power among the New Guinea Baruya*. New York: Cambridge University Press.

Goldstein, Donna. 1994. "AIDS and Women in Brazil: The Emerging Problem." *Social Science and Medicine* 39(7): 919–929.

———. 2003. *Laughter Out of Place: Race, Class, Violence, and Sexuality in a Rio Shantytown*. Berkeley and Los Angeles: University of California Press.

Goolsby, Rebecca. 1994. "Women, Work, and Family in a Northeastern Thai Provincial Capital." Ph.D. diss., University of Washington, Seattle.

Grahn, Judy. 1986. "Strange Country This: Lesbianism and North American Indian Tribes." *Journal of Homosexuality* 12(3/4): 43–57.

Green, James N. 1999. *Beyond Carnival: Male Homosexuality in Twentieth Century Brazil.* Chicago: University of Chicago Press.

Gremaux, Rene. 1993. "Woman Becomes Man in the Balkans." In Herdt 1993, 241–281.

Guest, Philip, and Jooean Tan. 1994. *Transformation of Marriage Patterns in Thailand.* Salaya, Nakornpathom, Thailand: Institute for Population and Social Research, Mahidol University.

Gutmann, Matthew C. 1996. *The Meanings of Macho: Being a Man in Mexico City.* Berkeley and Los Angeles: University of California Press.

———. 1997. "Trafficking in Men: The Anthropology of Globalization and Transnationalism." *Annual Review of Anthropology* 26: 385–409.

Guy, Donna. 1991. *Sex and Danger in Buenos Aires: Prostitution, Family, and Nation in Argentina.* Lincoln: University of Nebraska Press.

Haas, Mary R. 1964. *Thai-English Student's Dictionary.* Stanford, Calif.: Stanford University Press.

Halberstam, Judith. 1998. *Female Masculinity.* Durham, N.C.: Duke University Press.

Hale, Ann. 1984. "The Search for a Jural Rule: Women in Southeast Asia—the Northern Thai Cults in Perspective." Special issue, *Mankind* 14(4) (August): 330–338.

Halperin, David M. 1989. *One Hundred Years of Homosexuality and Other Essays on Greek Love.* New York: Routledge.

———. 1997. "A Response from David Halperin to Dennis Altman." *Australian Humanities Review,* no. 2 (July–August). http://www.lib.latrobe.edu.au/AHR/emuse/Globalqueering/halperin.html.

Hamilton, Annette. 1997. "Primal Dream: Masculinism, Sin, and Salvation in Thailand's Sex Trade." In Manderson and Jolly 1997, 145–165.

Hart, Donn V. 1992. "The Cebuano Bayot and Lakin-On." In Murray 1992d, 193–230.

Hawley, John C., ed. 2001. *Postcolonial, Queer: Theoretical Intersections.* Albany: State University of New York.

Hebdige, Dick. 1979. *Subculture: The Meaning of Style.* London: Methuen.

Hekma, Gert. 1993. "'A Female Soul in a Male Body': Sexual Inversion as Gender Inversion in Nineteenth-Century Sexology." In Herdt 1993, 213–239.

Heng, Geraldine, and Janadas Devan. 1995. "State Fatherhood: The Politics of Nationalism, Sexuality, and Race in Singapore." In Ong and Peletz 1995, 195–215.

Herdt, Gilbert. 1987a. *Guardians of the Flute: Idioms of Masculinity.* New York: Columbia University Press.

———. 1987b. *The Sambia: Ritual and Gender in New Guinea.* New York: Holt, Rinehart and Winston.

———. 1992. "Semen Depletion and the Sense of Maleness." In Murray 1992d, 33–68.

———, ed. 1993. *Third Sex, Third Gender: Beyond Sexual Dimorphism in Culture and History.* Repr., New York: Zone Books, 1996.

Herdt, Gilbert, and Robert J. Stoller. 1990. *Intimate Communications: Erotics and the Study of Culture.* New York: Columbia University Press.

Herzfeld, Michael. 1985. *The Poetics of Manhood: Context and Identity in a Cretan Mountain Village.* Princeton, N.J.: Princeton University Press.

Hobsbawm, Eric, and Terence Ranger, eds. 1983. *The Invention of Tradition.* New York: Cambridge University Press.

Howard, Richard Stephen. 1996. "Falling into the Gay World: Manhood, Marriage, and Family in Indonesia." Ph.D. diss., University of Illinois at Urbana—Champaign.

Irigaray, Luce. 1985. *The Sex Which Is Not One.* Trans. Catherine Porter with Carolyne Burke. Ithaca, N.Y.: Cornell University Press.

Irvine, Walter. 1984. "Decline of Village Spirit Cults and Growth of Urban Spirit Mediumship: The Persistence of Spirit Beliefs, the Position of Women, and Modernization." Special issue, *Mankind* 14(4) (August): 315–324.

Jackson, Peter. 1988. *Buddhasa: A Buddhist Thinker for the Modern World.* Bangkok: Siam Society.

———. 1989a. *Buddhism, Legitimation, and Conflict: The Political Functions of Urban Thai Buddhism.* Singapore: Institute of Southeast Asian Studies.

———. 1989b. *Male Homosexuality in Thailand.* Amsterdam: Global Academic Publishers.

———. 1995. *Dear Uncle Go: Male Homosexuality in Thailand.* Bangkok: Bua Luang Books.

———. 1996a. "One Gay Murder—Two Stories: Dual Discourses of Sex and the Complex Origins of Gay Identity in Pre-Stonewall Thailand." Paper presented at the Twentieth Anniversary Conference of the Asian Studies Association of Australia, La Trobe University, Melbourne, July 8–11.

———. 1996b. "The Persistence of Gender: From Ancient India *Pandakas* to Modern Thai *Gay-Quings.*" Australian Humanities Review, no. 1 (April–June 1996). http://www.lib.latrobe.edu.au/AHR/archive/Issue-April-1996/Jackson.html.

———. 1997a. "Beyond Bars and Boys: Life in Gay Bangkok." *Outrage* (July): 61–63.

———. 1997b. "Kathoey><Gay><Man: The Historical Emergence of Gay Male Identity in Thailand." In Manderson and Jolly 1997, 166–190.

———. 1997c. "Thai Research on Male Homosexuality and Transgenderism and the Cultural Limits of Foucauldian Analysis. *Journal of the History of Sexuality* 8(1): 52–85.

———. 1998. "From *Kamma* to Unnatural Vice: Male Homosexuality and Transgenderism in the Thai Buddhist Tradition." In W. Leyland, ed., *Queer*

Dharma: Voices of Gay Buddhists, vol 1, 55–89. San Francisco: Gay Sunshine Press.

———. 1999a. "Global Queering in Thailand: Peripheral Genders and the Limits of Queer Theory." Paper presented at the IASSCS Second International Conference, Manchester Metropolitan University, United Kingdom, July.

———. 1999b. "Tolerant but Unaccepting: The Myth of a Thai 'Gay Paradise.'" In Jackson and Cook 1999, 226–242.

Jackson, Peter, and Nerida Cook, eds. 1999. *Genders and Sexualities in Modern Thailand.* Chiang Mai, Thailand: Silkworm Books.

Jackson, Peter, and Gerard Sullivan, eds. 1999. *Lady Boys, Tom Boys, Rent Boys: Male and Female Homosexualities in Contemporary Thailand.* New York: Haworth Press.

Jaruwan Kanthanit. 1988. "Khwam-samphan rawang karn-puet-rap seu-muan-chon thatsanakhati tor reuang rak-ruam-pheet khorng nak-seuksaa nai krungtheep-mahanakhorn" (The relationships between mass media exposure and attitude toward homosexuality among Thai students in the Bangkok metropolitan area). Master's thesis, Chulalongkorn University, Bangkok.

Jitraporn Thammasarnsoonthon. 1995. "Kha-niyom lae thatsanakhati-thaang-pheet thii prakot nai nithayasarn phu-ying" (Sex values and sex attitudes in women [sic] magazines). Master's thesis, Chulalongkorn University, Bangkok.

Johnson, Mark. 1997. *Beauty and Power: Transgendering and Cultural Transformation in the Southern Philippines.* New York: Berg.

———. 1998. "Global Desirings and Translocal Loves: Transgendering and Same-Sex Sexualities in the Southern Philippines." *American Ethnologist* 25(4): 695–711.

Jolly, Margaret. 1997. "From Point Venus to Bali Ha'I: Eroticism and Exoticism in Representations of the Pacific." In Manderson and Jolly 1997, 99–122.

Jumphot Saisunthorn. 1993. "Thana thaang kotmaai khorng phu-rak-ruam-pheet" (The legal status of homosexuals). *Warasaan nitisaat* (Journal of law) 2(13): 60–69.

Kabilsingh, Chartsumarn. 1991. *Thai Women in Buddhism.* Berkeley, Calif.: Parallax Press.

Kamala Chodok. 1994. "Khwam-biang-been-thaang-pheet kab sangkhom mueang Thai" (Sexual deviance and Thai city society). *City Life,* no. 5 (July): 118–124.

Kaplan, Martha, and John D. Kelly. 1994. "Rethinking Resistance: Dialogics of 'Disaffection' in Colonial Fiji." *American Ethnologist* 21(1): 123–151.

Katrak, Ketu H. 1992. "Indian Nationalism, Gandhian 'Satyagraha,' and Representations of Female Sexuality." In Parker et al. 1992, 395–406.

Kearny, M. 1995. "The Local and the Global: The Anthropology of Globalization and Transnationalism." *Annual Review of Anthropology* 24: 547–565.

Kendall. 1999. "Women in Lesotho and the (Western) Construction of Homophobia." In Blackwood and Wieringa 1999, 157–178.

Kennedy, Elizabeth Lapovsky. 1994. "Living with Gay and Lesbian Identity and Community, Dreaming of Utopia." *American Anthropologist* 96(3): 697–700.

Kennedy, Elizabeth Lapovsky, and Madeline D. Davis. 1993. *Boots of Leather, Slippers of Gold: The History of a Lesbian Community.* New York: Penguin.

Keyes, Charles. 1984. "Mother or Mistress but Never a Monk: Buddhist Notions of Female Gender in Rural Thailand." *American Ethnologist* 12(2): 223–241.

———. 1986. "Ambiguous Gender: Male Initiation in a Northern Thai Buddhist Society." In C. Bynum, ed., *Gender and Religion: On the Complexity of Symbols,* 66–96. Boston: Beacon Press.

———. 1987. *Thailand: Buddhist Kingdom as Modern Nation-State.* Boulder, Colo.: Westview Press.

Khamini Tawanchaay. 1994. "Sex nai saai taa ying-chai: Khai dai-khrai sia?" (Sex in the eyes of women and men: Who gains and who loses?). *Satrithat* 10(28) (March–April): 22–30.

Khin Thitsa. 1980. *Providence and Prostitution: Image and Reality of Women in Buddhist Thailand.* London: Change International Reports.

Khin Thitsa, and Signe Howell. 1983. "Nuns, Mediums, and Prostitutes in Chiengmai: A Study of Some Marginal Categories of Women." In *Women and Development in Southeast Asia I.* Canterbury, University of Kent, Occasional Paper 1.

Kirati Chana, Aphirat Phetsiri, and Kittisak Prokati. 1993. "Karn aphi-prai reuang 'gay' lae kotmaai khana nitisaat maha-withayalai thamasat wan thii 18 kumphaphan ph.s. 2526" (The discussion panel on "Gays versus the Law" at the Law Faculty, Thammasat University, February 18, 1983). *Warasaan nitisaat* (Journal of law) 2(13): 96–149.

Kirsch, Thomas. 1982. "Buddhism, Sex-Roles, and the Thai Economy." In Van Esterik 1982b, 16–41.

———. 1985. "Text and Context: Buddhist Sex Roles/Culture of Gender Revisited." *American Ethnologist* 12(2): 302–320.

Kittisak Prokati. 1993. "Tamnarn rak-ruam-pheet" (The legends of homosexuality). *Warasaan nitisaat* (Journal of law) 2(13): 85–95.

Klausner, William J. 1987. *Reflections on Thai Culture.* 3rd ed. Bangkok: Siam Society.

Knauft, Bruce M. 1994. "Foucault Meets South New Guinea: Knowledge, Power, Sexuality." *Ethos* 22(4) (December): 391–438.

Kondo, Dorinne K. 1990. *Crafting Selves: Power, Gender, and Discoveries of Identity in a Japanese Workplace.* Chicago: University of Chicago.

Krafft-Ebing. 1965. *Psychopathia Sexualis: A Medico-Economic Study.* Trans. M. E. Wedeck. New York: G. P. Putnam's and Sons.

Krige, Eileen Jensen. 1974. "Woman-Marriage, with Special Reference to the Lovedu: Its Significance for the Definition of Marriage." *Africa* 44: 11–36.

Krisadawan, Hongladarom. 1999. "Competing Discourses on Hilltribes: Media Representations of Ethnic Minorities in Thailand." Paper presented at the Seventh International Thai Studies Conference, Amsterdam, July 4–8.

Kritaya, Archavanitkul, and Napaporn Havanon. 1993. "Situation, Opportunities, and Problems Encountered by Young Girls in Thai Society." In Yoddumnern-Attig et al. 1993, 293–311.

Kroeber, A. L. 1940. "Psychosis or Social Sanction." *Character and Personality* 8: 204–215.

Kulick, Don. 1998. *Travesti: Sex, Gender, and Culture among Brazilian Transgendered Prostitutes.* Chicago: University of Chicago Press.

Kulick, Don, and Margaret Willson, eds. 1995. *Taboo: Sex, Identity, and Erotic Subjectivity in Anthropological Fieldwork.* New York: Routledge.

Laclau, Ernesto, and Chantal Mouffe. 1985. *Hegemony and Socialist Strategy: Towards a Radical Democratic Politics.* London: Verso.

La-iat Chuprayuun. 1982. "Karn-seuksaa khwam-samphan rawang pheet khorng ruup waat nai khon prokati lae khon-khai thii rak-ruam-pheet" (The study of the relationship between the genders in illustrations [drawn by] normal people and homosexual patients). *Warasaan cit-tha-withaya khlinik* (Journal of clinical psychology) 13(2) (December): 37–46.

Lancaster, Roger N. 1995. "That We Should All Turn Queer: Homosexual Stigma in the Making of Manhood and the Breaking of a Revolution in Nicaragua." In Parker and Gagnon 1995, 133–156.

Landes, Ruth. 1940. "A Cult Matriarchate and Male Homosexuality." *Journal of Abnormal and Social Psychology* 35: 386–397.

Lang, Sabine. 1999. "Lesbians, Men-Women, and Two-Spirits: Homosexuality and Gender in Native American Cultures." In Blackwood and Wieringa 1999, 91–116.

"Lao chiwit mai khorng 'morm um' wiyada umarin" ["Morm Um" talks about her new life—Wiyada Umarin]. 1982. *Anuthin Khu Chiwit Dara Nak-rong* (Annals of the life of stars and singers) 12(133): 25–28.

Laothamatas, Anek. 1997. *Democratization in Southeast and East Asia.* Singapore: Institute of Southeast Asian Studies.

Leoprapai, Boonlert, and Michael J. Cook. 1978. *Labor Force Participation, Village Characteristics, and Modernism and Their Influence on Fertility among Rural Thai Women.* Salaya, Nakornpathom, Thailand: Institute for Population and Social Research, Mahidol University.

Lewin, Ellen. 1991. "Writing Lesbian and Gay Culture: What the Natives Have to Say for Themselves." *American Ethnologist* 18(4): 786–792.

———. 1993. *Lesbian Mothers: Accounts of Gender in American Culture.* Ithaca, N.Y.: Cornell University Press.

———. 1995. "Writing Lesbian Ethnography." In Behar and Gordon 1995, 322–335.

Lewin, Ellen, and William L. Leap, eds. 1996. *Out in the Field: Reflections of Lesbian and Gay Anthropologists.* Urbana: University of Illinois Press.

Lewis, Glen. 1996. "Thai Media Regionalisation: 'Thai-isation' or Transnationalisation?" In *Proceedings of the Sixth International Conference on Thai Studies. Theme 1—Globalization: Impact on and Coping Strategies in Thai Society,* October 14–17, Chiang Mai, Thailand, 127–142.

Lewis, Oscar. 1941. "Manly-Hearted Women among the North Piegan." *American Anthropologist* 43: 173–187.

Levy, Robert L. 1973. *Tahitians: Mind and Experience in the Society Islands.* Chicago: University of Chicago Press.

Lockard, Denyse. 1986. "The Lesbian Community: An Anthropological Approach." In Blackwood 1986b, 83–96.

Loos, Tamara. 1999. "Gender Adjudicated: Translating Modern Legal Subjects in Siam." Ph.D. diss., Cornell University, Ithaca, N.Y.

———. n.d.a. "Sex in the (Inner) City: Historicizing Female Same-Sex Sexuality in Thailand." Working paper.

———. n.d.b. "Subject Siam: Gender, Justice, and Colonial Modernity." Working book manuscript.

Lyttleton, Chris. 1999. "Changing the Rules: Shifting Bounds of Adolescent Sexuality in Northeast Thailand." In Jackson and Cook 1999, 28–42.

MacKay, Anne. *Wolf Girls at Vassar: Lesbian and Gay Experiences 1930–1990.* New York: St. Martin's Press.

MacKenzie, Gordene Olga. 1994. *Transgender Nation.* Bowling Green, Ohio: Bowling Green State University Popular Press.

Malinowski, Bronislaw. 1927. *Sex and Repression in Savage Society.* Chicago: Meridian Books, New American Library.

———. 1929. *The Sexual Life of Savages in North-western Melanesia.* New York: Hartcourt, Brace and World.

Mallet, Marian. 1978. "Causes and Consequences of the October '76 Coup." *Journal of Contemporary Asia* 8(1): 80–103.

Manderson, Lenore. 1997a. "Colonial Desires: Sexuality, Race, and Gender in British Malaysia." *Journal of the History of Sexuality* 7(3): 372–388.

———. 1997b. "Parables of Imperialism and Fantasies of the Exotic: Western Representations of Thailand—Place and Sex." In Manderson and Jolly 1997, 123–144.

Manderson, Lenore, and Margaret Jolly, eds. 1997. *Sites of Desire, Economies of Pleasure: Sexualities in Asia and the Pacific.* Chicago: University of Chicago Press.

Manitta Chanchai. 2003. "Khwam-phen-ekalak-thaang sangkhom khorng 'dee' lae konlayut nai karn-chai chiwit pracam wan khorng phu-ying thii mii khu-rak pen tom" (Social identity of *"dees"* and daily life strategies of women who have *tom* partners). Draft version of master's thesis, Thammasat University, Thailand.

Marcus, George, and Michael M. J. Fischer. 1986. *Anthropology as Cultural*

Critique: An Experimental Moment in the Human Sciences. Chicago: University of Chicago Press.

Marin, Malu. 1996. "Stolen Strands: The In and Out Lives of Lesbians in the Philippines." In Reinfelder 1996, 30–55.

Matthana Chetamee. 1995. "Withi-chiwit lae chiwit khropkhrua khorng ying-rak-ying" (Lifestyles and family life of women who love women). Master's thesis, Thammasat University, Thailand.

McCamish, Malcolm. 1999. "The Friends Thou Hast: Support Systems for Male Commercial Sex Workers in Pattaya, Thailand." In Jackson and Sullivan 1999, 161–192.

McCargo, Duncan. (1996). "The International Media and the Domestic Political Coverage of the Thai Press." In *Proceedings of the Sixth International Conference on Thai Studies. Theme 1—Globalization: Impact on and Coping Strategies in Thai Society*, October, Chiang Mai, Thailand, 159–181.

McClintock, Anne. 1995. *Imperial Leather: Race, Gender, and Sexuality in the Colonial Conquest*. New York: Routledge.

McIntosh, Mary. 1968. "The Homosexual Role." *Social Problems* 16 (fall 1968): 182–192.

McMorran, M. V. 1984. "Northern Thai Ancestral Cults: Authority and Aggression." Special issue 3, *Mankind* 14(4) (August 1984): 308–313.

Mead, Margaret. 1928. *Coming of Age in Somoa*. Repr., New York: Mentor Books, 1949.

———. 1949. *Male and Female: A Study of the Sexes in a Changing World*. New York: Morrow.

———. 1963. *Sex and Temperament in Three Primitive Societies*. New York: Morrow.

Miller, Neil. 1995. *Out of the Past: Gay and Lesbian History from 1869 to the Present*. New York: Vintage Books.

Mills, Mary Beth. 1992. "Modernity and Gender Vulnerability: Rural Women Working in Bangkok." In Van Esterik and Van Esterik 1992, 83–92.

———. 1993. "We Are Not Like Our Mothers: Migrants, Modernity, and Identity in Northeast Thailand." Ph.D. diss., University of California, Berkeley.

———. 1995. "Attack of the Widow Ghosts: Gender, Death, and Modernity in Northeast Thailand." In Ong and Peletz 1995, 244–273.

———. 1997. "Contesting the Margins of Modernity: Women, Migration, and Consumption in Thailand." *American Ethnologist* 24(1): 37–61.

———. 1999. *Thai Women in the Global Labor Force: Consuming Desires, Contested Selves*. New Brunswick, N.J.: Rutgers University Press.

Money, John, and Patricia Tucker. 1975. *Sexual Signatures: On Being a Man or a Woman*. London: Harrap.

Mongkhonvanit, Chollada. 2000. "The Characteristics of the Language Used, and the Reflection on Thai Culture in Thai Country Songs." Ph.D. diss., Mahidol University, Salaya, Nakornpathom, Thailand.

Moraga, Cherrie, and Gloria Anzaldua. 1981. *This Bridge Called My Back:*

Writings by Radical Women of Color. New York: Kitchen Table, Women of Color Press.

Morell, David, and Chai-anan Samudavanija. 1981. *Political Conflict in Thailand: Reform, Reaction, Revolution.* Cambridge, Mass.: Oelgeschlager, Gunn and Hain.

Moritz, Marguerite J. 1992. "How U.S. News Media Represent Sexual Minorities." In Dahlgren and Sparks 1992, 154–170.

Morris, Rosalind C. 1994. "Three Sexes and Four Sexualities: Redressing the Discourses on Gender and Sexuality in Thailand." *Positions* 2(1): 15–43.

———. 1997. "Educating Desire: Thailand, Transnationalism, and Transgression." *Social Text* 52/53, 15(3–4) (fall–winter): 53–79.

Morrison, Toni. 1992. *Playing in the Dark: Whiteness and the Literary Imagination.* London: Picador.

Mosse, George L. 1985. *Nationalism and Sexuality: Middle-Class Morality and Sexual Norms in Modern Europe.* Madison: University of Wisconsin Press.

———. 1990. *Fallen Soldiers: Reshaping the Memory of the World Wars.* New York: Oxford University Press.

———. 1991. *Nationalism of the Masses: Political Symbolism and Mass Movements in Germany from the Napoleonic Wars through the Third Reich.* Ithaca, N.Y.: Cornell University Press.

Muecke, Marjorie A. 1984. "Make Money Not Babies: Changing Status Markers of Northern Thai Women." *Asian Survey* 24(4): 459–470.

———. 1992. "Jane Richardson Hank's Work on Thai Gender." *Crossroads* 7(1): 21–26.

Murray, Alison J. 1991. *No Money, No Honey: A Study of Street Traders and Prostitutes in Jakarta.* New York: Oxford University Press.

———. 1999. "Let Them Take Ecstasy: Class and Jakarta Lesbians." In Blackwood and Wieringa 1999, 139–156.

Murray, Stephen O. 1992a. "Female Homosexuality in Pacific Societies: Introduction." In S. Murray 1992d, 397–405.

———. 1992b. "Male Homosexuality in Japan since the Meiji Restoration." In S. Murray 1992d, 111–150.

———. 1992c. "Vladimir Bogoraz's Account of Chukchi Transformed Shamans." In S. Murray 1992d, 313–339.

———. 1998. "'A Feeling within Me': Kamau, a Twenty-five-year-old Kikuyu." In Murray and Roscoe 1998, 41–65.

———, ed. 1992d. *Oceanic Homosexualities.* New York: Garland Publishing.

Murray, Stephen O., and Will Roscoe, eds. 1998. *Boy-Wives and Female Husbands: Studies in African Homosexualities.* New York: Palgrave.

Muscat, Robert J. 1994. *Fifth Tiger: A Study of Thai Development Policy.* Helsinki: United Nations University Press.

Myerhoff, Barbara, and Jay Ruby. 1992. "A Crack in the Mirror: Reflexive Perspectives in Anthropology." In M. Kaminsky, ed., *Remembered Lives: The*

Work of Ritual, Storytelling, and Growing Older, 307–340. Ann Arbor: University of Michigan.

Nagel, Joane. 1998. "Masculinity and Nationalism: Gender and Sexuality in the Making of Nations." *Ethnic and Racial Studies* 21(2) (March): 242–269.

Nanda, Serena. 1990. *Neither Man nor Woman: The Hijras of India.* Belmont, Calif.: Wadsworth.

———. 1993. "Hijras: An Alternative Sex and Gender Role in India." In Herdt 1993, 373–417.

Napat, Sirisambhand, and Alec Gordon. 1988. *Thai Rural Women and Agricultural Change: Approaches and a Case Study.* Bangkok: Women's Studies Program, Social Research Institute, Chulalongkorn University.

———. 1999. "Thai Women in Late Ayutthaya Style Paintings." *Journal of the Siam Society* 87(1–2): 1–16.

Narongsak Talaphat, Duangman Roeksamran, and Wanchai Chaysit. 1977. "Khropkhrua lae karn-op-rom liang-duu nai wai-dek kap rak-ruam-pheet" (The family, child rearing, and the problem of homosexuality). *Warasaan cit-tha-withaya khlinik* (Journal of clinical psychology) 8(1) (April): 24–35.

Nash, June. 1981. "Ethnographic Aspects of the World Capitalist System." *Annual Review of Anthropology* 10: 393–423.

Nederman, Cary J., and Jacqui True. 1996. "The Third Sex: The Idea of the Hermaphrodite in Twelfth-Century Europe." *Journal of the History of Sexuality* 6(4): 497–517.

Nelson, Cary, and Lawrence Grossberg, eds. 1988. *Marxism and the Interpretation of Culture.* London: Macmillan.

Nestle, Joan. 1987. *A Restricted Country.* Ithaca, N.Y.: Firebrand Books.

———, ed. 1992. *The Persistent Desire: A Femme-Butch Reader.* Boston: Alyson Publications.

Netchanok Buanark. 1989. "Khwam-samphan nai khropkhrua ruupbaep karn-seu-saan nai khropkhrua lae thatsanakhati thii mii tor ruang rak-ruam-pheet khorng nak-seuksaa nai kheet khrungtheep-mahanakhorn" (Family relations, communication patterns, and attitude toward homosexuality among students in the Bangkok metropolis). Master's thesis, Chulalongkorn University, Bangkok.

Newland, James Matthew. 1994. "The Images and Portrayals of Thai Masculinity: Through the History and Development of Politics, Buddhism, and Literature." Master's thesis, University of Oregon, Eugene.

Newton, Esther. 1972. *Mother Camp: Female Impersonators in America.* Chicago: University of Chicago Press.

———. 1984. "The Myth of the Mannish Lesbian: Radclyffe Hall and the New Woman." *Signs* 9(4): 557–575.

———. 1993. *Cherry Grove, Fire Island: Sixty Years in America's First Gay and Lesbian Town.* Boston: Beacon Press.

———. 2000. *Margaret Mead Made Me Gay: Personal Essays, Public Ideas.* Durham, N.C.: Duke University Press.

Nunthirat Kunakorn. 1989. "Phruettikam-thaang-pheet lae ceet-khati khorng wai-run koranee seuksaa rak-ruam-pheet kheet karn-seuksaa neung" (Sexual behaviors and attitude of adolescent students: A case study on homosexual behavior in Educational Region 1). Master's thesis, Mahidol University, Salaya, Nakornpathom, Thailand.

Oboler, Regina Smith. 1980. "Is the Female Husband a Man? Woman/Woman Marriage among the Nandi of Kenya." *Ethnology* 19: 69–88.

O'Brien, Denise. 1977. "Female Husbands in Southern Bantu Societies." In A. Schlegel, ed., *Sexual Stratification: A Cross-Cultural View,* 109–126. New York: Columbia University Press.

Oetomo, Dede. 1996. "Gender and Sexual Orientation in Indonesia." In Sears 1996, 259–269.

Ong, Aihwa. 1989. "State versus Islam: Malay Families, Women's Bodies, and the Body Politic in Malaysia." *American Ethnologist* 17(2): 258–276.

———. 1991. "The Gender and Labor Politics of Postmodernity." *Annual Review of Anthropology* 20: 279–309.

Ong, Aihwa, and Michael G. Peletz, eds. 1995. *Bewitching Women, Pious Men: Gender and Body Politics in Southeast Asia.* Berkeley and Los Angeles: University of California Press.

Ophat Thamwanich. 1984a. "Rak-ruam-pheet . . . pratheet caruen" (Homosexuality . . . in developed countries). *Athit Wiwat* pt. 1, vol. 1 [3], no. 43 [62] (November 3–9).

———. 1984b. "Rak-ruam-pheet . . . pratheet caruen" (Homosexuality . . . in developed countries). *Athit Wiwat* pt. 2, vol. 1 [3], no. 44 [63] (November 10–16): 42.

Opler, Marvin. 1965. "Anthropological and Cross-cultural Aspects of Homosexuality." In J. Marmor, ed., *Sexual Inversion: The Multiple Roots of Homosexuality,* 108–123. New York: Basic Books.

Ortner, Sherry B. 1990. "Gender Hegemonies." *Cultural Critique* (winter 1989–1990): 35–80.

Ortner, Sherry B., and Harriet Whitehead, eds. 1981. *Sexual Meanings: The Cultural Construction of Gender and Sexuality.* New York: Cambridge University Press.

P. Prin. 1988. "Pheet-thii-saam: saam rue sang-san" (The third sex: Degenerate or constructive?). *Nitayasaan karn-prachasongkror* (The journal of social work) 31(6) (November–December): 27–30.

Padgug, Robert. 1979. "Sexual Matters: On Conceptualizing Sexuality in History." *Radical History Review* 20 (spring/summer): 3–23.

Paga Sattayatam. 1973. "Karn-priap-thiap khwam-samphan nai khropkhrua thii hai karn-op-rom liang-duu khorng buk-khon thii rak-ruam-pheet kap buk-khon pokati" (A comparison of homosexual and normal people with respect to the relationships within their families). Master's thesis, Chula-longkorn University, Bangkok.

Parker, Andrew, Mary Russo, Doris Sommer, and Patricia Yaeger, eds. 1992. *Nationalisms and Sexualities*. New York: Routledge.

Parker, Richard. 1989. "Youth, Identity, and Homosexuality: The Changing Shape of Sexual Life in Contemporary Brazil." *Journal of Homosexuality* 17(3/4): 269–289.

————. 1999. *Beneath the Equator: Cultures of Desire, Male Homosexuality, and Emerging Gay Communities in Brazil*. New York: Routledge.

Parker, Richard, and John Gagnon, eds. 1995. *Conceiving Sexuality: Approaches to Sex Research in a Postmodern World*. New York: Routledge.

Payom Ingkatanuwat, M.D. 1978. "Karn mai yorm-rap pheet khorng ton" (Not accepting your own sex). *Klai-mor* (April 2): 34–35.

Phelan, Shane. 1993. "(Be)Coming Out: Lesbian Identity and Politics." *Signs* 18(4): 765–790.

Phongpaichit, Pasuk. 1982. *From Peasant Girls to Bangkok Masseuses*. Geneva: International Labour Office.

Phongpaichit, Pasuk, and Chris Baker. 1996. *Thailand's Boom*. Chiang Mai, Thailand: Silkworm Books.

Plummer, Kenneth, ed. 1981. *The Making of the Modern Homosexual*. Totowa, N.J.: Barnes and Noble Books.

Portelli, Alessandro. 1991. *The Death of Luigi Trastulli and Other Stories: Form and Meaning in Oral History*. Albany: State University of New York.

Porter, Mary. 1992. "Swahili Identity in Post-colonial Kenya: The Reproduction of Gender in Educational Discourse." Ph.D. diss., University of Washington, Seattle.

————. 1995. "Talking at the Margins: Kenyan Discourses on Homosexuality." In William L. Leap, ed., *Beyond the Lavender Lexicon*, 133–154. Amsterdam: Gordon and Breach.

Potter, Sulamith Heins. 1977. *Family Life in a Northern Thai Village: A Study in the Structural Significance of Women*. Berkeley and Los Angeles: University of California Press.

Prachakhom Lunachai. 1994. "Phu-ying laai chan" (A woman of many layers). *City Life*, no. 5 (July): 141–143.

Prakorn Siriwajon and Duangporn Khamnunwana. 1996. *Phu-chai khaai tua* (Men who sell their bodies). Salaya, Nakornpathom, Thailand: Institute of Language and Culture for Rural Development, Mahidol University.

Pramote, Prasarkul, Aphichat Chamratrithirong, Anthony Bennett, Ladda Jitwatanapataya, and Pimonpan Isarabhakdi. 1987. *Rural Adolescent Sexuality and the Determinants of Provincial Urban Premarital Adolescent Sex*. Salaya, Nakornpathom, Thailand: Institute for Population and Social Research, Mahidol University.

Pranee Wongthet. 1990. "Phu-ying siam botbaat lae sathanaphaap khorng phu-ying: Rorng roi caak phithi-kaam khwam-cheua" (Siamese women, the role and status of women: Clues from ritual and belief). *Sinlapa wattanatham* (Art and culture) 11(5): 183–191.

Pranorm Sarotman. 1981. "Rak-ruam-pheet" (Homosexuality). *Warasaan thammasat* (Thammasat University journal) (September): 164–179.

Praphaphan Wongsaroot. 1989. "Karn-phathanaa ekalak rak-ruam-pheet nai muu wai-run" (Homosexual identity formation among teenagers). Master's thesis, Thammasat University, Thailand.

Prieur, Annick. 1998. *Mema's House, Mexico City: On Transvestites, Queens, and Machos.* Chicago: University of Chicago Press.

Prizzia, Ross. 1985. *Thailand in Transition: The Roles of Oppositional Forces.* Asian Studies at Hawaii, no. 32. Honolulu: University of Hawai'i Press.

Program for Appropriate Technology in Health (PATH). 1994a. "Sut rak khorng ch. chai" (The formula of love for men). Bangkok: Bangkok AIDS.

———. 1994b. "Y. ying: Rak-pen" (Women know how to love). Bangkok: Bangkok AIDS.

Prudthatorn, Niramol. 1991. "Prostitution: Attitudes Are the Problem." *Friends of Women Newsletter* 2(1): 14–15.

Puar, Jasbir Kaur. 1999. "Transnational Sexualities in Trinidad: Modern Bodies, National Queers." Ph.D. diss., University of California, Berkeley.

Rabibhadana, Akin. 1984. "Kinship, Marriage, and the Thai Social System." In Aphichat Chamratrithirong, ed., *Perspectives on Thai Marriage*, 1–27. Bangkok: Institute for Population and Social Research, Mahidol University.

Radicalesbians. 1973. "The Woman Identified Woman." In A. Koedt, E. Levine, and A. Raponse, eds., *Radical Feminism*, 240–245. New York: Quadrangle.

Randall, Margaret. 1993. "To Change Our Own Reality and the World: A Conversation with Lesbians in Nicaragua." *Signs* 18(4): 907–924.

Rapp, Rayna Reiter, ed. 1975. *Toward an Anthropology of Women.* New York: Monthly Review Press.

Read, Kenneth. 1980. *Other Voices: The Style of a Homosexual Tavern.* Novato, Calif.: Chandler and Sharp.

Reid, Anthony. 1988. "Female Roles in Pre-Colonial Southeast Asia." *Modern Asian Studies* 22(3): 629–645.

Reinfelder, Monika, ed. 1996. *Amazon to Zami: Towards a Global Lesbian Feminism.* London: Cassell.

Reynolds, Craig J. 1994. "Predicaments of Thai History." *Southeast Asian Research* 2(1): 64–95.

———. 1999. "On the Gendering of Nationalist and Postnationalist Selves in Twentieth Century Thailand." In Jackson and Cook 1999, 261–274.

Rich, Adrienne. 1993 [1980]. "Compulsory Heterosexuality and Lesbian Existence." In Abelove, Barale, and Halperin 1993, 227–249.

Ringrose, Kathryn. 1993. "Living in the Shadows: Eunuchs and Gender in Byzantium." In Herdt 1993, 85–109.

Robertson, Jennifer. 1989. "Gender-Bending in Paradise: Doing 'Female' and 'Male' in Japan." *Genders* 5 (summer): 50–69.

Robinson, Richard H., and Willard L. Johnson. 1982. *The Buddhist Religion: A Historical Introduction*. Belmont, Calif.: Wadsworth.

Rorbakken, Sharon Kay. 2000. "Bar Belles: An Exploration of Gender Identity." Ph.D. diss., University of Iowa, Iowa City.

Rosaldo, Michele Z., and Louise Lamphere, eds. 1974. *Women, Culture, and Society*. Palo Alto, Calif.: Stanford University Press.

Roscoe, Will. 1988. "Strange Country This: Images of Berdaches and Warrior Women." In Will Roscoe, ed., *Living the Spirit*, 48–76. New York: St. Martin's Press.

———. 1991. *The Zuni Man-Woman*. Albuquerque: University of New Mexico Press.

———. 1993. "How to Become a Berdache: Toward a Unified Analysis of Gender Diversity." In Herdt 1993, 329–372.

Roseberry, William. 1988. "Political Economy." *Annual Review of Anthropology* 17: 161–185.

———. 1994. "Hegemony and the Language of Contention." In G. Joseph and D. Nugend, eds., *Everyday Forms of State Formation: Revolution and Negotiation of Rule in Modern Mexico*, 354–366. Durham, N.C.: Duke University Press.

Rubin, Gayle S. 1975. "The Traffic in Women: Notes on the 'Political Economy' of Sex." In Rapp 1957, 157–210.

———. 1984. "Thinking Sex: Notes for a Radical Theory of the Politics of Sexuality." In C. Vance, ed., *Pleasure and Danger: Exploring Female Sexuality*, 267–319. London: Pandora.

Russo, Vito. 1987. *The Celluloid Closet: Homosexuality and the Movies*. New York: Harper and Row.

Said, Edward. 1978. *Orientalism*. New York: Pantheon.

Saipin Suputtamongkol. 2000. *Khuk kap khon: Amnaat lae kaan-tor-taan khat-kheun* (Prison and people: Power and resistance). Bangkok: Thammasat University Press.

Saiprasert, Sirinan. 1993. "Gender Construction and Changing Nature of the Sexual Lifestyle of Thai Youth." In Yoddumnern-Attig et al. 1993, 312–332.

Salaff, Janet. 1981. *Working Daughters of Hong Kong*. Cambridge: Cambridge University Press.

Sankar, Andrea. 1986. "Sisters and Brothers, Lovers and Enemies: Marriage Resistance in Southern Kwangtung." In Blackwood 1986b, 69–82.

Schneider, David M. 1997. "The Power of Culture: Notes on Some Aspects of Gay and Lesbian Kinship in America Today." *Cultural Anthropology* 12(2) (May): 270–281.

Schofield, Michael. 1965. *Sociological Aspects of Homosexuality*. Boston: Little, Brown.

Sears, Laurie J., ed. 1996. *Fantasizing the Feminine in Indonesia.* Durham, N.C.: Duke University Press.

Sedgwick, Eve Kosofsky. 1990. *The Epistemology of the Closet.* Berkeley and Los Angeles: University of California Press.

Seidman, Steven. 1993. "Identity and Politics in a 'Postmodern' Gay Culture: Some Historical and Conceptual Notes." In M. Warner, ed., *Fear of a Queer Planet: Queer Politics and Social Theory,* 105–142. Minneapolis: University of Minnesota Press.

Shepherd, Gill. 1987. "Rank, Gender, and Homosexuality: Mombasa as a Key to Understanding Sexual Options." In Caplan 1987, 240–270.

Sinnott, Megan. 2000. "The Semiotics of Transgendered Sexual Identity in the Thai Print Media: Imagery and Discourse of the Sexual Other." *Culture, Health, and Sexuality* 2(4): 425–440.

———. 2002. "Transgender Identity and Same-Sex Relationships in Thailand: *Tom-Dee.*" Ph.D. diss., University of Wisconsin—Madison.

Sirinan Kittisuksathit. 1995. "Karn-wicai reuang phreuttikam thaang-pheet khorng wai-run nai pratheet thai: Pra-den pheet-samphan korn taeng-ngaan" (Research on sexual behavior of youth in Thai society: Sex before marriage). In documents from the seminar Direction of Research on Sexuality in Thai Society, October 12.

Siriyuvasak, Ubonrat. 1992. "Cultural Mediation and the Limits to 'Ideological Domination': The Mass Media and Ideological Representations in Thailand." *Sojourn* 6(1): 45–70.

———. 1994. "The Development of a Participatory Democracy: Raison d'Etre for Media Reform in Thailand." *Southeast Asian Journal of Social Science* 22: 101–114.

———. 1998. "The Ambiguity of the 'Emerging' Public Sphere and the Thai Media Industry." Paper presented at the Conference on the Production and Consumption of National and Local Cultural Products in the Age of Global Communication, National Chung-Cheng University, Taiwan, June.

Sitthiraksa, Sinith. 1992. "Prostitution and Development in Thailand." In Van Esterik and Van Esterik 1992, 93–108.

Smith-Rosenberg, Carroll. 1975. "The Female World of Love and Ritual: Relations between Women in Nineteenth-Century America." *Signs* 1(1): 1–29.

Sobieszcyk, Teresa Rae. 2000. "Pathways Abroad: Gender and International Labor Migration Institutions in Northern Thailand." Ph.D. diss., Cornell University, Ithaca, N.Y.

Somswasdi, Virada. 1994. *Women's Legal Position in Thailand.* Chiang Mai, Thailand: Women's Studies Center, Faculty of Social Sciences, Chiang Mai University.

Somswasdi, Virada, and Sally Theobald, eds. 1997. *Women, Gender Relations, and Development in Thai Society.* Vols. 1 and 2. Chiang Mai, Thailand: Women's Studies Center, Faculty of Social Sciences, Chiang Mai University.

Soonthorndhada, Amara. 1996. *Sexual Attitudes and Behaviors and Contraceptive Use of Late Female Adolescents in Bangkok: A Comparative Study of Students and Factory Workers.* Salaya, Nakornpathom, Thailand: Institute for Population and Social Research, Mahidol University.

Soonthorndhada, Kusol. 1991. "A Study of Employment and Fertility of Female Migrant Workers in the Manufacturing Industries of Bangkok and Periphery Areas." Ph.D. diss., Mahidol University, Salaya, Nakornpathom, Thailand.

Steedly, Mary Margaret. 1999. "The State of Culture Theory in the Anthropology of Southeast Asia." *Annual Review of Anthropology* 28: 431–454.

Stein, Edward, ed. 1992. *Forms of Desire: Sexual Orientation and the Social Constructionist Controversy.* New York: Routledge.

Stivens, Maila, ed. 1991. *Why Gender Matters in Southeast Asian Politics.* Monash Papers on Southeast Asia, no. 23. Clayton, Victoria: Monash University Centre of Southeast Asian Studies.

Stoler, Ann L. 1991. "Carnal Knowledge and Imperial Power: Gender, Race, and Morality in Colonial Asia." In di Leonardo 1991, 51–101.

———. 1995. *Race and the Education of Desire: Foucault's History of Sexuality and the Colonial Order of Things.* Durham, N.C.: Duke University Press.

Storer, Graeme. 1999. "Rehearsing Gender and Sexuality in Modern Thailand: Masculinity and Male-Male Sex Behaviors." In Jackson and Sullivan 1999, 141–160.

Suchitra Usaha. 1991. "Phreuttikam thaang-pheet lae cet-kha-ti khorng nak-rian wai-run: Koranii seuksaa phreuttikam rak-ruam-pheet" (Sexual behaviors and attitude of adolescent students: A case study on homosexual behavior in the Educational Region 4). Master's thesis, Mahidol University, Salaya, Nakornpathom, Thailand.

Sumalee Bumroongsook. 1993. "Khrai leuak khu: Phor mae reu bao-sao? Karn-plianplaeng withi-karn-leuak khu nai sangkhom thai phaak-klaang sa-mai ratanakosin" (Who chooses the partner: Parents or bride and groom? Change in the method of choosing partners in central Thailand society, Ratanakosin period). *Warasaan sukhothai thammathirat* (Journal of Sukhothai Thammathirat) 6(2) (August): 38–65. *See also* Bumroongsook, Sumalee.

Suphot Chaengrew. 1989. "Morm haam lesbian" (Royal concubines were "lesbians"). *Sinlapa wattanatham* (Art and culture) (November 22).

Surin, Maisrikrod. 1997. "The Making of Thai Democracy: A Study of Political Alliances among the State, the Capitalists, and the Middle Class." In Anek Laothamatas, ed., *Democratization in Southeast and East Asia,* 141–166. Singapore: Institute of Southeast Asian Studies.

Suwatthana Areephak. 1981. *Khwam-phit-pokati thaang-pheet* (Abnormal sexuality). Bangkok: Chulalongkorn University Press.

Swanson, Herbert R. 1988. "A New Generation: Missionary Education and

Changes in Women's Roles in Traditional Northern Thai Society." *Sojourn* 3(2): 187–206.

Talley, Colin L. 1996. "Gender and Male Same-Sex Erotic Behavior in British North America in the Seventeenth Century." *Journal of the History of Sexuality* 6(3): 385–408.

Tambiah, Stanley J. 1970. *Buddhism and Spirit Cults in Northeastern Thailand.* Cambridge: Cambridge University Press.

Tan, Beng Hui. 1999. "Women's Sexuality and the Discourse on Asian Values: Cross-Dressing in Malaysia." In Blackwood and Wieringa 1999, 281–307.

Tan, Michael L. 1995. "From Bakla to Gay: Shifting Gender Identities and Sexual Behaviors in the Philippines." In Parker and Gagnon 1995, 85–96.

———. 1997. "A Response to David Altman from Michael Tan in the Philippines." *Australian Humanities Review,* no. 2 (July–August). http://www.lib .latrobe.edu.au/AHR/emuse/Globalqueering/tan.html.

Tannenbaum, Nicola. 1999. "Buddhism, Prostitution, and Sex: Limits on the Discourse on Gender in Thailand." In Jackson and Cook 1999, 243–260.

Tansubhapol, Kulcharee. 1997. "Where Homosexuals Fear to Tread." *Bangkok Post,* Outlook, p. 1.

Tantiwiramanond, Darunee, and Shashi Ranjan Pandey. 1987. "The Status and Role of Thai Women in the Pre-Modern Period: A Historical and Cultural Perspective." *Sojourn* 2(1): 125–149.

———. 1991. *By Women, for Women: A Study of Women's Organizations in Thailand.* Research Notes and Discussions Paper no. 72. Singapore: Institute of Southeast Asian Studies.

Taywaditep, Kittiwut Jod, Eli Coleman, and Pacharin Dumronggittigule. 1997. "Thailand (Muang Thai)." In Robert T. Francoeur, ed., *The International Encyclopedia of Sexuality,* vol. 3, 1192–1265. New York: Continuum.

ten Brummelhuis, Han. 1999. "Transformations of Transgender: The Case of the Thai Kathoey." In Jackson and Sullivan 1999, 121–140.

Thammakiat Kan-ari. 1994. "Tamrap srichulakak sorn aray" (What do the works of Sri Chulalak teach us?). *Manager Magazine,* November 12–13.

Thaweesit, Suchada. 2000. "From Village to Factory 'Girl': Shifting Narratives on Gender and Sexuality in Thailand." Ph.D. diss., University of Washington, Seattle.

Thomson, Suteera. 1994. "Women Acting for Change: Towards an Equitable Society." Paper presented at the Friedrich Ebert Stiftung Conference on Women Acting for Change, June 13–14, Bonn, Germany. Bangkok: Gender and Development Research Institute.

Thomson, Suteera, and Sheila Thomson. 1993. *Women and Politics in Thailand: Options for the 1990s.* Bangkok: Gender and Development Research Institute.

Thongthiraj, Took Took. 1994. "Toward a Struggle against Invisibility: Love between Women in Thailand." *Amerasian Journal* 20(1): 45–58.

Thorbek, Susanne. 1987. *Voices from the City: Woman of Bangkok*. Atlantic Highlands: Zed Books.

Trumbach, Randolph. 1993. "London's Sapphists: From Three Sexes to Four Genders in the Making of Modern Culture." In Herdt 1993, 111–136.

Turton, Andrew. 1972. "Matrilineal Descent Groups and Spirit Cults of the Thai-yuan in Northern Thailand." *Journal of the Siam Society* 60(2): 217–256.

Udomsin Srisaengnam, M.D. 1989. *Pheet seuksaa thii naa ruu* (Sex education that you should know). Bangkok: Style Partnership Publishing.

van der Meer, Theo. 1993. "Sodomy and the Pursuit of a Third Sex in the Early Modern Period." In Herdt 1993, 137–212.

Van Esterik, Penny. 1982a. "Laywomen in Theravada Buddhism." In Van Esterik 1982b, 55–78.

———. 1992. "Thai Prostitution and the Medical Gaze." In Van Esterik and Van Esterik 1992, 133–152.

———, ed. 1982b. *Women of Southeast Asia*. Dekalb: Northern Illinois University, Center for Southeast Asian Studies, Occasional Paper 9.

Van Esterik, Penny, and John Van Esterik, eds. 1992. *Gender and Development in Southeast Asia*. Montreal: Council for Southeast Asian Studies.

VanLandingham, Mark, Chanpen Saengtienchai, John Knodel, and Anthony Pramualratana. 1995. *Friends, Wives, and Extramarital Sex in Thailand*. Bangkok: Institute of Population Studies, Chulalongkorn University; Ann Arbor: Population Studies Center, University of Michigan.

Vella, Walter F. 1978. *Chaiyo: King Vajiravudh and the Development of Thai Nationalism*. Honolulu: University of Hawai'i Press.

Vicinus, Martha. 1984. "Distance and Desire: English Boarding-School Friendships." *Signs* 9(4) (summer): 600–622.

———. 1992. "'They Wonder to Which Sex I Belong': The Historical Roots of the Modern Lesbian Identity." *Feminist Studies* 18(3) (fall): 467–498.

Wachara Khlainathorn. 1983. "Amnaat karn tat-sin-cai khorng satri nai khrop-khrua" (Decision-making power of women in the family). In *Ekasaan sam-ma-na thaang wichakan "sa-trii thai," kana sangkhom wittaya lae ma-nut-sa-ya wittaya* (Proceedings of the academic seminar Thai Women, at the faculty of sociology and anthropology), 62–64. Bangkok: Thammasat University.

Walker, Lisa M. 1993. "How to Recognize a Lesbian: The Cultural Politics of Looking Like What You Are." *Signs* 18(4): 866–890.

Walters, Delores M. 1996. "Cast among Outcastes: Interpreting Sexual Orientation, Racial, and Gender Identity in Yemen Arab Republic." In Lewin and Leap 1996, 58–69.

Wanlop Piyamanotham. 1992. "Tom gay tut dii" (*Tom*s, gays, *tut*s, *dee*s). In Wanlop Piyamanotham, *Kui kap nak-cit-tha-withaya* (Talking with a psychologist), 60–90. Bangkok: Baphitkanphim Publishing.

Wanpen Bunprakorb, M.D. 1983. "Korn ca pen lesbian, gay" (Before you become a lesbian or a gay). *Warasaan naenaew* (Nae Naew journal) (August–September): 59–64.

Wanthanee Wasikasin. 1983. *Phreuttikam-thaang-pheet khorng ma-nut kap ngaan sangkhom-song-khror* (Problems of human sexual behavior and social work). Bangkok: Thammasat University.

Waralaksana Thiramok. 1993. "Wan satrii sakon kap 'homosexuality'" (International Women's Day and homosexuality). *Chaiyapruek withayasaat* 40(273): 32–33.

"Wattanatham thai? Luuk-sao-haa-ngern, luuk-chai-chai-ngern" (Thai culture? Daughters make money, sons spend money). 1994. *Sinlapa wattanatham* (Art and culture) (April): 76–83.

Weeks, Jeffrey. 1977. *Coming Out: Homosexual Politics in Britain from the Nineteenth Century to the Present*. London: Quartet Books.

———. 1985. *Sexuality and Its Discontents: Meanings, Myths, and Modern Sexualities*. London: Routledge.

Weinrich, James. 1992. "Reality of Social Construction." In Stein 1992, 175–208.

Wekker, Gloria. 1999. "What's Identity Got to Do with It?: Rethinking Identity in Light of the *Mati* Work in Suriname." In Blackwood and Wieringa 1999, 119–138.

Werbner, Pnina. 1997. "Introduction: The Dialectics of Cultural Hybridity." In Werbner and Modood 1997, 1–24.

Werbner, Pnina and Tariq Modood, eds. 1997. *Multi-cultural Identities and the Politics of Anti-racism*. London: Zed.

Weston, Kath. 1991. *Families We Choose: Lesbians, Gays, Kinship*. New York: Columbia University Press.

———. 1993. "Lesbian/Gay Studies in the House of Anthropology." *Annual Review of Anthropology* 22: 339–367.

Wheelwright, Julie. 1989. *Amazons and Military Maids: Women Who Dressed as Men in the Pursuit of Life, Liberty, and Happiness*. Boston: Pandora.

Whitam, Frederick L., and Robin M. Mathy. 1986. *Male Homosexualities in Four Societies: Brazil, Guatemala, the Philippines, and the United States*. New York: Praeger.

Whitehead, Harriet. 1993. "The Bow and the Burden Strap: A New Look at Institutionalized Homosexuality in Native North America." In Abelove, Barale, and Halperin 1993, 498–527.

Whittaker, Andrea. 1999. "Women and Capitalist Transformation in a Northeastern Thai Village." In Jackson and Cook 1999, 43–62.

Wieringa, Saskia E. 1999. "Desiring Bodies or Defiant Cultures: Butch-Femme Lesbians in Jakarta and Lima." In Blackwood and Wieringa 1999, 206–231.

Wikan, Unni. 1991. "The Xanith: A Third Gender Role?" In *Behind the Veil in Arabia: Women in Oman*, 168–186. Chicago: University of Chicago Press.

Wilawan Kanjananpan. 1985. *A Study on the Relationship between Fertility Behavior and Size, Structure, and Functions of the Family in Thailand.* Salaya, Nakornpathom, Thailand: Institute for Population and Social Research, Mahidol University.

Williams, Raymond. 1976. *Keywords: A Vocabulary of Culture and Society.* New York: Oxford University Press.

———. 1977. *Marxism and Literature.* Oxford: Oxford University Press.

Williams, Walter. 1986a. "Persistence and Change in the Berdache Tradition among Contemporary Lakota Indians." In Blackwood 1986b, 191–200.

———. 1986b. *The Spirit and the Flesh: Sexual Diversity in American Indian Culture.* Boston: Beacon Press.

———. 1992. "Gay Self-Respect in Indonesia: The Life History of a Chinese Man from Central Java." In S. Murray 1992d, 375–386.

Wilson, Ara. 1997. "Women in the City of Consumption: Markets and the Construction of Gender in Bangkok, Thailand." Ph.D. diss., City University of New York.

Wilson, David. 1962. *Politics in Thailand.* Ithaca, N.Y.: Cornell University Press.

Winichakul, Thongchai. 1994. *Siam Mapped: A History of the Geo-Body of a Nation.* Honolulu: University of Hawai'i Press.

———. 2000. "The Others Within: Travel and Ethno-Spatial Differentiation of Siamese Subjects 1885–1990." In Andrew Turton, ed., *Civility and Savagery: Social Identity in Tai States,* 38–62. London: Curzon Press.

Wiphaan. 1984. "Kor phror plort-phai lae cai rak na-sii thueng pen saaw-dii lae num-tom" (We are *tom* and *dee* because it is safe and we like it). *Khruu Thai* (Thai teacher) (August 1984): 58–60.

Wit Thiangburanatham. 1994. *The New English-Thai Dictionary: Sentence and Phrase Structures Edition.* Bangkok: Ruamsan (1977).

Wolf, Diane Lauren. 1992. *Factory Daughters: Gender, Household Dynamics, and Rural Industrialization in Java.* Berkeley and Los Angeles: University of California Press.

Wolf, Margery. 1972. *Women and the Family in Rural Taiwan.* Stanford, Calif.: Stanford University Press.

Woodhouse, Annie. 1989. *Fantastic Women: Sex, Gender, and Transvestism.* London: Macmillan.

Wyatt, David K. 1982. *Thailand: A Short History.* New Haven, Conn.: Yale University Press.

———. 1994. *Studies in Thai History.* Chiang Mai, Thailand: Silkworm Books.

Yoddumnern-Attig, Bencha, Kerry Richter, Amara Soonthorndhada, Chanya Sethaput, and Anthony Pramualratana. 1992. *Changing Roles and Statuses of Women in Thailand: A Documentary Assessment.* Salaya, Nakornpathom, Thailand: Institute for Population and Social Research, Mahidol University.

Yoddumnern-Attig, Bencha, George Allen Attig, Wathinee Boonchalaksi, Kerry

Richter, and Amara Soonthorndhada, eds. 1993. *Qualitative Methods for Population and Health Research*. Salaya, Nakornpathom, Thailand: Institute for Population and Social Research, Mahidol University.

Yot Santasombat. 1987. "Sex pheua boriphook lae rook AIDS: Phu-ying gay lae udomkarn-amnaat" (Sex for consumption and AIDS: Women, gays, and the philosophy of power). *Baan-mai-ru-roi* 3(11): 42–50.

Young, Robert J. C. 1995. *Colonial Desire: Hybridity in Theory, Culture, and Race*. New York: Routledge.

Yuthana Thasanai. 1982. *Sex* (Sex). Bangkok: Phonphan.

Yuval-Davis, Nira. 1997. *Gender and Nation*. London: Sage Publications.

Zimmerman, Robert F. 1974. "Student 'Revolution' in Thailand: The End of the Bureaucratic Polity?" *Asian Survey* 14(6): 509–529.

INDEX

ABOUT THE AUTHOR

Megan Sinnott lived in Thailand for nearly a decade, teaching women's studies and international relations at Thammasat University and anthropology at Mahidol University. She also worked with Thai NGO's on issues of gender and labor rights. She received her Ph.D. from University of Wisconsin—Madison in 2002 and is presently an instructor at the Larry Kramer Initiative for Lesbian and Gay Studies at Yale University.

• BAKE *and* MAKE •

AMAZING

CAKES

Written by Elizabeth MacLeod
Illustrated by June Bradford

KIDS CAN PRESS

With lots of love to all my wonderful aunts:
Aunt Alix, Aunt Betty, Aunt Dorothy, Aunt Dot,
Aunt Louise, Aunt Marj, Aunt Mary Lou, Aunt Riek,
Aunt Tod, and in memory of Aunt Helen – E.M.

Text © 2001 Elizabeth MacLeod
Illustrations © 2001 June Bradford

KIDS CAN DO IT and the 🦫 logo are trademarks of Kids Can Press Ltd.

Kids Can Press acknowledges the financial support of the Government of Canada, through the BPIDP, for our publishing activity.

Published in Canada by
Kids Can Press Ltd.
29 Birch Avenue
Toronto, ON M4V 1E2

Published in the U.S. by
Kids Can Press Ltd.
2250 Military Rd.
Tonawanda, N.Y. 14150

Edited by Lori Burwash
Designed by Karen Powers
Photography by Frank Baldassarra
Cakes by June Bradford
Printed in Hong Kong by Wing King Tong Company Limited

The hardcover edition of this book is smyth sewn casebound.
The paperback edition of this book is limp sewn with a drawn-on cover.

CM 01 0 9 8 7 6 5 4 3 2 1
CM PA 01 0 9 8 7 6 5 4 3 2 1

Canadian Cataloguing in Publication Data

MacLeod, Elizabeth
Bake and make amazing cakes

(Kids can do it)
ISBN 1-55074-849-1 (bound)   ISBN 1-55074-848-3 (pbk.)

1. Cake — Juvenile literature. I. Bradford, June. II. Title. III. Series.

TX771.M333 2001   j641.8653   C00-931788-0

Kids Can Press is a Nelvana company

Contents

Introduction

*Stars, castles, tigers and dinosaurs —
it's easy to create cakes in all these shapes
and many more. Cakes make any
celebration special. Even an everyday
dinner becomes an occasion when you
finish it with a cake you've made and
decorated yourself. Cakes are wonderful
presents for friends and family, too.*

*Once you've made the cakes in this book,
try creating other cakes in whatever
shapes you like. You'll be surprised at how
easy it is to bake great-looking cakes —
you might say it's a piece of cake!*

CAKE RECIPES

Most projects in this book use one or
two cakes; a few use cupcakes. To make
the cakes and cupcakes, follow the easy
recipes on pages 32 to 36. Or use a
cake mix and follow the directions on
the package.

MIXING CAKES

For most cakes, you must beat the
batter with a hand or electric mixer to
make a light cake with a good texture.
If you don't have a mixer, beat the
batter by hand until it is smooth.

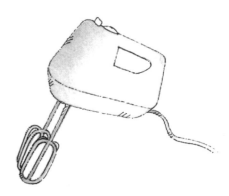

CAKE PANS

Cakes can be baked in almost any
container that safely goes in the oven.
It's a good idea to line the containers
with aluminum foil, shiny side up. The
foil makes the cakes easy to remove
from the pans, and the shiny surface
helps prevent the cakes from burning.

Line cupcake pans with cupcake papers. (Be sure to remove the papers before you cut and decorate the cupcakes.)

BAKING CAKES

Bake cakes in the center of your oven, no more than two at a time. To check if a cake is done, insert a toothpick or cake tester into the middle. If the toothpick comes out clean and dry, the cake is ready. Or gently touch the middle. If it springs back and the sides have shrunk away from the pan, the cake is done.

BAKING TIMES

Cooking times vary from oven to oven. Bake your cakes for the minimum time suggested, then test to see if they're done. If they're not, check them again in a few minutes. You may want to set a timer to remind you.

COOLING CAKES

Wearing oven mitts, remove the cake from the oven and place it on a cooling rack for at least 5 minutes. Then turn the cake upside down onto the cooling rack and remove it from the pan and foil. Let the cake cool completely before you cut and ice it.

Use a thick pair of oven mitts to handle hot cake pans. Always ask an adult to help you when moving cake pans into and out of the oven.

ICING CAKES

To make icing, follow the easy recipes on pages 37 and 38. Or buy ready-made icing or an icing mix and follow the directions on the package.

Before you begin icing, it's a good idea to cut the cake and let it stand for 1 to 2 hours. This allows the cut edges to dry out a little and makes the cake easier to ice.

To ice your cake, start by placing a dollop of icing on it. With a table knife, use short strokes to spread the icing from the top of the dollop — this keeps crumbs from getting in the icing. Continue adding dollops and icing this way until the cake is thickly covered. If your icing is hard to spread, dip the knife in hot water.

You can use icing to make the corners of your cake squarer, the edges straighter or the top rounder. (You can also use a knife to even out your cake before you begin icing.)

DECORATING CAKES

You can find candy, sprinkles, colored sugar and tinted icing at grocery stores, bulk-food stores or cake-decorating stores. Choose candies with strong colors. Light-colored candies look best on dark icing and dark candies look good on light-colored icing. See pages 39 and 40 for other decorating ideas and page 37 for how to tint icing.

MELTING CHOCOLATE

Use melted chocolate chips or bars of semisweet or milk chocolate to decorate your cake. If you break the bars into small pieces, the chocolate will melt faster.

Chocolate burns easily, so ask an adult to help you carefully melt it in a microwave or double boiler. Heat the chocolate just enough to melt it, then let it cool slightly before you use it. If the chocolate begins to harden before you are finished, melt it again.

DRAWING AND WRITING ON CAKES

It's easy to write a message or draw lines on your cake. Pour icing or slightly cooled melted chocolate into a small, heavy plastic bag, such as a freezer bag. When the bag is partly filled, snip off a tiny piece of one bottom corner.

Twist the bag closed and hold it firmly shut. Squeeze it until some chocolate or icing comes out. Cut a bigger hole if you want more to flow out.

DISPLAYING CAKES

Read each project and estimate how large your finished cake will be. If you can't find a plate or tray big enough to display your cake, use a large piece of heavy cardboard covered with aluminum foil.

FREEZING CAKES

Some projects call for only one round cake. You can save the other cake by freezing it. When the cake is completely cool, carefully wrap it in aluminum foil or plastic wrap and place it in a rigid container. Wrap and pack cupcakes the same way.

Sweet heart

Here's a special dessert for Valentine's Day, Mother's Day or Father's Day.

YOU WILL NEED

- 1 cake baked in a 20 cm (8 in.) round pan
- 1 cake baked in a 23 cm (9 in.) square pan
- 2 recipes of white icing, tinted pink
- decorations
- a large serrated knife (use only with an adult's help), a table knife

1 If the cakes aren't the same height, use the large knife to even them.

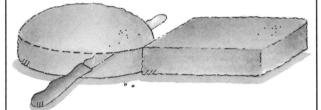

2 With the large knife, cut the round cake in half, as shown.

3 With the table knife, spread icing on both cut edges. Place one half so its cut side lies along one side of the square cake. Put the other half along an adjacent side of the square cake. If the cut edges of the halves are longer than the sides of the square cake, trim them.

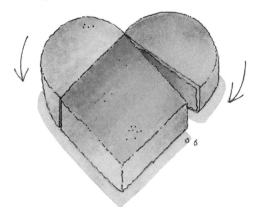

4 Ice and decorate the cake.

Terrific tiger

What a grrreat cake!
Try making any face you like.

YOU WILL NEED

- 1 cake baked in a
  20 cm (8 in.) round pan
- 1 recipe of white icing, tinted orange
- decorations, including 2 round cookies,
  2 large green gumdrops, black shoestring
  licorice, gumdrops, marshmallows,
  uncooked spaghetti,
  melted chocolate (page 7)
- a large serrated knife (use only with an
  adult's help), a table knife, a plastic bag

1 With the large knife, cut the cake diagonally, as shown.

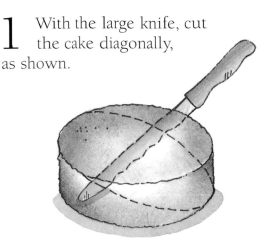

2 Stack the pieces so the thick edges are on top of each other.

3 Use the table knife to ice the cake.

4 Place the round cookies at the top of the cake for ears.

5 To make the eyes, see page 39.

6 Use gumdrops or other candies to make the nose and mouth. Put two marshmallows below the nose, and carefully stick pieces of spaghetti into them for whiskers.

7 Draw on stripes with the melted chocolate.

Lucky rainbow

Wish a friend happy birthday with this colorful rainbow.

1 With the large knife, cut the cake in half.

2 With the table knife, ice the top of one half and place the other half on top.

3 Stand the cake with the cut side down and ice all sides.

4 Using the candies, cover the cake in bands of each color.

10

OTHER IDEAS

• Make a puppy by following steps 1 to 3, using icing tinted yellow.

Add floppy paper ears, gumdrop eyes and nose and a shoestring licorice mouth and tail. If you like, cover the puppy in tinted coconut (page 39).

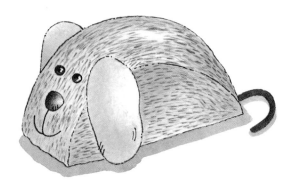

• You can make a cat, rabbit or mouse the same way.

• To make a watermelon, follow steps 1 and 2. Leave a small amount of the remaining icing white, tint a slightly larger amount green and color most of it pink. Ice the curved edge green, then stand the cake on that edge.

Ice a thin band white just inside the green icing.

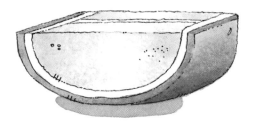

Ice the rest of the cake pink and add chocolate chips for watermelon seeds.

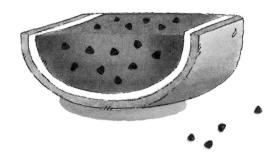

Bright butterfly

Make this fun, easy cake to celebrate a perfect summer day.

YOU WILL NEED

- 1 cake baked in a 20 cm (8 in.) round pan
- 1 recipe of white icing, tinted any colors you like
- decorations, including black shoestring licorice
- a kitchen knife, a table knife

1 With the kitchen knife, cut a pointed oval from the cake.

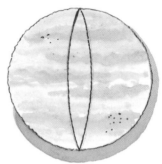

2 Place the larger pieces, cut sides out, on either side of the oval body.

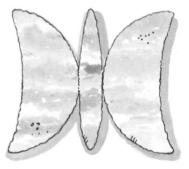

3 With the table knife, ice the body. Ice the wings a different color.

4 Decorate the cake, using the licorice as antennae.

OTHER IDEAS

- Make marble cakes by dividing half the batter for a white cake evenly into two prepared pans. Tint the remaining batter whatever color you like (page 33), then drizzle it in equal amounts into the two pans. With a table knife, lightly swirl the colored batter through the white.

Frothy mugcakes

When it's cold outside, serve these cupcakes with big mugs of cocoa.

YOU WILL NEED

- butter
- 1 recipe of cake batter
- 1 recipe of white icing
- ground cinnamon, miniature marshmallows
- 10 heavy ovenproof mugs, 2 shallow baking pans, a cooling rack, a table knife

1 Preheat the oven to 180°C (350°F).

2 Coat the inside of each mug with a thin layer of butter. Half fill each mug with batter.

3 Place the mugs in the baking pans. Have an adult place the pans in the oven and bake for 15 to 20 minutes or until done. Follow the directions for baking cakes on page 5, then place the mugcakes on the cooling rack.

4 When the mugcakes are completely cool, use the table knife to add a dollop of icing on top of each one, so that it looks like whipped cream.

5 Sprinkle cinnamon on the icing and add miniature marshmallows.

Cuddly cat

*You can make this cake look like
your favorite cat.*

YOU WILL NEED

- 2 cakes baked in
20 cm (8 in.) round pans

- 1 recipe of white icing,
tinted any color you like

- decorations, including 2 large green
or yellow gumdrops, black shoestring
licorice, a gumdrop, 2 round cookies

- a kitchen knife, a table knife

1   With the kitchen knife, cut one
cake as shown.

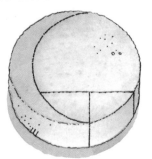

2   Arrange these
pieces around
the other cake
as shown.

3   With the table knife, use the
icing to "glue" the pieces
together, then ice the cake.

4   To make the eyes, see page 39.

5   Make a gumdrop nose, and use
the licorice for the mouth and
whiskers and the cookies for paws.

Cozy house

Welcome a new friend to your neighborhood with this house.

YOU WILL NEED

- 1 cake baked in a 23 cm x 33 cm (9 in. x 13 in.) pan
- 1 recipe of white icing, tinted any color you like
- decorations, including fruit leather; square, flat cereal; licorice; melted chocolate (page 7)
- a large serrated knife (use only with an adult's help), a table knife

1 With the large knife, cut the cake as shown.

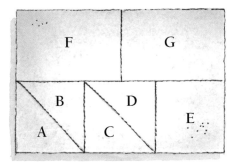

2 Assemble the pieces as shown. Use icing to glue the pieces together. Discard or eat the extra piece.

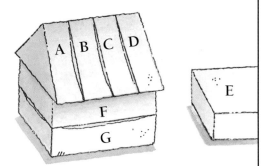

3 With the table knife, ice the whole house.

4 Decorate the house. If you like, add trees using upside-down ice-cream cones covered in green icing and green sugar or sprinkles.

OTHER IDEAS

- Use a half recipe of chocolate icing and a half of tinted white icing. Ice the roof with chocolate icing and the rest of the house with tinted icing.

Haunted castle

Don't be afraid to make this spooky cake.

YOU WILL NEED

- 1 cake baked in a
23 cm x 33 cm (9 in. x 13 in.) pan

- 2 recipes of chocolate icing

- decorations, including
fruit leather, 5 straight pretzels,
3 pointed ice-cream cones,
chocolate sprinkles,
caramels, a bar of chocolate
or cookies

- a large serrated knife
(use only with an adult's help),
a table knife, a kitchen knife

1 With the large knife, cut the cake as shown. Discard or eat one of the small pieces.

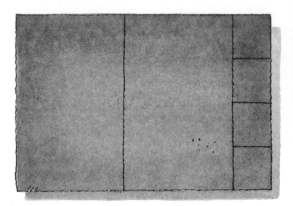

2 Assemble the cake as shown. With the table knife, use the icing to attach the small pieces.

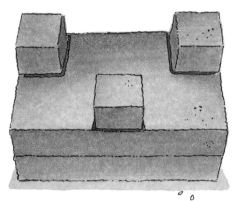

3 Set aside a small amount of icing for steps 4 and 5. With the rest, ice the entire castle, keeping any straight edges as straight as possible.

4 With the kitchen knife, cut a flag out of fruit leather and use icing to attach it to a pretzel. Gently poke the pretzel through the tip of an ice-cream cone. Repeat with the other cones.

5 Stand the ice-cream cones upside down on your work surface and ice them. Cover them with sprinkles.

6 Place the cones on the towers.

7 Arrange the caramels along the top of the castle.

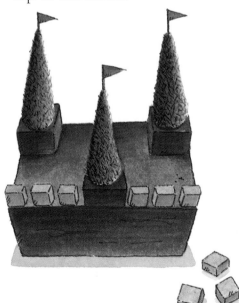

8 Decorate your castle. Make a drawbridge with a bar of chocolate or cookies. Use the remaining pretzels as drawbridge chains.

OTHER IDEAS

• Make a fantasy castle by icing the cake with white icing and decorating it with light-colored miniature marshmallows, sprinkles and other decorations.

Christmas tree

*Here's the perfect dessert for
a Christmas party.*

YOU WILL NEED

- 1 cake baked in a
23 cm x 33 cm (9 in. x 13 in.) pan
- 1 recipe of white icing, tinted green
- decorations
- a large serrated knife (use only with
an adult's help), a table knife

1 With the large knife, cut the cake into three triangles, as shown.

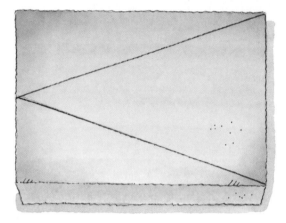

2 Form one large triangle with the two small triangles.

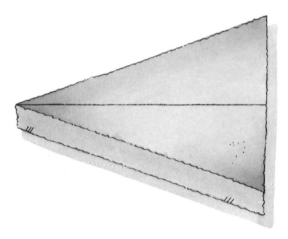

3 With the table knife, ice the top of this triangle.

4 Place the other triangle on top and ice the cake. If you like, sprinkle green sugar and sprinkles or coconut tinted green (page 39) over the cake.

5 Decorate the cake.

Spring flowers

Bake a whole bouquet of these pretty flowers.

YOU WILL NEED

- 12 cupcakes
- 1 recipe of white icing
- food coloring
- decorations
- a kitchen knife, a table knife

1 With the kitchen knife, cut six evenly spaced notches around a cupcake. Repeat with seven other cupcakes. Discard or eat the notches you cut away.

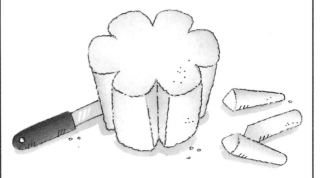

2 Tint two-thirds of the icing whatever color you'd like your flowers to be. You can make each flower a different color if you like. With the table knife, ice and decorate the flowers.

3 Cut one of the remaining cupcakes in half horizontally. Cut each half into two leaf shapes. Repeat with the other three cupcakes.

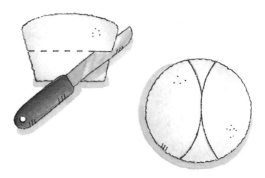

4 Tint the remaining icing green. Ice and decorate the leaves. Place two leaves with each flower.

Makes 8 flowers

Shining star

You'll be a star when you serve this terrific cake.

YOU WILL NEED

- 2 cakes baked in 20 cm (8 in.) round pans
- 1 recipe of white icing, tinted yellow
- decorations
- 10 toothpicks, a kitchen knife, a table knife

1 Evenly space five toothpicks around the edge of one cake. Place a circle of five toothpicks about 4 cm (1½ in.) inside the first circle, with each toothpick halfway between two outer toothpicks.

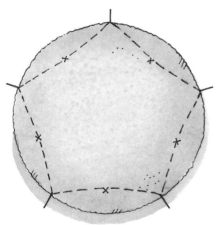

2 With the kitchen knife, cut from each outer toothpick to the two inner toothpicks closest to it. Remove the toothpicks and repeat steps 1 and 2 with the other cake. Discard or eat the pieces you cut away.

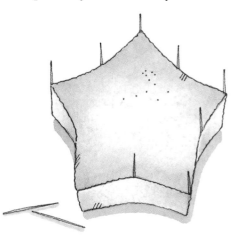

3 With the table knife, ice the top of one star and place the other star on top so that the points line up. Ice and decorate your cake.

Easter bunny

Celebrate Easter or spring with this bunny. Try making it with carrot cake and cream cheese icing, too.

YOU WILL NEED

- 2 cakes baked in 20 cm (8 in.) round pans
- 1 recipe of white icing
- food coloring
- decorations, including black shoestring licorice
- a kitchen knife, a table knife

1 With the kitchen knife, cut one cake as shown.

2 Arrange these pieces around the other cake as shown.

3 Tint a small amount of icing any color you like, and use the table knife to ice the bow tie.

4 Ice the rest of the cake with the white icing.

5 Use licorice and other candies to decorate your bunny. Decorate the bow tie, too.

Rolling bus

Beep! Beep!
Make way for this delicious cake!

YOU WILL NEED

- 1 cake baked in a
  23 cm x 33 cm (9 in. x 13 in.) pan
- 1 recipe of white icing, tinted yellow
- decorations, including 4 round cookies, fruit leather, black shoestring licorice, licorice sticks, 4 round candies
- a large serrated knife (use only with an adult's help), a table knife

1 With the large knife, cut the cake in half lengthwise, as shown.

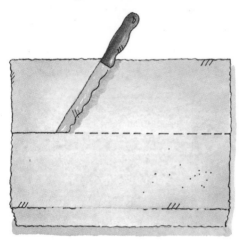

2 Cut about 7.5 cm (3 in.) off an end of one piece of cake.

From this small piece, cut a strip 2.5 cm (1 in.) thick.

Cut this strip in half lengthwise. Save one of these strips. Discard or eat the other one.

3 With the table knife, ice the top of the largest piece of cake. Place the next largest piece on top, lining up the pieces at one end. Ice one long side of the strip of cake from step 2. Place it, icing side down, at the other end of the top piece. Ice the cake.

4 Place the cookies around the cake base to make wheels.

5 Add windows using fruit leather. Make shoestring licorice wipers, and put shoestring licorice above and below the side windows.

6 Use two short pieces of licorice stick for the front grill and one long piece for the bumper.

7 Place two round candies on either side of the grill for headlights. Put lights on the top strip, too.

Jack-o'-lantern

*What a great centerpiece for a
Halloween party. Or make a face,
planet Earth, a ball — anything round!*

YOU WILL NEED

- 1 recipe of cake batter
- 1 recipe of white icing, tinted orange
- decorations, including
  black shoestring licorice
- a 1.5 L (6 c.) round glass casserole dish
  lined with aluminum foil, a cooling rack,
  a large serrated knife (use only with an
  adult's help), a table knife

1 Preheat the oven to 150°C
(300°F).

2 Pour the cake batter into the
dish and bake for 60 to 70
minutes or until done. Follow the
directions for baking and cooling
cakes on page 5.

3 With the large knife, slice the
cake in half horizontally.

4 With the table knife, ice the top
of the flat layer. Place the
rounded layer on top and ice the
whole cake.

5 Make lines in the icing to look
like the lines on a pumpkin.
Add the eyes, nose and mouth using
shoestring licorice and other candies.

Teddy bear

This un-bear-ably cute cake can also be decorated to look like a panda or a snowman.

YOU WILL NEED

- 2 cakes baked in 20 cm (8 in.) round pans

- 1 recipe of chocolate icing

- decorations, including 6 flat, round chocolate cookies; 1 white or chocolate marshmallow; 2 small, round candies; a red gumdrop; black shoestring licorice

- a kitchen knife, a table knife

1 With the kitchen knife, cut a shallow groove from one cake. Discard or eat the piece you cut away.

2 Arrange the cakes as shown.

3 With the table knife, ice the cake. If you like, sprinkle on chocolate sprinkles.

4 Place two cookies on the cake to make ears. Put smaller cookies on top if you like. Add cookie paws.

5 To make the eyes, see page 39.

6 Use the gumdrop for the nose and the licorice for the mouth and paws.

Delicious burger

A hamburger for dessert? Yum!

YOU WILL NEED

- 1 recipe of cake batter
- ½ recipe of white icing
- brown and yellow food coloring
- ½ recipe of chocolate icing
- 25 mL (2 tbsp.) strawberry jam
- round red gummi candies
- green fruit leather
- almonds, toasted (see "Note" on page 27)
- a 1.5 L (6 c.) round glass casserole dish lined with aluminum foil, a cooling rack, a large serrated knife (use only with an adult's help), a table knife, a kitchen knife, scissors

1 Preheat the oven to 150°C (300°F).

2 Pour the cake batter into the dish and bake for 60 to 70 minutes or until done. Follow the directions for baking and cooling cakes on page 5.

3 With the large knife, slice the cake horizontally into three equal layers.

4 Put aside a small amount of white icing. Tint the rest light brown. With the table knife, use about half the light brown icing to ice the sides of the bottom layer.

26

5 With the chocolate icing, ice the top of the bottom layer. Place the middle layer on top and ice its sides and top, also with chocolate icing.

6 Tint the white icing you set aside mustard yellow. Ice the edge of the middle layer to look like mustard.

7 Drizzle jam around the edge to add ketchup to your burger.

8 With the kitchen knife, cut gummi candies to look like tomato slices. Place around the edge of the middle layer.

9 For shredded lettuce, cut the fruit leather into thin strips with the scissors and place around the edge.

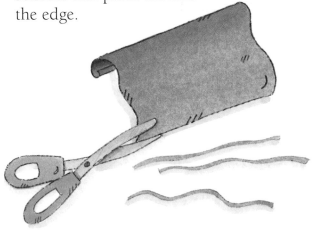

10 Place the rounded layer on top and ice it with the remaining light brown icing. Sprinkle on the almonds.

Note: *To toast almonds, preheat the oven to 150°C (300°F). Place the almonds on a cookie sheet and toast them for 3 minutes or until they are golden brown. Watch the almonds carefully — they burn easily.*

Creeping caterpillar

Did you ever think you'd eat a caterpillar?

YOU WILL NEED

- 12 cupcakes
- 1 recipe of white icing, tinted any colors you like
- decorations, including colored sugar or tinted coconut (page 39), black shoestring licorice, 2 lollipops
- a table knife

1 Arrange the cupcakes in a wavy line, tops down.

2 With the table knife, ice the cupcakes. You can make each cupcake a different color if you like. Cover them with colored sugar or tinted coconut.

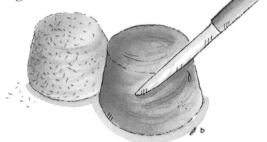

3 Decorate your caterpillar. Use candies for a face, shoestring licorice for feet and lollipops for antennae.

OTHER IDEAS

- Use icing to stick the tops of two cupcakes together. Ice and decorate to look like an apple.

Sun hat

This hat is good enough to eat!
What other hats can you make?

YOU WILL NEED

- 2 cakes baked in
20 cm (8 in.) round pans

- 1 recipe of white icing,
tinted any color you like

- decorations, including
fruit leather or shoestring licorice,
marshmallow flowers
and leaves (page 39)

- a large serrated knife
(use only with an adult's help),
toothpicks, a kitchen knife, a table knife

1 With the large knife, slice one cake in half horizontally, as shown. Put one half aside for step 3. Discard or eat the other half.

2 Place a ring of toothpicks 2.5 cm (1 in.) in from the edge of the other cake. With the kitchen knife, cut along the ring. Remove the toothpicks. Discard or eat the cake you cut away.

3 With the table knife, ice the top of the piece of cake from step 1. Place the other piece on top, in the center, and ice the whole cake.

4 Place a band of fruit leather or shoestring licorice around the hat. Add marshmallow flowers and leaves.

Scary dinosaur

*Decorate this cake to look like
your favorite dinosaur.*

YOU WILL NEED

- 2 cakes baked in
  20 cm (8 in.) round pans
- 1 recipe of white icing, tinted green
- decorations, including a licorice stick
- a kitchen knife, a short wooden skewer
  or long match with head removed,
  a table knife

1 With the kitchen knife, cut one
cake as shown.

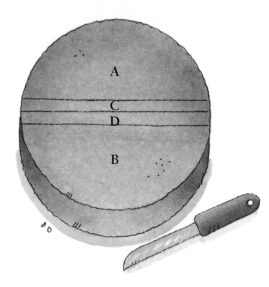

2 Cut off one-third of the other
cake. From this piece, cut a
curved strip about 2.5 cm (1 in.) wide.
Cut a piece 7.5 cm (3 in.) long from
this strip for the head and neck.

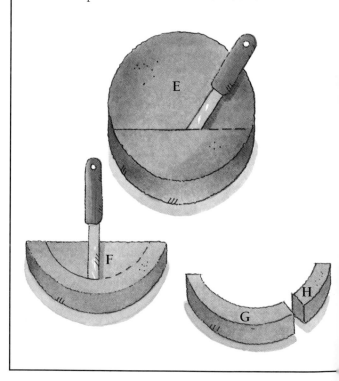

3 Cut a notch from the large piece of cake from step 2, as shown. Save the large piece and discard or eat the small piece.

5 With the table knife, ice the dinosaur, then decorate it. Use two short pieces of licorice for arms (you may have to fasten them to the cake with toothpicks).

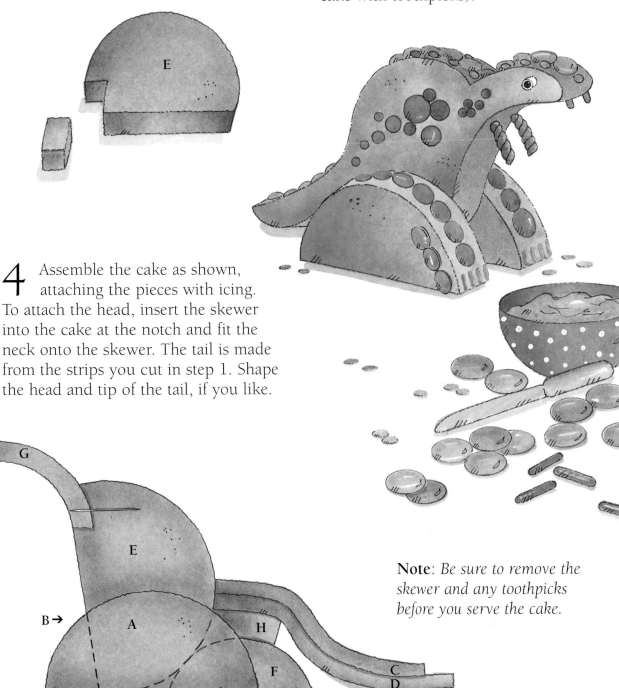

4 Assemble the cake as shown, attaching the pieces with icing. To attach the head, insert the skewer into the cake at the notch and fit the neck onto the skewer. The tail is made from the strips you cut in step 1. Shape the head and tip of the tail, if you like.

Note: *Be sure to remove the skewer and any toothpicks before you serve the cake.*

RECIPES

When you're baking cakes, it's very important to measure accurately and follow the instructions carefully.

ABBREVIATIONS

The following abbreviations have been used in the recipes:

L = liter
mL = milliliter
cm = centimeter
°C = degrees Celsius
c. = cup
tbsp. = tablespoon
tsp. = teaspoon
in. = inch
°F = degrees Fahrenheit

MEASURING INGREDIENTS

Both the metric and imperial systems of measurement are used in this book. The systems vary, so choose one and use it for all your measuring.

Dry ingredients and wet ingredients require different measuring cups. A dry measuring cup is flat across the top so you can level off the dry ingredients with a knife for a really accurate measure.

A wet measuring cup has a spout to make pouring easier. Be sure to match your ingredients with the correct type of measuring cup.

White cake

450 mL	white sugar	1¾ c.
150 mL	butter or margarine, at room temperature	⅔ c.
2	eggs	2
10 mL	vanilla	2 tsp.
750 mL	all-purpose flour	3 c.
12 mL	baking powder	2½ tsp.
2 mL	salt	½ tsp.
375 mL	milk	1½ c.

measuring cups and spoons,
a large and a medium mixing bowl,
a hand or electric mixer, a sifter,
cake pan(s) lined with aluminum foil,
a cooling rack

1 Preheat the oven to 180°C (350°F).

2 In the large bowl, use the mixer to cream the sugar and butter until they are smooth and light in color. Add the eggs and vanilla. Blend well.

3 Sift together the flour, baking powder and salt into the medium bowl.

4 Add one-third of the dry ingredients to the wet mixture and mix well. Add half the milk and blend. Repeat, then add the remaining flour mixture and mix well.

5 Pour the batter into the pan(s) and push it out to the sides. Tap the pan(s) lightly to remove large air bubbles.

6 Place the pan(s) in the oven and bake for 30 to 40 minutes or until done (see "Baking Times" on page 5). Follow the directions for baking and cooling cakes on page 5.

Makes one 23 cm x 33 cm (9 in. x 13 in.) cake, two 20 cm (8 in.) round cakes, two 23 cm (9 in.) square cakes or 24 cupcakes

• To tint this batter, use food coloring. Start by adding three drops and keep adding drops until you create the color you want. Or stir about 50 mL (¼ c.) colored sugar into the batter.

• You can flavor this batter with extracts and flavorings, available at the grocery store. Start by adding three drops and keep adding drops until you create the flavor you want.

Chocolate cake

YOU WILL NEED

500 mL	white sugar	2 c.
150 mL	butter or margarine, at room temperature	2/3 c.
2	eggs	2
10 mL	vanilla	2 tsp.
625 mL	all-purpose flour	2½ c.
175 mL	cocoa powder	3/4 c.
12 mL	baking powder	2½ tsp.
2 mL	salt	½ tsp.
375 mL	milk	1½ c.

measuring cups and spoons,
a large and a medium mixing bowl,
a hand or electric mixer, a sifter,
cake pan(s) lined with aluminum foil,
a cooling rack

1 Preheat the oven to 180°C (350°F).

2 In the large bowl, use the mixer to cream the sugar and butter until they are smooth and light in color. Add the eggs and vanilla. Blend well.

3 Sift together the flour, cocoa, baking powder and salt into the medium bowl.

4 Add one-third of the dry ingredients to the wet mixture and mix well. Add half the milk and blend. Repeat, then add the remaining flour mixture and mix well.

5 Pour the batter into the pan(s) and push it out to the sides. Tap the pan(s) lightly to remove large air bubbles.

6 Place the pan(s) in the oven and bake for 30 to 40 minutes or until done (see "Baking Times" on page 5). Follow the directions for baking and cooling cakes on page 5.

Makes one 23 cm x 33 cm (9 in. x 13 in.) cake, two 20 cm (8 in.) round cakes, two 23 cm (9 in.) square cakes or 24 cupcakes

Banana cake

50 mL	milk	¼ c.
15 mL	lemon juice	1 tbsp.
300 mL	white sugar	1¼ c.
125 mL	butter or margarine, at room temperature	½ c.
2	eggs	2
5 mL	vanilla	1 tsp.
500 mL	all-purpose flour	2 c.
5 mL	baking soda	1 tsp.
250 mL	mashed bananas (about 2 medium)	1 c.

measuring cups and spoons;
small, large and medium mixing bowls;
a wooden spoon; a sifter;
cake pan(s) lined with aluminum foil;
a cooling rack

1 Preheat the oven to 180°C (350°F).

2 In the small bowl, combine the milk and lemon juice. Set aside.

3 In the large bowl, use the wooden spoon to cream the sugar and butter until they are smooth and light in color. Add the eggs and vanilla. Beat until light and fluffy.

4 Add the milk mixture to the batter and beat well.

5 Sift together the flour and baking soda into the medium bowl.

6 Add one-third of the dry ingredients to the wet mixture and mix well. Add half the bananas and blend. Repeat, then add the remaining flour mixture and mix well.

7 Pour the batter into the pan(s) and push it out to the sides. Tap the pan(s) lightly to remove large air bubbles.

8 Place the pan(s) in the oven and bake for 40 to 50 minutes or until done (see "Baking Times" on page 5). Follow the directions for baking and cooling cakes on page 5.

Makes one 23 cm x 33 cm (9 in. x 13 in.) cake, two 20 cm (8 in.) round cakes, two 23 cm (9 in.) square cakes or 24 cupcakes

Carrot cake

YOU WILL NEED

250 mL	white sugar	1 c.
250 mL	brown sugar	1 c.
125 mL	butter or margarine, at room temperature	1/2 c.
3	eggs	3
125 mL	vegetable oil	1/2 c.
10 mL	vanilla	2 tsp.
500 mL	all-purpose flour	2 c.
10 mL	baking soda	2 tsp.
5 mL	cinnamon	1 tsp.
2 mL	salt	1/2 tsp.
500 mL	grated carrots	2 c.
125 mL	walnuts, chopped (optional, see "Note")	1/2 c.
125 mL	raisins (optional)	1/2 c.

measuring cups and spoons,
a large mixing bowl,
a wooden spoon, a sifter,
cake pan(s) lined with aluminum foil,
a cooling rack

Note: *If you want to use walnuts, first make sure no one is allergic to them.*

1 Preheat the oven to 180°C (350°F).

2 In the bowl, use the wooden spoon to cream the sugars and butter until they are smooth. Add the eggs, oil and vanilla. Blend well.

3 Sift together the flour, baking soda, cinnamon and salt into the wet mixture and mix.

4 Mix in the carrots, walnuts and raisins.

5 Pour the batter into the pan(s) and push it out to the sides. Tap the pan(s) lightly to remove large air bubbles.

6 Place the pan(s) in the oven and bake for 60 minutes or until done (see "Baking Times" on page 5). Follow the directions for baking and cooling cakes on page 5.

Makes one 23 cm x 33 cm (9 in. x 13 in.) cake, two 20 cm (8 in.) round cakes, two 23 cm (9 in.) square cakes or 24 cupcakes

White or chocolate icing

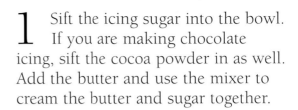

1 Sift the icing sugar into the bowl. If you are making chocolate icing, sift the cocoa powder in as well. Add the butter and use the mixer to cream the butter and sugar together.

2 Add the milk and vanilla. Beat until smooth.

3 If the icing is too thin, add more icing sugar. If the icing is too thick, add a little more milk.

• If you want to tint white icing, use butter when making it — the coloring in margarine may affect the coloring you add. Use food coloring or icing color paste. If you use food coloring, start by adding three drops and keep adding drops until you create the color you want. If you use icing color paste, use a toothpick to add a very small amount of the paste. Add a little more until you create the color you want.

• You can flavor white and chocolate icing with extracts and flavorings, available at the grocery store. Start by adding three drops and keep adding drops until you create the flavor you want.

Icing will keep in a covered container in your refrigerator for about two weeks. Mix well before using and add a little milk or water if necessary.

Makes about 500 mL (2 c.)

Cream cheese icing

YOU WILL NEED

250 mL	cream cheese, at room temperature	1 c.
125 mL	butter or margarine, at room temperature	½ c.
1 L	icing sugar	4 c.
5 mL	vanilla	1 tsp.
5 mL	milk or orange juice	1 tsp.

measuring cups and spoons,
a hand or electric mixer,
a large mixing bowl, a sifter

1 Using the mixer, cream together the cream cheese and butter in the bowl.

2 With the mixer turned on, slowly sift the icing sugar into the bowl. Beat the mixture until there are no lumps.

3 Add the vanilla and milk. Beat until smooth.

4 If the icing is too thin, add more icing sugar. If the icing is too thick, add a little more milk.

If you like, add 15 mL (1 tbsp.) grated lemon or orange peel for extra flavor. Or add 125 mL (½ c.) chopped pecans.

This icing will keep in a covered container in your refrigerator for about one week. Mix well before using and add a little milk or water if necessary.

Makes about 500 mL (2 c.)

DECORATING IDEAS

MAKING EYES

• Make cat or tiger eyes by using a kitchen knife to slice the bottom off two green or yellow gumdrops. Place the slices on the face. Add a short piece of black shoestring licorice to each eye to make the center.

Or shape two round, black-centered licorice allsorts and place each on a candy fruit slice.

• To make teddy bear eyes, slice a marshmallow in half and place each half, cut side down, on a flat, round chocolate cookie. Place a small, round candy on each marshmallow.

TINTING COCONUT

• To tint coconut, place about 250 mL (1 c.) flaked coconut and 2 drops of food coloring in a jar. Tightly screw on the lid and shake the jar until the coconut is evenly tinted. Repeat with more food coloring if you want a darker color. To make brown coconut, use 15 mL (1 tbsp.) cocoa powder.

MAKING FLOWERS

• To make marshmallow flowers, use scissors to cut a marshmallow into five rounds, as shown. Use the pieces as petals to make flowers. Cut green marshmallows the same way for leaves.

USING CANDIES, NUTS AND OTHER DECORATIONS

• Birthday candles become really special when you place candy rings on top of your cake and insert each candle into a ring.

• For a fun birthday cake, use fruit leather to wrap a cake as if it's a present. Be sure to add a big bow!

• It's easy to decorate a cake by sprinkling nuts on the top or sides or both. (Before you do, make sure no one is allergic to nuts.) You can also crush peppermint candy or other hard candy and sprinkle it on your cake.

• Decorate a round cake to look like a drum. Add round lollipops for drumsticks.

• For a safari cake, ice the cake and place animal cookies around the outside and on top. Use coconut tinted green for grass.

CUTTING SHAPES

• Cut a cake into interesting shapes using large cookie cutters.

• Or cut the cake as shown. What other shapes can you cut?

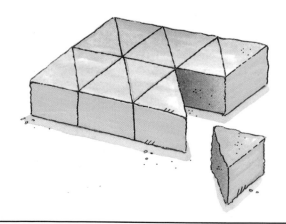